Michelle Lovric is the authn
Venice: *Carnevale, The Floating*   -
nationally bestselling antholog   *of*
Passion. She lives in London and Venice.

ALSO BY MICHELLE LOVRIC

Carnevale

The Floating Book

The Virago Book of Christmas

The Remedy

Venice
Tales of the City

Selected and Introduced by
MICHELLE LOVRIC

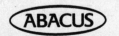

ABACUS

First published in Great Britain in 2003 by Little, Brown
This edition published in 2005 by Abacus
Reprinted 2005

The editor would like to thank the following people for their invaluable
assistance and good humour with translating the original Venetian and
Italian material in this book: Ornella Tarantola, Susie and Bruno
Palmarin, Lucio Sponsa and, most particularly, Elena Marcarini; for help
with research, sincere thanks are due to Kristina Blagojevitch and to
Daniel Pordes; for kindly checking the manuscript, Howard Fitzpatrick,
of Venice Art.

Acknowledgements on pp. 436–9 constitute an extension
of this copyright page.

A CIP catalogue record for this book
is available from the British Library.

ISBN 0 349 11899 x

Printed and bound in Great Britain
by Bookmarque Ltd, Croydon, Surrey

Abacus
An imprint of
Time Warner Books Group UK
Brettenham House
Lancaster Place
London WC2E 7 N

Contents

Introduction

City of the Soul
SOME INTRODUCTIONS

The Watery City
BUILDING THE MYTHICAL TOWN

City of the Venetians
THE CHARACTER OF THE VENETIANS

The Merchant City
PICTURESQUE TRADES

City Afloat
GONDOLAS AND GONDOLIERS

City at Play
CARNEVALE AND OTHER DIVERSIONS

Contents vii

City of Sights
FOREIGNERS

City of Forgotten Voices
THE VENETIANS' VENETIANS

Dark Side of the City
CRIMES AND PUNISHMENTS

City of Love
AFFAIRS OF THE HEART AND THE
BUSINESS OF LOVE

City of Arts
ARTISTS AND WRITERS

City of Flavours
DINING IN VENICE

The Haunting City
SADNESS AND MADNESS

City of Birds and Beasts
CATS, RATS AND MYTHICAL CREATURES

The Past and Future City
SOME CONCLUSIONS

Introduction

Venice seldom goes begging for praise — or anthologies. Most of the latter are compiled by foreigners from the words of foreigners. They present Venice as a quaint curiosity, a dilapidated snow-dome of gondolas and Gothic, to be held up and viewed for outsiderly amusement, poignant with memories of grandeur long past. Reading these accounts of a muted, tragic *Serenissima*, one would never suspect that they are describing a living, eating, love-making, swearing, laughing city.

But reports of her demise have been greatly exaggerated. Just a short distance from the tourist nodes, the secret life of Venice continues as vibrantly as it ever did. It can still be heard in the droll blandishments of the fruitmen at the Rialto, in the throbbing music of the late-night open-air dancing contests at San Giacomo dell'Orio, in the passionate editorials of the town newspapers, in the wry exchanges over 6 a.m. coffees in backstreet bars.

If Venice is a museum, her rooms are the most beautiful in the world, and her exhibits still very much inhabited. In this anthology, the voices of today's Venetians mingle with those of their ancestors, just as they still do on the streets of the city. Recite a few words from Arnaldo Fusinato's 1849 masterpiece 'Addio a Venezia' and almost any Venetian will declaim not just the rest of the stanza but the whole stirring poem, reproduced here in English for the first time. The laments of the fifteenth-century diarist Marino Sanudo are today repeated in *Il Gazzettino*, almost word for word, week by week. The Venetians are still well served by their vast repertoire of ironic and earthy proverbs. The warning cries of the gondoliers are the same; the greeting gestures the locals reserve for their own kind are unchanged; identical seasonal delicacies, *frittole*, *galani*, musk melons, perfume the air at the same times of year.

It is these things, and the pleasure Venetians have taken in them since time immemorial, that are the stuff of this book. Where possible, they are described by native writers, in hymns to hot chocolate, paeans to dried cod, private letters, diaries and memoirs.

Who better to conjure up the hedonism of eighteenth-century Venice than notorious native sons Lorenzo da Ponte, Carlo Goldoni and Giacomo Casanova? Or to describe the pretensions of Venetian literary life than Goldoni's arch-rival Carlo Gozzi? Who else but Baffo could describe San Marco as the place to find 'bitches of all breeds/who go there to wag their tails', parading themselves in such a manner that the poet can scarcely restrain himself from pinching them?

And who better than Doge Francesco Morosini and historian Pompeo Molmenti to describe the fantastical origins of their own city? The bluestocking *Dogaressa* Giustina Renier Michiel explains why pigeons haunt San Marco to this day. Riccardo Calimani describes the near-extinction of the Venetian Jews in the Holocaust.

Other voices, some now long forgotten, describe uniquely Venetian joys and tribulations. Here are the astonishing lyrics to the songs the workers sang as they drove down the piles that form the foundation of the floating city. A sixteenth-century merchant bemoans his six-year run of unspeakable ill-fortune on the high seas. Veronica Franco, the courtesan-poetess, implores a friend not to set her daughter up as prostitute in Venice . . . 'do not allow the flesh of your poor daughter to be slaughtered and sold, and to become yourself her own butcher'.

The secret city also reveals herself in her ancient documents: the original 'wanted' poster for the perpetrators of a legendary crime, the brutal murder attempt on the saintly Paolo Sarpi; a Renaissance treatise on how to detect the signs of possession by demons (if someone cannot eat the flesh of a goat for thirty days, for example). In the expense-book of the artist Lorenzo Lotto we see what it costs to undress a potential life-model 'only to look'.

Also included are pieces that were written for the entertainment of the Venetians themselves: the tale of the wicked nuns and their exhausted gardener; the original and much darker account of the Moor of Venice upon which Shakespeare based his *Othello*.

Far too many visiting poets have slathered the city with the effluvia of their sentimental raptures. But there are those, like Anthony Hecht and Octavio Paz, who have brought new and delicate sensibilities to the city. Their work is extracted here.

In some ways the greatest kindness a foreigner can show is *not* to take Venice too seriously. Mark Twain, Théophile Gautier and Thomas Coryate have enriched the literary legacy of Venice with laughter. Some of their tongue-in-cheek accounts are included.

There are visitors who have adored Venice with such commitment that they have come to stay for some time, such as George Sand, Byron and William Dean Howells, or even for the rest of their lives, like Pietro Aretino, Ezra Pound and Horatio F. Brown: their writings are given precedence among the foreigners included in this book.

And, of course, the Venetians have their own thoughts on the foreigners who come to look at their city. Paolo Barbaro and Piero Pazzi explain how it feels to live in a place where the locals numbering less than sixty thousand face an annual influx of fourteen million tourists.

Many of the extracts in this anthology are here translated into English for the first time. For their help in allowing the Venetians, ancient and modern, to have their say, I have pleasure in thanking Clara Caleo-Green, Bruno and Susie Palmarin, Lucio Sponsa, Ornella Tarantola, Cinzia Viviani and most particularly Elena Marcarini.

Michelle Lovric
2003

City of the Soul

SOME INTRODUCTIONS

See Naples and die — See Venice and tell!

He who never sees Venice
can never know her beauty.

He who is lord of the sea is also lord of the land.

Names for the city:
Heneti, Venecia, Veneciae, Venegia, Venessia, Veneti, Venetia,
Venetiae, Venetici, Venetie, Venettia, Venexia, Venezia,
Veniesia, Veniexia, Venitiano, Venegia, Vinetia, Viniziani.

If Venice had no bridge, Europe would be an island.

MARIO STEFANI

Every time I describe a city I am saying something about Venice.

ITALO CALVINO

The scholars of the world were sweating over their quills, trying to find praises sufficient to describe our unsurpassable city. In fact, their noble souls, indoctrinated by experience, after making a tour and seeing the universe, finally ending in this triumphant realm, denominate her thus:

> Noble Emporium
> Unique Virgin of the Universe
> Queen of the Sea
> Safe House of Inner Liberty
> Home of Honest Living
> Wonder of the World . . .

VINCENZO CORONELLI

The abuse which the city suffers derives . . . from its own fatal gift for manufacturing endlessly seductive clichés.

JONATHAN KEATES

. . . the stones of Venice are now covered with, completely obliterated by, the shining tracks of those who have crawled among them so often and for so long.

OSBERT SITWELL

Thus, paintings, poems, romances, and alas! Many histories have combined to create a purely conventional Venice.

FERDINAND ONGANIA

Venice was more beautiful than romances had feigned.

GEORGE ELIOT (MARY ANN EVANS)

Other cities had admirers, Venice alone has lovers.

PAUL DE ST VICTOR

The truth is that we must number Venice among the 'cities of the soul' . . . she has the fatal gift to touch the imagination, to awaken a permanent desire.

HORATIO F. BROWN

. . . do you know of any other place in the world like Venice, in its power of stimulating at certain moments all the powers of human life, and of exciting every desire to the point of fever?

GABRIELE D'ANNUNZIO

The Watery City

BUILDING THE MYTHICAL TOWN

If God had wanted Venetians to be fish
he would have given us an aquarium and not a city.

Water carries no stains.

Turbulent water doesn't make a mirror.

Is there anyone who doesn't know how to swim?

VENETIAN PROVERBS

'But where do the people walk?' inquired I of my gondolier.

HANS CHRISTIAN ANDERSEN

. . . she sided with the poets and decided to be built on water.

PAUL MORAND

. . . the fawning sea
Licked her white feet.

DAVID GRAY

It is a great oddity – a city for beavers.

RALPH WALDO EMERSON

Receive from my hand this ring, and let it be the sign of the lordship that you hold over the sea. Take her in marriage every year, you and your successors, in order that posterity may know that she, the sea, belongs to you by right of victory, and shall be subject unto you as the wife unto the husband.

POPE ALEXANDER III'S LEGENDARY BEQUEST TO DOGE SEBASTIANO ZIANI IN 1173, THE ORIGIN OF THE CEREMONY OF THE *SPOSALIZIO*, WHEREBY THE DOGE DROPPED A GOLDEN RING INTO THE SEA EACH YEAR ON ASCENSION DAY.

It is situated in a place which is not land, nor water, nor sky . . . it is inhabited by mortal creatures, a fact that obviously denies its possible belonging to the realms of the sky. It is not land, because . . . here one does not see growing above the waters anything else than buildings and temples and splendid palaces for the exclusive use of human beings. Besides, it is clear that it cannot be called water either, since one can see towering around fantastic buildings, and superb houses, which are a heavy burden on the soft shoulders of the water. Therefore, I do not know whether it should be called motionless sea, or earthly sky or celestial heart.

DOMENICO MARTINELLI

There is a freshness of wonder that attends every part of the progress through this floating world . . .

FRANCES TROLLOPE

. . . each palace has a mirror in which to gaze at its beauty, like a coquettish woman.

THÉOPHILE GAUTIER

But, close about the quays and churches, palaces and prisons: sucking at their walls, and welling up into the secret places of the town: crept the water always. Noiseless and watchful: coiled round and round it, in its many folds, like an old serpent . . .

CHARLES DICKENS

The channels (which are called in Latin *euripi* or *estuaria*, that is, pretty little armes of the Sea . . .) are very singular ornaments to the citie, through which they runne even as the veynes doe through the body of a man . . .

THOMAS CORYATE

Life on the lagoon was good for his soul as well. It crystallized
determination: it sifted out the urgencies of desires.

FREDERICK ROLFE, 'BARON CORVO'

> And see! What heroes it drew here
> To build themselves palaces and temples,
> From the rise and fall of oars in the waves.

COUNT AUGUSTUS VON PLATEN-HALLERMUNDE

Francesco Morosini

(1619–94)

A hard-earned and tender pride suffuses Francesco Morosini's account of his aquatic city. A member of one of the great patrician families, he devoted his life to fighting Venice's traditional enemies, the Turks. His naval expeditions are recorded in a beautiful sequence of paintings in the Correr Museum.

However, success was not always Morosini's lot. As 'Captain General of the Sea' he presided over the ignominious 1469 surrender of the Cretan city of Candia, which for four hundred years had been a Venetian possession. Betrayed by their French allies, the Venetians had little choice but to end their nine-year resistance to the Ottoman siege, but Morosini returned home to face trial and ostracism: Venetian commanders were usually the scapegoats for any defeat.

Fourteen years later, Morosini was restored to power, appointed *generalissimo* in yet another war against the Turks. He reconquered Attica and the Peloponnese, bringing back as booty two of the famous lions now at the Arsenale.

His own eponymous *palazzo* is to be found in Campo San Stefano (also known as Campo Francesco Morosini) and he is buried in the church of Santo Stefano. Appointed Doge in 1488, Morosini wrote a journal of the Turkish campaigns, which includes his own laudation of the city, as well as neatly explaining its geographical situation, its early history, and the organisation of the state he served so faithfully.

In the year of Christ, 421, the inhabitants of Aqulteia [sic] and Padua, though dread of the Hunns, and finding their own Cities destroy'd, betook themselves to Flight, and made themselves Masters of the Islands of the Adriatic Sea; and retiring first to the upper Shoar, now call'd the Rialto, there laid the Foundations of Venice. The City itself is seated in the inmost recess of the Adriatick Bay, containing almost Sixty Islands, at a very small distance one from another, divided by narrow Eddies running between, which a small Mount (provided by Provident Nature) defends from the Violence of the Sea. It is stor'd with convenient Rivers, which import all things as well for Delight, as for the Necessities of Mankind.

The whole City consists of three Ranks of People, the Patricians, or Gentlemen, the Citizens, and Mechanics. The Supream Power of Government is in the hands of the Patricians . . .

Upon the Front that looks toward the Shoar, stand two very vast Pillars, the one bearing the Winged Lion of St. Mark, and the other the Statue of St. Theodorus; and in the Space between, all Malefactors are Executed. The Cathedral of St. Mark is a most Sumptuous and Magnificent Structure, all of Marble. The Streets are divided with small Channels, or Canales, joined together with several Bridges, part of Wood, and part of Stone, to the Number of 440.

The Arsenal is a place every way surrounded with strong Walls, wherein Four hundred Workmen are continually employ'd in preparing Materials for the Building of Galleys, and the Reparation of the Bridges, who are every Week paid their Wages to the value of 2000 Crowns.

In a word, Venice is the Queen of all the Cities in the World, and which is more, never Subdu'd to Foraign Subjection. This is She, that has for so many Centuries of Years been the Bulwark of Christendom, against the Power of the Turks; being Marry'd to the Sea every Year, by the Ceremony of throwing a Gold Ring into the Neighbouring Ocean upon Ascension-Day. In a word, such is the strength of her Situation, such the Constitution of her Government, such the strict Observance of her Constitutions, and so exact the Fidelity of her Subjects under an easie and gentle Rule, that she may well be counted the most Renowned City in the Universe.

Francesco Sansovino

(1521–83)

Those who adopt Venice as their home often add the gloss of wonder to their love of the city. Another who sang her praises was the writer and publisher Francesco Sansovino, born in Rome. He came to Venice in 1527 and stayed there for the rest of his life. Sansovino, son of the sculptor and architect Jacopo, was ready to attribute even longevity and beauty of complexion to the health-giving 'ayre' of the watery city.

~~~

The ayre of *Venice is* exceedingly good, because it is continuallie purged with the ebbing and flowing of the tydes, carrying every six howres away with it whatsoever is corrupt or uncleane, besides the multitude of fiers dissolveth al noysome vapours, and the free scope of the windes blowing every where unhindered, maketh the ayre most sounde and holesome: besides much is attributed to the saltnes, which being by nature more hot, & lesse colde, engendreth a most equall and sweete temperature, for that strangers with great amazement do not any where beholde men more venerable and of greater age, full of flesh, straight bodyed, of goodly presence, and more vigorous constitution. But above all other thinges this is most straunge, that this aire by a speciall priveledge of nature doth agree with the complections of all such straungers, as resorte thither, of what nation, or under what climate soever they bee borne.

The Venetian Piledrivers

(Traditional)

It's a pleasurable thought that the building of Venice, as described by Morosini and Domenico Martinelli, had its musical accompaniment: the men who drove the wooden piles into the subsoil of the lagoon sang while they worked. The nineteenth-century historian, Horatio F. Brown, fortunately recorded some of their robust lyrics before they could be lost.

The foundation piles were usually made of oak. Brown observed that it was not in fact mud into which the workman drove their poles but a stratum of clay, the hardness of which varies throughout the city. Near the Frari, for example, it is softer and saturated with water, but on the Dorsoduro, as the name implies, the clay is hard as bone. Below the clay lies a deep layer of watery sand, creating a hydraulic resistance to the downward pressure of the buildings.

The effort entailed in the work of piledriving, even before the advent of steam-power, must have been incredible. These choruses with their short phrases and their thumping exclamations, wonderfully reflect the breathing rhythms of men strenuously at work.

The American poet Amy Clampitt described the Venetian piles as 'stilts for the stupendous/masquerade of history'. Some of the words below show how ancient are these refrains. The frequent mentions of the Turk hark back to the war of Candia and the Battle of Lepanto in 1571.

Up with it well,
Up to the top,
Up with it well,
Up to the summit.
Saint Joseph, he
Was an old fellow,
With his adze he,
Plane and hammer he,
Went for to make
A great ship,
All for to fight
The great Sultano,
The great Sultano,
Him of the Turks,
Those fools of Turks,
All for to get
Hold of his treasure,
All for to seize
All he had pride in . . .
Down till it finds there
All its companions:
Down in the caverns
Awful and gloomy;
Down in the caverns
Grots full of horror.
Drive we amain then,
Give it her hot then,
Give it her strong then,
Aye, let them feel it

Up to the very gates,
Gates of the arsenal,
Whence there will come forth
Vessels and ships too,
Whence there will come forth
Brigs and our schooners,
Bound, as we all know,
Bound for the battle,
Bound for to battle
E'en with the great Turk,
Aye, with the great Turk.

Ezra Pound

(1885–1972)

The American poet Ezra Pound claimed Venice as his 'magnetic centre'.

Born in Idaho and brought up near Philadelphia, he travelled in Europe after graduating from university. His first volume of poetry, *A Lume Spento*, was published in Venice in 1908, following three months spent in the city. He visited again in 1910 and 1913.

He moved to Rapallo, on Italy's Amalfi coast, in 1925, but from the 1930s onwards he spent his summers in Venice, alternately inspired and discouraged by the 'completedness' of her art and architecture.

After involving himself with the Fascist movement, Pound was granted an official audience with Mussolini in 1933. His broadcasts on behalf of the Fascists brought him notoriety, and after the war he was escorted back to the United States to be tried for treason. However, he was certified insane and sent to a mental hospital.

After his release in 1958 the poet returned to Venice where he lived six months of each year, writing on literature, music, art and economics, and translating from French, Italian, Chinese and Japanese. He lived above a bakery at San Vio and later in the Calle dei Frati, and particularly enjoyed café life on Zattere. His own poetry, much of which is informed with Venetian imagery, was acclaimed and awarded. He is also to be credited with reviving modern interest in the long-forgotten Venetian composer Vivaldi.

Pound was one of the few people honoured with a permanent grave on the cemetery island of San Michele.

A great experimenter in verse, Pound was a founding member of the Imagist movement, which sought clarity of expression through the use of precise images. 'Night Litany', a sweet and solemn hymn to the watery city, comes from an early collection, *A Quinzaine for This Yule*, published in 1909.

O Dieu, purifiez nos coeurs!
Purifiez nos coeurs!

Yea, the lines hast thou laid unto me
          in pleasant places,
And the beauty of this thy Venice
          hast thou shown unto me
Until is its loveliness become unto me
          a thing of tears.

O God, what great kindness
          have we done in times past
          and forgotten it;
That thou givest this wonder unto us,
          O God of waters?

O God of the night
          what great sorrow
Cometh unto us,
          that thou thus repayest us
Before the time of its coming?

O God of silence,
          Purifiez nos coeurs,
          Purifiez nos coeurs,
For we have seen
The glory of the shadow of the
          likeness of thine handmaid,

Yea, the glory of the shadow

of thy Beauty hath walked
Upon the shadow of the waters
In this thy Venice.
And before the holiness
Of the shadow of thy handmaid
Have I hidden mine eyes,
O God of waters.

O God of silence,
Purifiez nos coeurs,
Purifiez nos coeurs,
O God of waters,
make clean our hearts within us
And our lips to show forth thy praise.
For I have seen the
Shadow of this thy Venice
Floating upon the waters,
And thy stars

Have seen this thing out of their far courses
Have they seen this thing,
O God of waters.
Even as are thy stars
Silent unto us in their far-coursing,
Even so is mine heart
become silent within me.

(Fainter)
Purifiez nos coeurs
O God of the silence,
Purifiez nos coeurs
O God of waters.

Sean O'Faolain

(1900–91)

Though half a century old, the Irish writer Sean O'Faolain's lilting description of Venice is one of the freshest to be found. He devotes a significant part of his book, *A Summer in Italy*, to the floating city.

During his weeks wandering the *calli* of Venice – 'There is no end to this crapulous and lovely labyrinth' – O'Faolain amused himself by 'Going Corvo' – imagining the life of one of the town's more eccentric expatriates, Frederick Rolfe, the self-styled Baron Corvo, whose preposterous novel *The Desire and Pursuit of the Whole* thinly disguises his own traumas, including near-starvation, near-drowning and well-deserved social ostracism by his peers. Only the love of his faithful gondolier (a girl disguised as a boy – possibly) saves Corvo from perishing in a geyser of dangerously melodramatic self-pity.

O'Faolain gently extracts the truth from the hyperbole, combining and synthesising his own observations with Corvo's and those of many other writers, for the Irishman is nothing if not well read in the history and literature of Venice. But he wears his scholarship lightly, musing and smiling rather than lecturing or sneering, two tendencies which ruin many writings on Venice by outsiders.

This extract, the introduction to a chapter about the influence of water on the 'amphibians' who live in Venice, gives a flavour of O'Faolain's delectable writing style.

Although one may read the greater part of everything that has ever been written about Venice since its hey-day, from Goldoni to Corvo, one will never get any other feeling but that this exquisite and magnificent, this solid and squalid city conjured out of the wraiths of the sea is, for them all, still sea-wraithed, still sea-veiled as with the iridescent spray and the spume of the goddess-mouth that blew it from her conch. None of us who write of it can stop ourselves from so glorifying this creation of the past that its dawns, its days and its nights become intimations of immortality . . .

Reason, by this time flying distraught from me, perhaps to the island of San Lazzaro to study Armenian with the Mechitarists, or to study lunacy in the islet of San Servolo where the mad are housed, snarls at me over its shoulder: 'I suppose you know, dotty, what all this comes from? Water! Merely water!' And Reason is quite right and, as it so often is, it is also very silly. Merely water? One might as well say merely history. Everything Venetian has been dictated by the sea: her origin, her power, her architecture, the temper of her people, her ruin and her final transfiguration into an object of delight.

Paolo Barbaro (Ennio Gallo)

(1922–)

A native Venetian writer here furnishes a completely different take on the theme of the waterlogged city. Paolo Barbaro wrote *Venice Revealed* on returning to his home town after a number of years away, and being struck anew by her disturbing magic.

The book charts this Venetian's journey of self-knowledge, describing his traumas and misunderstandings, the surreal dramas of trying to move home or restore a house in Venice, the difficulties of reconnecting with old friends who've never left the town, the everyday fantastical realities of modern life there. Everywhere, Barbaro asks questions with a childlike persistence and is anguished, overjoyed or merely bemused by the grim or humorous answers he receives from his fellow citizens.

In this extract from *Venice Revealed* Barbaro describes an evening during *Carnevale* when an unexpected *acqua alta* begins to flood the square outside his home, where he is giving a party.

This piece vividly conveys how native Venetians react to the ever-increasing phenomenon of finding themselves islanded and stranded within their own city. Unlike foreigners, who seem to find the floods thrilling, the Venetians respond wearily, explaining the ways and means of *acqua alta* to their Swiss friend Kramer.

~~~

This is what happens at our house this evening. It's Fat Tuesday, *martedì grasso*, so we've invited over all our friends, filling the house for a change. We've even managed to persuade Kramer to come back. Some are wearing masks and costumes, others not; the resident cat studies the situation, as astounded as we are.

After a while, a masked friend I don't recognize at the moment walks up to the window overlooking the courtyard and notices that the waters are rising, welling up through the stones. The tide has decided to participate in the party, sweeping into the court-yard, gurgling and calling, right down here among the stones and geraniums. *Acqua alta* is rare at this time of year; but here it is anyway, in the dead of winter, in full *Carnevale*.

'It's been brooding for a few days now,' explains Daniela (I see that it's her now, behind the mask), 'and tonight, since it's *martedì grasso*, the tide has made up its mind.'

I telephone the weather and water information center: *1,35 sul mediomare* is the technical response. Meaning that very shortly half the city will be flooded.

Immediately our friends divide up into three groups:

1. Those who take flight swiftly and at once. It's not pleasant to have to wade home with soaked feet in winter, especially in sewer water. (So: We can kiss this evening good-bye.)
2. Those who decide to stay on until it's subsided – that is, until three in the morning. (So: They'll ruin my night.)

3. Those who hope the forecast is wrong, who remove themselves from the question entirely, who prefer not to think about it, as if it weren't happening – as if the tide didn't exist.

However, every once in a while the Daniela-mask glances restlessly out the window: 'It's risen, it's still rising.'

In other words, the evening's a bust. Even more so when someone remembers that we're more or less – give or take a month – in the *trentennale*: thirty years ago the *acqua alta* reached an incredible height and lasted two days and two nights. Since then . . .

'Since then it's never really stopped,' I say to Kramer. 'In a certain sense it continues to rise every day, and life in the city is getting worse all the time.'

'But has the tide ever gotten that high again?' he inquires.

'Not quite,' I tell him, 'but last year San Marco and other low points were submerged forty to fifty times. Our own courtyard, right here, was flooded thirty-nine times in one year. And it can always happen again. They've been working on it, on and off, for the past thirty years – but we're still in the hands of God.'

Discussion becomes more and more animated. But in only a few minutes . . . Damn! The water in the courtyard is already so high there's no getting through it; it's lapping at the stairs.

'How can it rise so fast?' asks Kramer, astonished.

'Because now,' I have to tell him, 'after they excavated those new canals for the oil tankers in the lagoon, the tide has become very swift. It sweeps into the city, the courtyard, the houses much faster than it ever did before. You have to decide right away: stay here or go now!'

'It's even worse when the water's dropping, ebbing back out,' our friends inform dear Kramer, 'from the lagoon to the sea. It does that much faster than it used to, too, and drags a lot more earth with it. So the houses "walk,"' they explain, grimacing, caught between unease and hopes of a miracle. 'Even this one, where we are right now.' We listen to the creaking of the walls as they shudder. 'They're moving up and down,' say my friends, and they're right; more cracks appear with each high and low tide.

But the moment of enchantment has arrived, down in the courtyard brimming with water. Sewer water no longer, it is (or seems) a limpid gift from the sea. Beneath the full moon laughing at us — after all, she's responsible for all this — I can clearly see from my window the paving stones of the courtyard and the blossoms of the geraniums through the crystalline water. As the minutes tick by, it splashes up stair after stair, lapping at the second floor of the house.

The full moon, a little oblique now, lights up our small, submerged world like a lamp, shedding a milky radiance on the courtyard and stairs. Then Kramer descends into the courtyard, takes off his shoes, and begins to dance. This Swiss, this citizen of Zurich, has gone suddenly crazy and is dancing in the water with the moon.

City of the Venetians

THE CHARACTER OF THE VENETIANS

First Venetians, then Christians.

The Venetians are born tired and live to sleep.

The old house never lacks a rat.
(The noble families always have their black sheep).

VENETIAN PROVERBS

The Bible speaks of the flood and of Noah and his ark . . . But the Bible passes over in silence the fact that there must have been a chronicler aboard the ark.

I am the chronicler of the ark, of the floor drowning my city, the city in the flood. I am a Venetian.

HANS HABE

There have perhaps been no more than three million true Venetians in all the history of the place: and this grand insularity, this isolation, this sense of queerness and crookedness has preserved the Venetian character uncannily, as though it was pickled like a rare intestine or mummified in lotions.

JAN MORRIS

Venice, as a city, was a foundling, floating upon the waters like Moses in his basket among the bulrushes. It was therefore obliged to be inventive, to steal and improvise.

MARY MCCARTHY

There's a strange spirit of inquisitiveness reigns among the Venetians; they know every little trifle. Perhaps in hearing a thousand frivolous things, they meet with one that may be of some concern to them.

JOSEPH SPENCE

Whether for good or ill, they are always up to something together.

JOHANN WOLFGANG VON GOETHE

Those Pantaloons!

SEVENTEENTH-CENTURY FRENCH AMBASSADOR

They were the first to have the sense of luxury, to appreciate the refinements of life, the first to delight in sumptuous houses and tissues, in the splendour of gems and the sheen of pearls.

CHARLES YRIARTE

. . . it resembles a garden transplanted with the flower of Italian nobility.

DOMENICO MARTINELLI

There was enough innovation during the Renaissance to last another thousand years or so. Ancestral inventiveness suffices here . . .

MARLENA DE BLASI

At present a much-used form of address to any gentleman in the city is 'Your Magnificence'.

MARINO SANUDO

In Venice the mildness of the climate, which encourages sensuality, the frequent sirocco, the moist airs, all contribute to make the blood run languid in the veins, and loosen the muscles and render them unfit for daily strenuous toil . . . But this lack of firmness in the body is, as frequently happens, accompanied by a remarkable mobility of nerves.

POMPEO MOLMENTI

With so many creatures who seem like roses
It is a place marked out by God . . .

ANDREA CALMO

A lord is born to the world.

VENETIAN SAYING, when a native child is born

William S. Rose

(1775–1843)

One of the great genteel Grand Tourists, the Englishman William Rose kept a correspondence with the Whig historian Henry Hallam about the state of Italy after Napoleon. He visited Venice in 1817 and his letters about the town are richly informative on a wide variety of subjects, including music, poetry, architecture and history.

In this extract he explains how he was forced to cast aside his grim presuppositions about the Venetians, finding them affectionate, open and spontaneous, where he had expected to see the city full of spies and divisions, and thoroughly 'depressed under the iron crown of France and the leaden sceptre of Austria'.

In fact, the only division he found was the traditional one between the Castellani and the Nicolotti, the two excitable tribes of working-class Venice.

(I except the case of the *Castelani* and the *Nicoloti*,) but am ready to maintain that I never visited any country, where the people seemed equally linked in love. You cannot walk the town for a day without being struck by this universal spirit of kindness. The young man, who is perhaps loaded with a burden, if he desires an old man to make way for him, addresses him by the title of *father*, the old man answers him with that of *son*, and you hear continually '*caro pare*' and '*caro fio*' from the mouth of the lowest of the mob. Your servant calls the kitchen-maid his sister, and she hails him as her brother. The Venetians really give you the idea of being members of one great family. It is true that throughout Italy you may observe the inhabitants of every petty city hang together more than in any other country, a consequence undoubtedly of their affections being centered within a narrow focus: But this fact is peculiarly remarkable in Venice.

Charles de Brosses
(1709–77)

The city has never opened herself freely to outsiders, and the French writer and politician Charles de Brosses here paints a still recognisable picture of Venetian hospitality.

De Brosses's passion for the Latin classics inspired him to travel to the classical world. His resulting *Letters from Italy* by far eclipsed in popularity his more serious works on navigation, etymology and history. The first edition of *Letters* appeared in 1839 and the good-humoured malice and fun of its observations quickly won it an appreciative audience.

I find it more difficult to describe the private life of Venice, as strangers are not easily admitted into the social part of Venetian life. The gentry come in the evening to the cafés, where they meet us, and are most sociable and pleasant; but as to asking us to come to their houses, that is quite another pair of shoes. Besides, there are but few houses here in which the hosts receive, and when they do their receptions are neither amusing nor attractive to a stranger. One has not even the resource of card-playing, for to know the cards we should have to be exceedingly clever, since they are neither like ours in their fashion nor do they bear the same names. The Venetians, with all their show and their palaver, do not understand the first rudiments of hospitality. I have looked in sometimes at the conversazione of the Marchesa Foscarini, who lives in a superb palace; she is a most gracious dame, but for refreshments we were offered at three o'clock (that is to say, at eleven o'clock P.M. by our time), by twenty varlets, a large pumpkin, cut into quarters, on a silver dish, which they call here a water-melon — a most loathsome vegetable. This is followed by piles of silver plates; everyone seizes a portion, takes therewith a little cup of coffee, and returns home with an empty stomach to have supper at midnight . . .

You must expect, when on your travels, to satisfy the eyes, but to leave the heart empty — to get as much amusement and novelty as possible, but no social happiness.

Fabio Mutinelli

(19th century)

A distinguished man of letters, Fabio Mutinelli was appointed to manage the state archives in 1847 and it was he who persuaded the Austrians not to pillage the Venetian state papers they coveted for their own museums.

Mutinelli made good use of the materials he had conserved, producing many volumes of historical works about the city.

In his *Del costume veneziano* (1831), he looks beneath outer appearances to distil some truths about his fellow citizens.

According to what has been asserted by highly esteemed historians, who wrote in various centuries, Venetian people were tall, with blonde hair, but prone to go white early in their life although both sexes would live very long lives . . . All women enjoy beautiful features in different ways, and they have a way of talking which is, as Denina pointed out, very suitable to express passion, and have sweet and pleasant manners. Men have an easy intelligence and a big heart and dress simply. They are generous with the Church, and do not waste their time. They have composed manners and serious voices even when exchanging views in their homes, and behave and speak in a courteous way. It is common knowledge that they only pretend to forgive, and that they are accustomed to love without much discrimination, consuming themselves once for one woman and soon after for another, and that they do not know any constancy in love.

Margaret Oliphant
(1828–97)

The Edinburgh-born novelist Mrs Oliphant is best known for her family sagas and romantic dramas such as *The Primrose Path* (1878). But a penetrating scholarship shines through her non-fiction tome, *The Makers of Venice: Doges, Conquerors, Painters and Men of Letters*, published in 1887.

In this extract, Mrs Oliphant points out the very remarkable lack of famous individual personalities in Venice compared to the number of well-known Florentines who had cast their particular shadows on the past. Even Byron, she explains, could find only the tragic Doges Foscari and Faliero as material for his Venetian dramas.

~~~

After the bewitchment of the first vision, a chill falls upon the inquirer. Where is the poet, where the prophet, the princes, the scholars, the men whom, could we see, we should recognise wherever we met them, with whom the whole world is acquainted? They are not here. In the sunshine of the Piazza, in the glorious gloom of San Marco, in the great council-chambers and offices of state, once so full of busy statesmen, and great interests, there is scarcely a figure recognisable of all, to be met with in the spirit – no one whom we look for as we walk, whose individual footsteps are traceable wherever we turn. Instead of the men who made her what she is, who ruled her with so high a hand, who filled her archives with the most detailed narratives, and gleaned throughout the world every particular of universal history which could enlighten and guide her, we find everywhere the great image – an idealisation more wonderful than any in poetry – of Venice herself, the crowned and reigning city, the centre of all their aspirations, the mistress of their affections, for whom those haughty patricians of an older day, with a proud self-abnegation which has no humility or sacrifice in it, effaced themselves, thinking of nothing but her glory. It is a singular tribute to pay to any race, especially to a race so strong, so full of life and energy, loving power, luxury, and pleasantness as few other races have done; yet it is true.

Horatio F. Brown

(1854–1926)

Not to be confused with the other famous expatriate Rawdon Lubbock Brown, the Englishman Horatio F. Brown also lived in Venice for many years, from 1879, and devoted himself to studying the city.

Brown delved into many subjects too esoteric for more conventional researchers, undertaking among other things a serious study of the early printing industry, translating popular poetry, and researching the *osele*, commemorative silver pieces struck by each Doge.

Brown's 1884 publication, *Life on the Lagoons*, was described by the *Whitehall Review* as 'delightful, gossipy, yet learned'. Robert Louis Stevenson, on his sickbed, loved it so much that he dashed off a quick poem in its praise.

In this extract from *Life on the Lagoons* (which he dedicated to his gondolier Antonio Salin), Brown explains some of the picturesque traditions and superstitions surrounding childbirth in Venice.

As soon as the birth of his godchild, or *fiozzo*, is announced, the *compare* must send to the mother a pound of meat, a fowl, and two eggs in a box. Then the day for the baptism is settled. The baby is swathed in bands of white linen; round its neck is fastened a charm; and all over its swaddled feet are pinned half moons, hearts, charms, and medals of silver, to keep away the witch Pagana, who is especially on the look-out for unbaptized infants. The baby is laid on a long shallow tray and covered over by a large glass case, which has blue silk curtains round the outside. In this way the *creatura*, as everybody calls it, is carried to church by the midwife, accompanied by its father and its *santolo*, or godfather. Out of three names the *santolo* has the right to bestow two, and one is given by the Church. The Church always gives the same names, John for boys, and Mary for girls; so every Venetian is either John or Mary, the reason being that those who bear these names are less exposed to the power of the witches. If the *santolo* stumbles in saying the Creed, then the child that is being baptized will be liable to see ghosts . . .

The ghosts themselves, who have the power 'to visit the glimpses of the moon,' are also limited. They are those spirits who are in purgatory; those in heaven or in hell are barred from all appearance on the earth. These limitations reduce Venetian ghosts and ghost stories to very scanty numbers. Yet the dread of ghosts is lively, and the Venetians are scrupulous never to say anything that may offend the dead. The belief prevails that on the vigil of All Souls' the dead leave their graves in the island of San Michele and cross the lagoon to the city. They pass in procession through every street, and as each ghost arrives at his former home, he enters and seats himself, unseen, by the kitchen fire. It is of the worst possible luck for one who has the power to see ghosts to be looking out of his window when the ghostly train goes by.

The belief in witches is still alive in Venice though hidden away, and chiefly confined to women. In most quarters of the city there are certain families who have the reputation of being hereditary witches; and it is not uncommon for those who have been robbed, or crossed in love, or have other cause for hatred, to consult these witches to the undoing of their enemy.

October is the witches' favourite month; and on Thursday nights they comb their hair and preen themselves, and Friday is their field-day. It is only on Christmas-eve that new witches can be made. The witches assemble in the house of their chief; the novice is introduced and placed before a looking-glass; then three words, which witches only know, summons the demon and the pact is made and signed. Once a witch always a witch. No witch can die while pictures of the saints are on the wall. The demon draws them away, but they cannot go until the saints are turned with their face to the wall, and then they die in peace. Their chief delight is to make long journeys between midnight and cockcrow. They unchain the gondolas and put to sea; and Alexandria is their favourite destination.

Children may be spellbound by a look, by a kiss, by fruit and sweetmeats, by bread and wine. But the most effective and terrible way is this: the witch procures the hair of the person to be bewitched, and with this hair she binds a scorpion and buries it in a pot full of sand, which must be covered with earth, and the spell pronounced; as the scorpion slowly dies so the bewitched likewise.

The Merchant City

PICTURESQUE TRADES

Money is our second blood.

Before acquiring, you'd better acquire some money.

With truth and lies, you sell the merchandise.

Money makes money and lice make lice.

When there's no money you should spend, and when there is some, you should save.

A man without money is a corpse that walks.

VENETIAN PROVERBS

And in this city nothing grows, yet whatever you want can be found in abundance.

MARINO SANUDO

To Venice come the oils of Apulia, the saffrons of the Abruzzo, the malmseys of Crete, the raisins of Zante, the cinnamon and pepper of the Indies, the carpets of Alexandria, the sugar of Cyprus, the dates of Palestine, the silk, wax and ashes of Syria, the cordovans of the Morea . . . the caviar of Caffa.

GIOVANNI BOTERO

She is still gay, flourishing and fresh, and flowing with all kinds of bravery and delight, which may be had at cheap rates . . .

JAMES HOWELL

Venice seems to have itself a licence to rip off everyone, even Venetians.

MATT FREI

The shopkeepers and gondoliers, the beggars and the models, depend upon it for a living; they are the custodians and the ushers of the great museum – they are even themselves to a certain extent the objects on exhibition.

HENRY JAMES

The Fair of the Sensa is a beautiful egg
Pierced by four doors
Through which everyone passes,
Nobles, rich, poor and scoundrels,
Gentlemen, pawns,
Greatcoats and whores,
Inside and out it is well stocked
By the craving for rich and
Beautiful things.

DON ANTONIO DALLA ROVERE,
on Bernardino Maccaruzzi's circular set for the
annual fair in San Marco

The articles best worth purchasing at Venice are gold chains, seals, &c., sold by weight, according to the price of gold – necklaces, and other personal ornaments, made with very small beads of various colours – wax candles – Mocha coffee – chocolate – books and maps.

From *Information and Directions for Travellers
on the Continent*, 1824, MARIANA STARKE

I wrote you a long [letter] from Venice but the laudable love of gain (*buscare* as they call it – i.e. gaining their livelihood) which burns with zealous heat in the breast of every Italian caused the hotel keeper to charge the postage & to throw the letter in the fire together with several others.

MARY SHELLEY

Good morning to the Day; and, next, my Gold:

From *Volpone*, 1607, BEN JONSON (spoken by the
Venetian title character)

Pompeo Molmenti

(1852–1928)

The written past of Venice would be sadly lacking in panache without the works of Pompeo Molmenti, the energetic Venetian lawyer and great professor of history. Among his many books, the key work is probably the acclaimed classic, the monumental *La storia di Venezia nella vita privata dalle origini alla caduta della Repubblica* (Venice: Its Individual Growth from the Earliest Beginnings to the Fall of the Republic).

In spite of his success, the indefatigable Molmenti never ceased excavating the archives for new material. He was ahead of his time in maintaining that historical works, no matter how learned, should be vivified with facsimiles of documents from the archives and illustrations from art.

In this extract, Molmenti describes one of the most notorious trades of the merchant city – that in human flesh. He recounts how the Venetians even opened a slave market in Rome, transporting there a large cargo destined for servitude among the Saracens. Pope Zaccaria, horrified at the thought of Christians being sold into pagan slavery, bought and liberated the entire consignment. Several laws were passed against the slave-traders, but to no avail. Between 1393 and 1491 there are records of 150 sales of young slaves in Venice.

The iniquitous traffic in slaves was also a source of gain to Venice. It flourished up to the eighth century. Slaves, for the most part Tartars, Russians, Saracens, Mingrelians, Bosniacs, Greeks, *de genere avogassorium*, – that is, Circassians, – *de genere alanorum* (Teutons), were purchased from Slav or Saracenic pirates, and were resold – in spite of the *graves poenas contrafacientibus* recorded by Andrea Dandolo – at public auction both at San Giorgio and at Rialto. A woman, whether Circassian, Georgian, or from those parts, if twelve, fourteen, or sixteen years of age and certified *sane ed integre dei loro membri occulti e manifesti*, young boys, and grown men were sold, in the fourteenth century, for prices which ranged from sixteen golden ducats, equal to about 322, to eighty-seven ducats, equal to 2093 ducats. In the archives at Venice there are entire volumes containing nothing but deeds relating to the sale and purchase, exchange, cession, and donation of slaves. These documents go back as far as the twelfth century and it is curious to note that some were drawn up by notaries who were actually priests, in defiance of the State, of Popes, and of councils.

Pietro Casola

(1427–1507)

'The soul's Rialto hath its merchandise,' Elizabeth Barrett Browning would observe after her visit to the city. The more spiritual traveller to Venice has always been bemused by the flaunting materialism of the city, and none more so than the Milanese Canon Pietro Casola.

In 1490 Casola published an Ambrosian breviary, later re-issued in the smaller octavo format for the use of travelling priests. No doubt tucking one of his own volumes into his trunk, Casola set off on a pilgrimage to Jerusalem, arriving in Venice on 20 May.

As usual, the pilgrim galley to Jaffa was delayed: a cunning Venetian device to keep the tourists shopping and expensively accommodated while they waited, usually until just after the great fair of the *Sensa*. Casola threw himself into industrious tourism.

The beauty of the city and the splendour of the palaces and churches so much overwhelmed him that he struggled to find enough superlatives, not just for Venice but for her magnificently attired inhabitants.

In this extract he describes the opulence of the merchandise to be found at Rialto.

Something may be said about the quantity of merchandise in the said city, although not nearly the whole truth, because it is inestimable. Indeed it seems as if all the world flocks there, and that human beings have concentrated there all their force for trading. I was taken to see various warehouses, beginning with that of the Germans – which it appears to me would by itself suffice to supply all Italy with the goods that come and go – and so many others that it may be said that they are innumerable. I see that the special products for which other cities are famous are all to be found there, and that what is sold elsewhere by the pound and the ounce is sold there by canthari and sacks of a moggio each. And who could count the many shops so well furnished that they also seem warehouses, with so many cloths of every make – tapestry, brocades and hangings of every design, carpets of every sort, camlets of every colour and texture, silks of every kind; and so many warehouses full of spices, groceries and drugs, and so much beautiful white wax! These things stupefy the beholder, and cannot be fully described to those who have not seen them. Though I wished to see everything, I saw only a part, and even that by forcing myself to see all I could.

William Thomas

(1507–54)

The first English travel book on Italy was written in 1549 by the colourful Welshman William Thomas.

Educated at Oxford, Thomas enjoyed success in his career as a civil servant, but was suddenly plunged into trauma at the age of forty when he became a fugitive, decamping to Venice with some monies belonging to his patron Sir Anthony Browne. The English diplomatic agent in Venice had Thomas arrested and the stolen letters of exchange were forcibly recovered. Apparently Thomas showed great remorse for his actions, which had been brought on by an inveterate addiction to gambling. He was pardoned by the Privy Council, but did not return home immediately.

During some three years in Italy he travelled widely, studying the language and culture. The result was *The History of Italy* in 1549 and *Principal Rules of the Italian Grammar* the following year. Both books were quickly reprinted.

The History of Italy, a vivid and scholarly work, makes clear the fact that, although Henry VIII had dissolved the links with the Church of Rome, for educated Britons the cultural attractions of Italy had never waned. Thomas considered Italy to be the most civilised nation in the world, and this view marked the beginning of the English admiration for Italy that became a passion for the Elizabethans and has lasted through the centuries.

While the author's views flourished, Thomas himself suffered an untimely end. He had returned to England, where he was appointed tutor to the new young King Edward VI, but he later joined the rebellion against Queen Mary's marriage to the King of Spain, and was arrested and hanged at Tyburn in February 1554.

In this extract from *The History of Italy* Thomas describes the rampant greed of the Venetian state that allowed nothing to be traded at Rialto without taking a tariff.

As I have been credibly informed by some gentlemen Venetians that have had to do therein, they levy of their subjects little less than four millions of gold by the year, which (after our old reckoning) amounted to the sum of ten hundred thousand pounds sterling – a thing rather to be wondered at than believed, considering they raise it not upon lands but upon customs, after so extreme a sort that it would make any honest heart sorrowful to hear it. For there is not a grain of corn, a spoonful of wine, a corn of salt, egg, bird, beast, fowl, or fish bought or sold that payeth not a certain custom. And in Venice specially, the customer's part in many things is more than the owner's. And if anything be taken by the way uncustomed, be it merchandise or other, never so great or small, it is forfeited. For those customers keep such a sort of prollers [prowlers] to search all things as they come to and fro that I think Cerberus was never so greedy at the gates of hell as they be in the channels about Venice. And though they in searching a boat find no forfeiture, yet will they not depart without drinking money. And many times the meanest laborer or craftsman throughout all their dominion payeth a rate for the poll by the month. Insomuch that a Candiot, my friend (one that had dwelled in Constantinople), sware to me by his faith the Christians lived a great deal better under the Turk than under the Venetians.

Zuane di Andrea Zane

(16th century)

Life in the merchant city was not always as balmy as the tourists painted it. Venetian traders were vulnerable to reverses of fortune, as shown by this sad list of vicissitudes suffered by the Zane family.

In July 1550, when Zuane di Andrea Zane and his brothers petitioned for aid after a six-year run of truly evil fortune, the Senate was clearly moved by this appeal and granted the Zane brothers pensions of ten ducats a month each.

The Prince Doria described in the petition is Andrea Doria, first citizen of Genoa, Prince of Melfi and admiral in the French fleet, at that time allied to Venice in the wars against the Turk.

We will not count among our losses the damage inflicted by the Rialto fire, nor what the sea took from us at that time, nor yet the large sums borne away by debtors, nor yet the marriage portions of our three sisters and a natural daughter of the late Missier Maphio our brother – although these things amount to a great deal of money. We will speak only of the disasters which have overtaken us since the year 1524. In April of that year we sent a ship of 1300 butts to England, and our brother Beneto was aboard it, armed with the most ample safe-conduct from the Most Christian King [of France]. On its return voyage from England in May this ship was attacked off Cádiz by a French captain named Gioan Fiorin and captured after a lengthy fight. In defending himself our brother received seventeen wounds, and, being so dreadfully torn and mutilated, he was taken prisoner. It was not God's will that he should die then, but ill fortune kept a far worse fate in store for him. Upon that ship were our wools, kerseys, cloths and tin, and a large sum in cash to buy salt at Ibiza if other business should be lacking – so that, taking account of the ship itself, equipped as it was with guns and with everything else necessary to sailing such seas and encountering so many different peoples, and taking account too of our own merchandise and money, the loss amounted to over 22,000 ducats. We say nothing of the cargo of sugar we were due to take on in Cádiz and the profit expected from the merchandise and from various freight charges of more than 8000 ducats, and there was a clear loss of another 11,000 ducats and more – a thing one shudders even to hear about, let alone suffer oneself . . .

Never ceasing to trade in order to live and earn our living, we kept in the Morea our brother Missier Alvise as our man of business in the whole of that region, and he sent to Venice great quantities of corn (in some years more than 30,000 stara), and many oak-galls [*valonie*], which greatly swelled the customs revenue, and various other goods which proved to be of great profit and benefit to this city. In these activities we sustained several very severe losses. It happened that Prince Doria went with the imperial fleet to take Coron, and on his return he took great plunder at Patras in the Gulf of Lepanto, and it fell to us to have our marine warehouses pillaged. In these we had great quantities of raisins, not yet stored in sacks or barrels, and we also had wrought copper and quantities of soap, and they robbed us of almost everything. And, because we saved our house at Patras by a gift of 400 gold ducats to a captain of foot soldiers, the Turks began to suspect us of being in league with Prince Doria. Fearful of the danger, our brother went off by himself to Zante, leaving our merchandise and credits in the hands of agents. One of these, Marco Cucholino, entered the Gulf to lade a ship of ours with corn, and on account of this suspicion he was taken from our ship and for no good reason beheaded by Huctu Bey, commander of the [Turkish] fleet which was then at Lepanto, and they robbed him of a hoard of 350 gold ducats belonging to us, which he had taken with him to provide for his release, and many other things as well, and they sent the ship back empty, to our own great loss.

War with the Turks then followed. Before this happened we sent Missier Piero Marcello, our nephew, to take charge of our affairs, and from the very start he suffered great trouble and loss. On the outbreak of war, his house and stores were pillaged and everything removed, including the books and documents which recorded our great credits with many persons in that land, and we were despoiled and deprived of everything, and our nephew enslaved and clapped in irons, and he spent almost four years in that harsh servitude between Patras and Constantinople. Hence our brother [Alvise], seeing that he and all of us were ruined and without the means of recovery, and in debt to the extent of 5000 ducats and more, was overcome by grief and melancholy, and so died . . .

James Howell

(c. 1594–1666)

For a thousand years the merchant city has traded heavily on her most delicate export: glass. The oldest document relating to the glass industry is from 1292 – a decree of the Grand Council to demolish the furnaces at Rialto and remove them to the island of Murano, in order to reduce the loss of life and property through fire. On Murano the glassblowers flourished, the secrets of their manufacture protected by law.

This description of the glassworks at Murano was written by the Englishman James Howell, who came to Venice in 1621 and quickly fell almost carnally in love with the place: 'I protest unto you at my first landing I was for some days ravished with the high beauty of this maid . . .'

He was fascinated by the lustrous perfection of Murano's glass-wares, asserting that 'some impute it to the quality of the circumambient air that hangs over the place, which is purified and attenuated by the concurrence of so many fires that are in those furnaces day and night'.

The art of glass-making here is very highly valued; for, whosoever be of that profession are gentlemen *ipso facto*, and it is not without reason; it being a rare kind of knowledge and chemistry to transmute dust and sand (for they are the only main ingredients) to such a diaphanous pellucid dainty body as you see a crystal glass is, which hath this property above gold or silver or any other mineral, to admit no poison; as also that it never wastes or loses a whit of its first weight, though you use it never so long. When I saw so many sorts of curious glasses made here I thought upon the compliment which a gentleman put upon a lady in England, who having five or six comely daughters, said he never saw in his life such a dainty cupboard of crystal glasses; the compliment proceeds, it seems, from a saying they have here, 'That the first handsome woman that ever was made, was made of Venice glass,' which implies beauty, but brittleness with all (and Venice is not unfurnished with some of that mould, for no place abounds more with lasses and glasses) . . .

Mary Braddon

(1837–1915)

Mary Braddon was born in London, was educated privately, and began writing at an early age. Her novel *Lady Audley's Secret*, published in 1862, was an immediate best-seller, with nearly a million copies printed.

Her novel *The Venetians*, published in 1892, tells the tale of the Englishman Vansittart who, captivated by the Venetian temptress Fiordelisa, kills her insufferable 'protector' in a brawl. In this extract Braddon describes in delicious detail all the irresistible frippery set out for the unwary shopper in Venice.

Théophile Gautier described similar temptations in 1850: 'The Frezzeria is one of the most animated streets of the city . . . It is in this street chiefly that are to be found the goldsmiths who manufacture those delicate little golden chains as tenuous as hairs, which are called *jaserons* . . .'

Mary McCarthy has observed tartly that in modern times 'the Venetian crafts have become sideshows'. Today it seems that every month one more traditional shop closes, only to reopen as yet another mask and glass emporium, stocked with products whose provenance is as likely to be the Far East or Eastern Europe as Venice herself. But for the dedicated shopper there are still extraordinary purchases to be made of products unique to Venice.

At the Atelier Rolando Segalin in Calle Fuseri, they can make a customised pair of exquisite gondola-shaped shoes. Or at Livio de Marchi in San Samuele one can buy wooden *trompe l'oeil* objects from the man who recently carved a life-size wooden Volkswagen and drove it up the Grand Canal. And there is the gentle and elegant Alberto Valese, in San Stefano, who makes unique marbled papers, with tulips, trees and fish worked subtly into the stippled backgrounds. To create his effects, he uses seaweed, gelatine and egg-tempera paints weighted with different amounts of oxgall: techniques developed after much research in Turkey. Marbling originated in Japan and spread to Persia and finally, in the sixteenth century, to Western Europe. But nowhere does the watermarked paper seem more appropriate than in this watermarked city.

The touters were touting at the shop doors, with that smiling persistence which makes the *Procuratie Vecchie* odious, and recalls Cranbourne Alley in the dark ages. Lisa made a dead stop before a shop where gaudy wooden negroes, garish with crude colour and much gilding, were grilling in the glare of the gas. It was a kind of bazaar, half Venetian, half Moorish, and one window was full of bead necklaces and barbaric jewels. At these Lisa looked with such childish longing eyes that Vansittart would have been hard as a stone if he had not suggested making a selection from that sparkling display of rainbow glass and enamel.

The spider at the door was entreating the flies to go into his web, a young Venetian with great, smiling black eyes and a Jewish nose – a lineal descendant of Jessica, perhaps – a very agreeable young spider, entreating the Signora and Signorina to go in and look about them. There would be no necessity for them to buy. 'To look costs nothing.'

They all three went in. Fiordelisa fastened upon a tray of jewels, and lost herself in a bewilderment as to which of all those earrings, brooches, and necklaces she most desired. Vansittart was interested in the Moorish things – the bronze cups, the gold and scarlet slippers, the embroidered curtains, and, most of all, the daggers, of which there were many curious shapes, in purple-gleaming Damascus steel.

While Fiordelisa and her aunt were choosing brooches and necklaces – necklaces which by a double twist became bracelets – Vansittart was cheapening daggers, and, as a young man of ample means, ended by buying the dearest and perhaps the best, a really serviceable knife, in a red velvet sheath.

He paid for as many things as Lisa cared to choose; for a bead necklace and an enamel brooch; for a square of gold-striped gauze to twist about her head and shoulders; for a dainty little pair of Moorish shoes which might admit Lisa's toes, but which would certainly leave the major part of her substantial foot out in the cold; for a gilded casket to hold her jewels – for a fan – for a gilt thimble – and for a little set of Algerian coffee-cups for her aunt.

City Afloat

GONDOLAS AND GONDOLIERS

A clean boat is not an earner.

If you want a big noise,
go to where the women and the boatmen are.

Better to drown yourself in a big sea
(i.e. do it in style).

VENETIAN PROVERBS

. . . nobody ever thinks of walking in Venice. It is poor policy to do so.

From *COOK'S HANDBOOK*, 1875

The gondola is a natural production of Venice, an animated being having its special and local life, a kind of fish which can only subsist in the water of a canal . . . The city is a Madrepore of which the gondola is the mollusc.

THÉOPHILE GAUTIER

How daintily it sits upon the water! How like a knowing swan it bends its head . . .

FRANCIS HOPKINSON SMITH

Have you swam in a gondola? . . . If you have not, there is a wide difference between us.

FRANCES TROLLOPE

Ah,
Life should be as the gondola!

ARTHUR HUGH CLOUGH

For my part, as I have said before, I should wish God to change me into a gondola when I die, or if that is considered beyond my deserts, into one of its oars or a cleaning rag. A sponge would be still more appropriate.

PIETRO ARETINO

It would be difficult to discover any greater provocative to utter idling . . . That was surely a work of supererogation which the Venetian doctor undertook when he addressed a treatise to his English friend upon the art of sitting in a gondola. The art is all too easy to learn; it consists in yielding yourself to the cushions and the boat.

HORATIO F. BROWN

The gondola waits at the wave-washed steps, and if you are wise you will take your place beside a discriminating companion. Such a companion in Venice should of course be of the sex that discriminates most finely. An intelligent woman who knows her Venice seems doubly intelligent, and it makes no woman's perceptions less keen to be aware that she can't help looking graceful as she is borne over the waves.

HENRY JAMES

Had tiresome little attack of sickness after dinner, brought on, it seemed to me, by intense disgust at gondolier's horrible Santa Lucia done twice over.

JOHN RUSKIN

And Toni is paying attention only
To plying his oar.
He does not look, he does not hear,
He is a man of stucco.
He is a fool.
He just keeps rowing . . .

PIETRO BURATTI

Charles de Brosses

(1709–77)

Like all travellers of his time, de Brosses first came to Venice by water. He made his way from Padua down the Brenta Canal on the Bucentaure, 'but a very small child of the true Bucentaure [the Doge's ceremonial boat], but it is the prettiest little infant in the world'. He describes the luxury of the cabin, hung with Venetian brocade, equipped with leather chairs and well supplied with viands and Canary wine. He was so comfortable, gazing on the passing panorama of the Venetian nobles' country villas, that he had almost no wish to reach his journey's end.

Of course, on arriving in Venice and transferring to a gondola, he was literally transported into ecstasies. De Brosses' rhapsody on his floating carriage is one of the best to be found and any modern-day traveller would recognise the sensations, physical and visual, that he describes: apart from the *felze* or cabin, the sinuous black boats of his day were exactly the same as the modern ones. Excessive decoration of the noblemen's boats had led to the introduction of a sumptuary law in 1633 decreeing that every gondola should be painted black. To this day it is rare to see a gondola of any other colour.

~~~

No carriage in the world can equal a gondola in comfort. It reminds me in its shapes of a shark; there is room for two people at the end of the boat, and for others on either side, and you can open or shut the little cabin in the centre as you please. The prow is armed with a large bit of iron shaped like the neck of a stork, garnished with six large teeth — this helps to steady the boat. The entire boat is painted black and is varnished, and is furnished with black velvet and cloth, and with leather cushions of the same hue. Not even the greatest nobles are allowed any other decorations, nor are theirs different from those of the humblest individual; so that one cannot guess who is inside a closed gondola. One sits within as in one's own room, in which one can read, write, talk, make love, eat, drink, &c., while making a round of visits in the town. Two men of proved fidelity are in front; another behind conducts the vessel, without being able to see you if you do not wish to be seen. I do not expect to feel comfortable again in a carriage after having tried this mode of progression. I was told that there was never the crush with gondolas that one has with one's carriage in Paris; on the contrary, nothing is more frequent, especially in the narrow canals and under the bridges; but they certainly do not last long.

Tita Merati

(18th century)

While de Brosses waxed lyrical about the sixty thousand souls said to make their living by their oars, either as gondoliers or sailors, the Venetians themselves saw their aquatic professions in a far more practical light.

Giambattista ('Tita') Merati served as a Benedictine abate on the island of San Giorgio. For his literary works, he used the anagrammatical pseudonym Tati Remita. His *Saggi Metrici* includes poems on such subjects as the wise man who, despite all his philosophies, trembles like a coward in the face of death, the perfumed, shaven man who proves ineffectual in his duties, and the sophisticated Venetian who perishes from boredom in the countryside.

The following sonnet, called 'The True Venetian Boatman', is considered one of his best, illustrating the honest creed of the boatmen of Venice. Today it seems just as appropriate to the *motoscafisti* who ply the canals in their James Bond-style water taxis, their *telefonini* clamped to their improbably tanned ears.

Know the ways of the water, live within your means,
Row straight, without thrashing the waves,
Moor not in the narrow canals,
Scuffle not with other boats, rather pull back;
    Count only men of honour among your friends;
Greet all whom you pass in the street,
Take care of yourself, threaten no one
Without reason, provoke nothing;
    Treat your wife kindly, and be sure that
Your boat does not become your family's religion,
Be discreet, don't take advantage of idiots;
    Do not make the tavern your kitchen,
Nor your bank the Ghetto, don't let the lottery feed on you.
This is the true boatman. Look for him!

Antonio Lamberti

(1757–1832)

Lamberti, the ultimate portraitist of voluptuous eighteenth-century Venice, could trace his ancestry back to the original citizenry of the town. Although not particularly handsome, Lamberti seems to have had an attractive personality. Genial, musical, socially accomplished and universally liked by women, he was the friend of many doctors, poets and scholars. He was also popular among the cultured elements of the Venetian nobility. He was a charming performer of pieces of his own composition and an acute mimic. He turned the Venetian dialect to good advantage in his work, careful to use it not as mere pastiche but when and where it was appropriate and natural.

Lamberti's 'La Biondina in Gondoleta' is the song any tourist to Venice is most likely to hear floating across the Grand Canal. In fact 'La Biondina' is a 'song à clef' about the vivacious aristocrat Marina Quirini Benzona, described as being of a carnation complexion, golden hair and azure eyes. She was much admired by Lord Byron, Stendhal and others. She kept a *conversazione*, or literary salon, rivalled only by that of the Countess Albrizzi, and was visited as a curiosity by all upmarket tourists.

Marina Benzona was notorious for the fact that on the fall of the Republic in 1797, she was to be seen dancing around the 'liberty tree' in San Marco, wearing an 'Athenian petticoat' split to the thigh. She died in old age, monstrously fat, having acquired another less flattering nickname: '*El Fumeto*'. Translated as 'The

Steaming Lady', this referred to her penchant for going about in winter with lumps of hot polenta between her breasts.

Frances, Lady Shelley, visited La Benzona when she was sixty years of age and her charms, though not her lively mind, had somewhat decomposed. Lady Shelley observed tartly that, in terms of feminine beauty, it was 'better to be a has-been than a never-was'.

Lamberti's verses for 'La Biondina' (The little blonde lady) conjure a kinder period in La Benzona's life.

The other night I took
A little blonde lady in my gondola,
Such was her pleasure that the girl
Fell suddenly asleep.

She was sleeping leaning on her arm.
I woke her up every now and then,
But the boat was rocking her,
And she kept falling asleep once more.

In the sky, the moon was half hidden
Between the clouds,
The lagoon was very calm
And the wind was very soft.

Just a tiny breeze
Was blowing through her hair,
And lifting the veil from her bodice
So that her breast was no longer hidden.

Contemplating very carefully
The features of my love
That face so smooth
That mouth and that breast,

I felt in my heart
An ardour, a confusion,
An intensity of happiness
That I could never explain.

The Hunchback Song
(Traditional)

Tourists believe that the songs of the gondoliers are largely local confections. This is not true. Most of them, including the inescapable 'O Sole Mio', hail from Naples, home of the love-dirge.

The song extracted below is known all over Italy: a Venetian version has local variations in which, for example, two hunchbacks duel at two o'clock in the morning on the Rialto. It can sometimes be heard, sung to a rollicking rhythm by the gondoliers, but it is also a song very popular at celebrations, particularly when the wine has been flowing.

This translation is very literal, failing to do justice to the Venetian, but the difficulties of attempting to do so are similar to those of translating cockney: the essence of the humour tends to evaporate.

His father's a hunchback
His mother's a hunchback
Even the kid of his sister's a hunchback
Everyone has their little hump
That's the hunchback fam-i-ly!

And at the wedding,
There's the choir
And all of them hunchbacks, too!
All of them, hunchbacks too
That's the hunchback fam-il-y!

And nine months later
There's a beautiful baby
Also with his little hump
Also with his little hump —
That's the hunchback fam-il-y!

And when it came that the hunchback died
They had a fine coffin made for him,
And even that had its little hump
Even that had its little hump
That's the hunchback fam-il-y!

Hunchbacks sit down!
On the big chair!
Sabion!

Countess Giustina Renier Michiel

(1755–1832)

Giustina Renier Michiel was the niece of the Doge Paolo Venier who scandalously married a Greek dancing girl he had met in Constantinople. So Giustina took the role of his official consort, the *Dosetta* or *Dogaressa*, and performed all the necessary duties from 1779 till 1788.

She married very young. A charming domestic portrait of the Michiel family by Pietro Longhi shows her, tiny and homely, holding the hands of two of her little daughters while a *balia*, or wetnurse, holds up the third. However, all was not as serene as it appeared, for in 1784, just after the painting was finished, Giustina Renier divorced her husband, Marcantio Michiel, on the grounds of 'vexatious cohabitation'.

The *Dosetta* held a salon at the Corte Contarina at San Moisè. Rossini, Foscolo, Canova and Madame de Staël were among those who patronised it, Countess Michiel being something of an intellectual. She was a translator of Shakespeare, biographer of Madame de Sévigné, an expert in physics, botany and chemistry, and the author of *Origine delle Feste Veneziane*, a history of the many ceremonies and celebrations unique to the city.

Lady Sydney Morgan visited the Michiel *conversazione* in 1819 but felt that its pretensions did little to mask the passive indifference of the Venetians to the overthrow of their Republic twenty years before. Lady Morgan observed: 'In her elegant little work on the *Feste Veneziane*, Madame Michiel struggles to hide the degradation of Venice, by a recurrence to its former glory and freedom, and all the primitive virtues that accompanied them.'

In this extract from her sturdy six-volume work, Michiel describes one of the red-letter days of the Venetian year. In a city devoted to pleasureful display, the modern-day version of this event, the *Regatta Storica* in early September, remains perhaps the most picturesque of her ceremonies.

~~~

It's hard to describe the ardour generated in all classes by the announcement of an imminent *Regatta* and the effort that went into filling it with pomp and enjoyment. The champions, as they are today, were the *gondolieri* . . . a class of people who, although today quite different from what they used to be, still deserve the attention of the attentive philosopher because they retain, more than any other class, the hues of the primitive national character. *Gondolieri* are usually full of spirit, of finesse, of perceptiveness; they are skilled and cheerful; the vivacity of their answers and of their expressions is enjoyable and enchanting. In particular they have the reputation of having straight, loyal and open hearts; of being discreet, faithful and very fond of their masters. Almost all of them can read and are gifted with an extraordinary memory. It was a real pleasure to see them at times standing at the back of their *gondoletta*, pushing it lightly around the Grand Canal and to listen to them, imitating the Greek prosodists, reciting the amorous strophes of our Homer – Tasso – with their own particular musical rhythm . . .

Mark Twain (Samuel Langhorne Clemens)
(1835–1910)

The watery city of Venice was bound to captivate the American Mark Twain, whose two masterpieces, *Tom Sawyer* (1876) and *Huckleberry Finn* (1884), draw on his childhood experiences of life beside the Mississippi River.

Twain was apprenticed to a printer but later worked as a riverboat pilot, a job he held until the outbreak of the Civil War. (His pen-name is the pilots' jargon for 'mark two fathoms', the term used when taking soundings in shallow waters.) He moved around the United States, trying his hand at goldmining in Nevada and journalism in San Francisco and Buffalo, before settling in Connecticut.

Twain arrived in Venice on 20 July 1867, the night of the first *Redentore* festival since Venice's liberation from the Austrians. Like most well-heeled travellers of his time, he stayed at the Grand Hotel near San Moisè and put himself through all the expected paces, but in a way quite unlike any other observer of the town. He professed to see Venice through the eyes of a romantic lusting after glorious decadence and tragic desolation but, throughout his account, his wicked humour gushes up like the water in San Marco.

He returned ten years later with his wife and two daughters and, on that trip, was given the benefit of the company of William Dean Howells, the American consul. A second book, *A Tramp Abroad* (1880), showed a matured view of Venice.

The extract below, however, comes from Twain's tongue-in-cheek observations as a gauche wise-*and*-foolish Venice virgin, on his first trip. This article later became part of his famous travel book *The Innocents Abroad* (1869). Twain's mock-hostility towards the gondola and gondoliers is typical of his bristly but intrinsically affectionate portrait of Venice. Despite his initial resistance, he soon succumbs to the charm of the *Redentore* spectacle of lanterned boats full of feasting Venetians and confesses himself utterly seduced by the music he initially scorned. Incidentally, Twain's vision of the gondola as a hearse has been visited by far too many other writers.

We reached Venice at eight in the evening, and entered a hearse belonging to the Grand Hotel d'Europe. At any rate, it was more like a hearse than anything else, though, to speak by the card, it was a gondola. And this was the storied gondola of Venice! – the fairy boat in which the princely cavaliers of the olden time were wont to cleave the waters of the moonlit canals and look the eloquence of love into the soft eyes of patrician beauties, while the gay gondolier in silken doublet touched his guitar and sang as only gondoliers can sing! This the famed gondola and this the gorgeous gondolier! – the one an inky, rusty old canoe with a sable hearse-body clapped on to the middle of it, and the other a mangy, barefooted gutter-snipe with a portion of his raiment on exhibition which should have been sacred from public scrutiny. Presently, as he turned a corner and shot his hearse into a dismal ditch between two long rows of towering, untenanted buildings, the gay gondolier began to sing, true to the traditions of his race. I stood it a little while. Then I said:

'Now, here, Roderigo Gonzales Michael Angelo, I'm a pilgrim, and I'm a stranger, but I am not going to have my feelings lacerated by any such caterwauling as that. If that goes on, one of us has got to take water. It is enough that my cherished dreams of Venice have been blighted forever as to the romantic gondola and the gorgeous gondolier; this system of destruction shall go no farther; I will accept the hearse, under protest, and you may fly your flag of truce in peace, but here I register a dark and bloody oath that you shan't sing. Another yelp, and overboard you go.'

I began to feel that the old Venice of song and story had departed forever. But I was too hasty. In a few minutes we swept gracefully out into the Grand Canal, and under the mellow moonlight the Venice of poetry and romance stood revealed. Right from the water's edge rose long lines of stately palaces of marble; gondolas were gliding swiftly hither and thither and disappearing suddenly through unsuspected gates and alleys; ponderous stone bridges threw their shadows athwart the glittering waves. There was life and motion everywhere, and yet everywhere there was a hush, a stealthy sort of stillness, that was suggestive of secret enterprises of bravoes and of lovers; and, clad half in moonbeams and half in mysterious shadows, the grim old mansions of the Republic seemed to have an expression about them of having an eye out for just such enterprises as these at that same moment. Music came floating over waters — Venice was complete.

William Dean Howells

(1837–1920)

The new American consul who arrived in Venice in 1861 was just twenty-four years old. It was a glamorous and confusing appointment for the sociable, charming William Dean Howells. Nothing in his New World background had prepared him for the unique difficulties of making a life in Venice.

Born in Ohio, he was the son of a journalist of Welsh extraction. By the age of nine he was working as a compositor in his father's office. He began to write poetry, which he contributed to *Atlantic Monthly*, the journal he later edited (1871–81). He wrote thirty-five novels and supplied a regular column to *Harper's* magazine from 1900 to 1920.

During his five years in Venice Howells began to keep a personal diary. Letters about his experiences, initially published in the *Boston Advertiser*, eventually formed the backbone of his book *Venetian Life*, published in 1866.

Howells' Venice is a depressed one. The Austrians are in occupation, the *Carnevale* is extinguished. The city is in disarray and disrepair, and these problems are miniaturised in the domestic difficulties Howells encounters at home. The ways of his staff are Byzantine. The 'treasure' Giovanna, hired to run the household, ends up tyrannising it, and to escape her clutches the family is forced to move from their residence in Ca' Falier to another *palazzo* on the Grand Canal.

In *Venetian Life*, which has been described as the best book ever written about Venice, Howells displays a beautiful turn of phrase, describing, for example, the *terrazzo* flooring of most *palazzi* as 'petrified plum-pudding'.

He had great respect for the gondoliers, declaring them the most intelligent and quick-witted of the populace; not truculent but amiable. He observed that 'a faint prospect of future employment purifies them of every trait of dishonesty'. In this extract he recounts three of the gondoliers' favourite tales: those of the cannibal sausage-maker (whose restaurant was supposed to have existed in the sixteenth century at the Riva di Biasio), the innocent baker boy Pietro Fasiol, and the hanging of the murderess Veneranda Porta.

The first of these legends is that of a sausage-maker who flourished in Venice some centuries ago, and who improved the quality of the broth which the *luganegheri* make of their scraps and sell to the gondoliers, by cutting up into it now and then a child of some neighbor. He was finally detected by a gondolier who discovered a little finger in his broth, and being brought to justice, was dragged through the city at the heels of a wild horse. This uncomfortable character appears to be the first hero in the romance of the gondoliers, and he certainly deserves to rank with that long line of imaginary personages who have made childhood so wretched and tractable. The second is the Innocent Baker-Boy already named, who was put to death on suspicion of having murdered a noble, because in the dead man's heart was found a dagger fitting a sheath which the baker had picked up in the street, on the morning of the murder, and kept in his possession. Many years afterwards, a malefactor who died in Padua confessed the murder, and thereupon two lamps were lighted before a shrine in the southern façade of St. Mark's Church, — one for the murdered nobleman's soul, and the other for that of the innocent boy. Such is the gondoliers' story, and the lamps still burn every night before the shrine from dark till dawn, in witness of its truth. The fact of the murder and its guiltless expiation is an incident of Venetian history, and it is said that the Council of the Ten never pronounced a sentence of death thereafter till they had been solemnly warned by one of their number with '*Ricordatevi del povero Fornaretto!*' (Remember the poor Baker-Boy!) The poet Dall 'Ongaro has woven the story into a touching tragedy; but I believe the poet is still to be born who shall take from the gondoliers their Veneranda Porta, and place her historic figure in dramatic literature. Veneranda Porta was a lady of the days of the Republic, between whom and her husband existed an incompatibility. This was increased by the course of Signora Porta in taking a lover, and at last it led to the assassination of the husband by the paramours. The head of the murdered man was found in one of the canals, and being exposed, as the old custom was, upon the granite pedestal at the corner of St. Mark's Church, it was recognized by his brother, who found among the papers on which the long hair was curled fragments of a letter he had written to the deceased. The crime was traced to the paramours, and being brought before the Ten, they were both condemned to be hanged between the columns of the Piazzetta. The gondoliers relate that when the sentence was pronounced, Veneranda said to the Chief of the Ten, 'But as for me the sentence will never be carried out. You cannot hang a woman. Consider the impropriety!' The Venetian rulers were wise men in their generation, and far from being balked by this question of delicacy, the Chief replied, solving it, 'My dear, you shall be hanged in my breeches.'

Dorothy Menpes

(1883–1973)

One of the most luxurious books on Venice is a father–daughter collaboration. *Venice*, published in 1904, combines the gentle watercolours of the acclaimed Australian-born artist Mortimer Menpes with the lively text of his daughter Dorothy.

Born in England, Dorothy accompanied her father on his many travels, including painting trips to Venice, Japan and South Africa. Similar books appeared as a result.

Dorothy Menpes adored gondolas, insisting, 'Like most characteristic objects appertaining to Venice, it is suitable to the place: in fact, it is the outcome of the place.' In this extract she describes the working calls and vengeful profanities of the gondoliers.

Few people have any knowledge of the real meanings of the gondoliers' cries, some of which are peculiarly sweet and characteristic. When a man wants to pass on the left, and does not intend to use the backward stroke, he cries 'Premi!' If, on the other hand, he wishes to pass on the right, he cries, 'Stali!' Sometimes, if when turning a dangerous corner he wishes to be especially emphatic, he cries, 'Premi! Premi!' and 'Stali! ah, Stali!' The gondola can be stopped immediately, however great the rate at which it is travelling, by placing the blade in front of the fork. If a man is really expert he stops his gondola very suddenly, making a great deal of foam with his oar. When stopping a gondola thus the gondolier cries, 'Sciar!' As you approach the landing-stage a crowd of ragamuffins, old and young, called 'crab-catchers,' come forward, holding in their hands staffs, with bent nails attached, with which to secure your gondola as you place your foot on shore.

The gondolier is a voluble, gossiping person. He loves to have a chat at the top of his voice with another of his kind, and to scream repartee across the water. He enjoys nothing more than a quarrel, especially with a man who is across the canal. Invariably they pass from pertinent observations on their personal appearances to defamation of their women. If such language were used at close quarters on either bank they would come to blows. I once saw two gondolas hook on to each other by mistake with their iron axes, and I shall never forget the discussion that ensued. It made one's blood literally curdle! The men looked like two angry sea-birds pecking at each other as they pulled and pulled in their endeavour to release themselves. When this had been accomplished they stood upright, each on his own poop, brandishing their oars as though they longed to kill. As a matter of fact, there is rarely any violence among Venetians except in language. 'Body of Bacchus!' one shouts. 'Blood of David!' the adversary answers. These mythological oaths being not sufficiently comforting, they continue: 'Low crab!' 'Sea-lion!' 'Dog!' 'Son of a cow!' 'Ass!' 'Son of a sow!' 'Assassin!' 'Ruffian!' 'Spy!' Having reached the worst taunt in their vocabulary, they take to cursing the rival saints. 'The Madonna of thy landing is a street-walker who is not worth two candles!' one will cry. 'Thy saint is a rascal who does not know how to make a decent miracle!' the other will rejoin. The profanity becomes more terrible as the distance between them increases. Possibly next time they meet they will drink a glass of wine together without remembering the quarrel.

Piero Pazzi

(1958–)

In recent years a stylish black-and-white calendar featuring portraits of gondoliers has been available at all good *edicole*.

The *Calendario dei Gondolieri* is the brainchild of Piero Pazzi, an energetic Venetian who occupies himself with the promotion of the traditional Venetian skills and values.

The glamorous calendar, he explains, was in fact conceived as his mouthpiece 'for denouncing the errors and omissions of the Italian and Venetian administrations when they behave irresponsibly towards my city . . . a Calendar of the Disgraces and Problems of Venice would not exactly be a great success.'

Instead, since 2002, Pazzi has been publishing his selection of good-looking young gondoliers. His aim, he says, is to attract the interest of the feminine public who, after looking at the photographs, will then read his passionate text and learn something about the truly parlous state of affairs in Venice.

Here are some of Pazzi's comments from the 2003 edition. He explains that there are today around four hundred gondoliers working in Venice from twelve stations, or *traghetti*, adding that a gondolier is probably the best-informed and friendly private guide a tourist could want.

~~~

I now present to the public the *Calendar of the Gondoliers.*

Its main goal is to stop the prejudice, born of misinformation, which has been directed against gondoliers . . .

I am convinced that after your journey in a gondola you will recommend the experience to your friends. May this calendar be a reminder of your stay: with it you will take home the faces of some of the gondoliers and so surely remember Venice in a pleasing light.

A last and disinterested piece of advice: if it is possible, don't come to Venice with a group. It's the worst way of visiting the city. How can you appreciate its artistic treasures, its civility, when you are in a herd of cows? Groups, where the time is counted by the minutes when you are visiting a museum, eating and, especially, when you are pushed into the shops where they sell the so-called 'Venetian handicrafts'.

Venice must be visited with sensibility and intelligence. If you don't believe me, buy a video and stay at home. It's the best thing you can do. We already have too many tourists and we don't need one like you!

If you must go in a group, there are plenty of other places: Lourdes or Fatima, for example, where, if you know how to ask, you can obtain the graces of the Virgin Mary. Here, on the other hand, you are actually breaking the balls and compromising the fragile equilibrium of a little city that was built on a human scale and not for oceanic crowds!

City at Play

CARNEVALE AND OTHER DIVERSIONS

Novelty pleases those who have nothing to lose.

The first sin is to be born desperate.

He who expects to get help at the gaming table
will grow long hair like a bear.

Fortune is like a cow:
to some she shows her good side; to others her backside.

VENETIAN PROVERBS

Venice plays at being a town and we play at discovering it.

RÉGIS DEBRAY

. . . that marvellous yet futile puppet theatre, Venice.

GIORGIO BUSETTO

All the world repaire to Venice to see the folly and madness of the Carnevall.

JOHN EVELYN

Every one is now in *maschera*, and one great convenience is, that if you fasten your mask on your hat you have the privilege of not taking off your hat when any one speaks to you; and you never address them by name, but always as '*Servitore umilissimo, Signora Maschera!' Cospetto di Bacco!* That is fun!

From *Carnevale*, WOLFGANG AMADEUS MOZART, 1771

Pleasure and vice are not only allowed but managed and promoted politically among them; 'tis one of the main hinges of their government.

JOSEPH SPENCE

Moreover these frequent festivals – which today would only mean laziness and foolish orgies – were at that epoch one of the means for assisting the development of industry by tempting foreigners to the city . . .

POMPEO MOLMENTI

Gallant *cavalieri* and grave *cittadini*; soldiers of Dalmatia, and seamen of the galleys; dames of the city, and females of lighter manners; jewellers of the Rialto, and traders from the Levant; Jew, Turk, and Christian; traveller, adventurer, *podesta*, valet, *avvocato*, and gondolier, held their way alike to the common centre of amusement. The hurried air and careless eye; the measured step and jealous glance; the jest and laugh; the song of the *cantatrice*, and the melody of the flute; the grimace of the buffoon and the tragic frown of the *improvisatore*; the pyramid of the grotesque, the compelled and melancholy smile of the harpist, cries of the water-sellers, cowls of monks, plumage of warriors, hum of voices, and the universal movement and bustle, added to the more permanent objects of the place, rendered the scene the most remarkable in Christendom.

JAMES FENIMORE COOPER

We are in the agonies of Carnival's last days, and I must be up all night again . . .

GEORGE GORDON, LORD BYRON

I have just got back from the Tragedy and am still laughing.

JOHANN WOLFGANG VON GOETHE

I have better health and spirits than many younger ladies, who pass their nights at the *ridotto* and their days in spleen for their losses there.

MARY WORTLEY MONTAGU

Joseph Addison

(1672–1719)

The English writer (co-founder of the *Spectator*) and politician Joseph Addison visited Venice during an extended Grand Tour of Europe (1699–1703) in preparation for a diplomatic career. He was shocked and delighted by Venice and her *Carnevale*.

Carnevale. *Carnem levare*. Farewell to Meat. Forbid the Flesh, in the carnal as well as alimentary sense. For forty days before Lent's abstinence and penitence, Venice had *Carnevale* – forty days of rioting in the flesh.

Most cultures have sought to mark the end of winter with a great party. But the Venetian *Carnevale* has always been different from all the others. In their island state, the Venetians always considered themselves free of the strictures of Rome. They prided themselves on being more gallant, more irreverent and more secretive, with stronger stomachs for debauchery and more picturesque resources than anyone else.

The first *Carnevale* probably took place in 1094, and ever after the great *campi* of the city were seasonally devoted to minstrels, actors, competitions, balls and pageantry.

In the fifteenth century groups of young noblemen, *Compagnie della Calza*, took on the organisation of parties and entertainments, particularly readings of erotic poetry. Their name originated in their preferred costume: tight stockings (*calze*) in gorgeous stripes and embroideries. We can still see just how these effete young men looked: their smooth-buttocked, blond, lithe figures populate the paintings of the contemporary artist Victor Carpaccio.

It was the *Compagnie della Calza* that introduced the mask, a novelty that quickly became a prerequisite. The imperious Lords of Fun insisted that for *Carnevale* everyone must have an alternative face, another identity, in place of their everyday one. The Venetians liked to turn their social world upside down during *Carnevale*. Noblemen dressed as country bumpkins. Maids got themselves up as great ladies and were treated as such.

There was a mask for every personality, from the little black muzzle of the *Moretta*, which had to be clenched between the teeth, to the beaky white *Bauta* with its inbuilt leer. Then there were all the characters of the *commedia dell'arte:* the greedy servant Arlecchino in his chequerboard costume with the hare's foot flopping on his cap (Punch is his descendant), Doctor Graziano in the black robe, and Pulcinella playing the bagpipes.

But *Carnevale* was already in decline by the end of the sixteenth century when even the hedonist Venetians were forced, at least in name, to observe the austerities imposed by the Council of Trent. *Carnevale* revived itself a little but was put to bed again by Napoleon, who considered mask-wearing and licentiousness serious security risks. For nearly two hundred years after that, *Carnevale* lay almost dormant, erupting only in small pockets of playfulness, until the 1950s when Charles Bestegui, a rich foreigner, tried to reanimate it. The Church and the Communists condemned his lavish parties and *Carnevale* slept again until the 1980s when a group of enterprising entertainers brought it back to life, reviving as many of the ancient traditions as were legally possible.

So the *Carnevale* of today is a pastiche of old and new, not exactly folkloric archaeology, and not quite Disneyland. When

Carnevale comes back to Venice, so does the past. In a city that has not changed its appearance time is stretchable. It never jolts at any time of year to see people in eighteenth-century costume selling concert tickets on street corners. It's the tourists in their jeans who look out of place.

At San Marco a huge stage is erected in the middle of the Piazza and the revellers come to see and be seen. At dusk the costumed contenders promenade between the arches in front of the famous Caffè Florian, allowing themselves to be photographed, but with the utmost disdain, self-contained in their own glory.

There are more spectators than participators, unlike the old days of *Carnevale*. Charles de Brosses in the eighteenth century could scarcely credit reports that Venice received thirty thousand visitors a year. Yet these days, San Marco has been known to host one hundred thousand tourists on one *Carnevale* afternoon.

Joseph Addison described the senate as one of the wisest councils in the world but despaired of the corrupt principles that motivated it, and he noted the decline in numbers of the ruling noblemen. His tut-tutting description of the *Carnevale* and its associated entertainments mirrors the feeling of other contemporary writers such as Edward Gibbon, who declared, 'Of all the towns in Italy, I am the least satisfied with Venice . . . the worst architecture I ever yet saw . . .'

As a lover of the classics, and the author of the tragedy *Cato*, Addison took exception to the liberties taken by the Venetian dramatists in the festival season.

The carnival of Venice is everywhere talked of. The great diversion of the place at that time, as well as on all other high occasions, is masking. The Venetians, who are naturally grave, love to give in to the follies and entertainments of such seasons, when disguised in a false personage . . . These disguises give occasion to abundance of love-adventures; for there is something more intriguing in the amours of Venice than in those of other countries, and I question not but the secret history of a carnival would make a collection of very diverting novels. Operas are another great entertainment of this season. The poetry of them is generally as exquisitely ill, as the music is good. The arguments are often taken from some celebrated action of the ancient Greeks or Romans, which sometimes looks ridiculous enough; for who can endure to hear one of the rough old Romans squeaking through the mouth of an eunuch, especially when they may choose a subject out of courts where eunuchs are really actors, or represent by them any of the soft Asiatic monarchs? . . .

The comedies that I saw at Venice, or indeed in any other part of Italy, are very indifferent, and more lewd than those of other countries. Their poets have no notion of genteel comedy, and fall into the most filthy double-meanings imaginable, when they have a mind to make their audience merry.

M. R. Lovric

(1959–)

The editor's first novel, *Carnevale*, describes the life and loves of Cecilia Cornaro, a fictional Venetian portrait painter who conducts love affairs with both Casanova and Byron.

In this preamble to her story, Cecilia explains the breathless spirit abroad in Venice in the second half of the eighteenth century as the city partied herself into depletion and the cold embrace of Napoleon Bonaparte.

The joyful paintings of Gabriel Bella and Pietro Longhi (now at the Querini Stampalia and the Ca' Rezzonico) show how the *Carnevale* of Cecilia's time consumed the whole city. Maskers patrolled San Marco. In mock regattas at Rialto, they ran about with decorated wheelbarrows, instead of boats. The Riva degli Schiavoni was the sideshow of the *Carnevale:* here performed the mountebanks, ballad singers, rope-dancers, jugglers, snake-charmers, freaks and conjurers. A fortune-teller would whisper his predictions down a long silver trumpet. Quack doctors proffered their noxious nostrums. In the animal enclosures were every kind of dancing dog and bear. Tottering through all of this was the *forza d'Ercole*, a human pyramid of twenty-six men with a tiny child on top. On Maundy Thursday the *saltamartino* slid head-first down a rope from the top of the Campanile.

In those days, *Carnevale* ended in style. The *Calabresi* with their lighted caps would carry the coffin of the old feast to San Marco, followed by wheelbarrows of limp bodies wearing the hideous death mask of a face covered with syphilitic sores. Even Lent would be interrupted by the *segavecchia: a* decrepit dummy of an old woman, symbolising famine and deprivation, would be put on trial on a stage. She stood accused of killing the *Carnevale* and was condemned to be sawn in two. As the saws sliced through her torso, sweets and fruit fell from her belly and the crowd would fight for them.

There is a Venetian story about a Turkish sailor who arrived there on Ash Wednesday. He had heard that the Venetians were crazy six months at a time but on one particular day of the year a flaky grey powder could cure them of their madness immediately and this cure lasted forty days to the day.

As *Carnevale*'s Cecilia Cornaro explains, nothing could be further from the truth. Until Napoleon arrived to put their pleasures to bed, there was no stopping the Venetians of the eighteenth century in their pursuit of absolute and heedless bliss.

Before I can tell you about Casanova, there are some things you must know about Venice. I need to tell you how she was in the days when my account begins, for in her gaunt and ghostly decline, as you *poverini* must see her, you would not recognise the city of perfervid happiness which spawned both me, Cecilia Cornaro, and Giacomo Casanova, and our story.

Ah, we were a happy city! It was our entire occupation to be happy. We were mad with happiness, stuffed with it like truffles. When I think of Venice as she was in 1782, I think of a hundred thousand souls all devoted to pleasure. Souls like that become insubstantial and faintly luminous. You see, we were in the *phosphorescent* stage of decay.

We were a happy city. We were harmless and slightly worn out, loose and languid in our frisks. We had a child's sense of fun, latterly a tired child's. We were always up to something. There was no viciousness in us, only the irresponsible trespasses that unfortunately happen when pleasure runs wild. We loved practical jokes. We were constantly in that exquisite, perilous state of happiness, the gasping moment before the belly-laugh jumps out of the belly. We were so happy that we could not bear tragedies in our theatres. The one sad play they tried was a tremendous flop. In the comedies, when the villains were despatched, we cheered the corpses: *Bravi i morti!*

The deepest of our philosophies was this:

> In the morning a little mass,
> In the afternoon a little gambling,
> In the evening a little lady.

We gambled like lunatics. In Venice people staked their clothes and walked home naked. Others staked their wives or daughters. The poorer we were, the more extravagant we became. We lost the concept of the value of money because we did not earn it. At Arsenale, where we should have been building ships to defend ourselves, fountains of wine ran continually. We forgot how to sleep: we merely fell into stupors. We rose to start our routs when civilised cities were going to bed. Our masses were like gala concerts. Our very beggars spoke in poetry.

Yes, we were a happy city. Our morals were indeed somewhat *nimble*. And our dress might be called immodest, but this was because we considered it our *duty* to show the world every beautiful part of ourselves. And yes, our pleasures were spiced with a few picturesque depravities. Actually, we were ripe as old fish! There were lewd acts engraved upon our snuffboxes and calling cards. Certainly, we took no nonsense from our priests. Think on this: there were ten times as many courtesans as noble or respectable bourgeois wives like my mother . . .

Everything was decoration in that happy city. Luxury became us. In Venice, we were mesmerised by our own entrancing vision in the mirror: the mirrors of the water and the speckled mirrors in our sumptuous bedrooms. In Venice, every boat wore at the point of its prow a lacy little spume of foam. As the world closed in upon us, we used our depleted stocks of gunpowder not to arm ourselves but for fireworks! Fortunately, we were so beautiful that we *frightened* our enemies; they did not think themselves good enough to conquer us. When you hear that it was necessary to forbid the Venetian *laundry women* to wear velvet, satin and black fox fur, you start to understand what kind of city we were then.

Ah, we were a happy city! Venice had become so old that she had fallen into her second childhood and laughed at everything.

We were voluble as parrots. Our hands conducted simultaneous conversations, eloquent as a pair of poets. With a flourish, we welcomed in all the self-styled counts and virgins, the fortune-tellers and the snake-oil salesmen. The very men who swept the streets sent the dust dancing in graceful arcs, tendering their brooms like slender ballerinas. We even made joy of *acqua alta*! We pirouetted over the *passerelle* with the water clucking underneath us like an old governess. We splashed and giggled even as the sea dragged our chairs and our underwear into the lagoon . . .

We had *Carnevale* six months of the year. In our strange and beautiful masks we always had a choice of who to be. In our masks, we were accountable to no one, and we took full advantage of this. In those days Venice kept eight hundred and fifty mask-makers in business. For our masks were not merely for *Carnevale*. They were for the fairy tale of the everyday, to be worn every night.

We ate foolish foods: *møringata* and towering confections of spun sugar. We were so spoiled we thought cherries fell from the trees without stones. We drank pomegranate sherbet from Araby and herbed raspberry kvass. Afterwards we dabbed the corners of our greedy mouths with silk handkerchiefs and threw them away! We ground the detritus of our pleasures into the paving stones until they made a harlequinade of orange peel, confetti and pumpkin seeds under our slippered feet. In the crowds, the women were liberally fondled.

You start to have an idea of us, now perhaps. But don't even try to imagine the joy of being *born* Venetian in the time when Venice was a happy city. You would not come close to the truth. These things I knew in my bones about Venice before this story began, even though I myself lived in a family that tried to hold itself aloof from the happy city, that tried very hard not to be happy, but, instead, to be good.

George Gordon, Lord Byron

(1788–1824)

George Gordon, Lord Byron, had always dreamed of Venice, describing her as the greenest island of his imagination. When he arrived there in November 1816 he sought not a casual but an intimate relationship with the town. He lived in Venice for three years, becoming fluent in the dialect and pleasurably scandalising the town with his succession of colourful local mistresses from all levels of society.

Cold-shouldered out of London after his own failed marriage and the scandal of his passionate relationship with his half-sister, Byron found the easy-going Venetian morality much to his taste. He immediately took full advantage of the fashionable system of open marriages, whereby each wife also had at least one regular admirer.

The *cicisbeo* or extramural husband is the theme of Byron's rollicking poem, *Beppo*, composed in Venice. It is supposed, ironically, to be based on a tale told to him by the husband of his first Venetian mistress, Marianna Segati, in whose house he lodged when he arrived in Venice.

When he tired of Segati, Byron moved to the imposing Palazzo Mocenigo on the Grand Canal where he installed a menagerie of pets, his illegitimate daughter Allegra and, for a short period, 'La Fornarina', the baker's wife and the most fiery of his mistresses. He also rented a villa on the Brenta, rode horses along the Lido beach and memorably swam from the Lido to the Grand Canal, beating an Italian competitor 'all to bubbles'.

In 1819 Byron found himself taking the role of *cicisbeo* in a more profound way than he had ever imagined. He fell in love with the Countess Teresa Guiccioli and followed her to Ravenna, effectively ending his romance with Venice. Instead, he took up with the Italian nationalist cause and in 1823 he travelled to Greece where he joined the insurgents fighting against Turkish rule. He died of a fever there, without seeing any action.

As well as *Beppo* (1818), Byron began writing his mock-epic *Don Juan* in Venice. Today his poetry, which once seemed exotic and thrilling, can sound crude and lacking in depth. Certainly, he has bestowed upon Venice some of her most well-worn and emptiest clichés. His letters, in contrast, reveal a man full of searing humour and self-mocking vanity, giving a far better insight into his extraordinary personal charisma – and his feelings about the city – than the posturing of his verse.

The facetious tone of this extract from *Beppo* reflects Byron's enjoyment of his early period in Venice and the fun he extracted from his first *Carnevale*. It borrows heavily from the style of the fifteenth-century Italian writer, Luigi Pulci.

'Tis known, at least it should be, that throughout
    All countries of the Catholic persuasion,
Some weeks before Shrove Tuesday comes about,
    The people take their fill of recreation,
And buy repentance, ere they grow devout,
    However high their rank, or low their station,
With fiddling, feasting, dancing, drinking, masking,
And other things which may be had for asking.

The moment night with dusky mantle covers
    The skies (and the more duskily the better),
The time less liked by husbands than by lovers
    Begins, and prudery flings aside her fetter;
And gaiety on restless tiptoe hovers,
    Giggling with all the gallants who beset her;
And there are songs and quavers, roaring, humming,
Guitars, and every other sort of strumming.

And there are dresses splendid, but fantastical,
    Masks of all times and nations, Turks and Jews,
And harlequins and clowns, with feats gymnastical,
    Greeks, Romans, Yankee-doodles, and Hindoos;
All kinds of dress, except the ecclesiastical,
    All people, as their fancies hit, may choose,
But no one in these parts may quiz the clergy, –
Therefore take heed, ye Freethinkers! I charge ye . . .

Of all the places where the Carnival
  Was most facetious in the days of yore,
For dance, and song, and serenade, and ball,
  And masque, and mime, and mystery, and more
Than I have time to tell now, or at all,
  Venice the bell from every city bore, —
And at the moment when I fix my story,
That sea-born city was in all her glory.

Benjamin Disraeli

(1804–81)

Novelist and influential English Prime Minister of the Victorian era, Benjamin Disraeli is better remembered for his statesmanship than his literary success. However, his *Contarini Fleming*, about an Englishman of Venetian ancestry returning to *La Serenissima* to answer the calls of his blood, is as taut a confection of suspense and sentimentality as any contemporary romantic novelist could muster. Perhaps the fact that Disraeli's own grandfather was Italian perfumes the text with a stronger flavour of authenticity. Disraeli, who became the first Earl of Beaconsfield, always claimed that his ancestors settled in Venice after the exodus of Jews from Spain in 1492, but in fact there is no record of the family there until 1821.

Subtitled 'A Psychological Autobiography', *Contarini Fleming* also gives a good portrait of the city. In the scene that follows, our hero conducts one of those terse, oblique, innuendo-loaded conversations with a complete stranger that are seemingly obligatory at masked balls.

In the old days such balls, known as *i festini*, were the great enchantment of *Carnevale*. Unlike today, when tickets cost as much as £250, anyone could enter provided that they wore a mask. The location was signalled by a lantern garlanded with flowers. There was always music, a cello and spinet, and people danced the fashionable dances of the time: the *ciaccona*, the minuet, the gavotte and the *gagliarda*. From time to time during the dancing, the owner of the house would pass among his guests, who would reach into their pockets and hand over a modest sum. Some balls were sumptuous, proclaiming the power and wealth of the hosts.

The state tried to intervene to rein in the enormous waste of money and effort, as well as the moral standards of the dancers, who competed with one another in licentious behaviour.

The poor of the city also held dances: in their houses, in the streets and, particularly, in the *sestiere* of Castello where the boldest of the women would dance the erotically charged *furlana*.

The ball of *Contarini Fleming* is a much more restrained affair . . .

During the last nights of the Carnival it is the practice to convert the Opera House into a ball-room, and, on these occasions, the highest orders are masqued. The scene is indeed very gay and amusing. In some boxes, a supper is always ready at which all guests are welcome. But masqued you must be. It is even strict etiquette on these occasions for ladies to ramble about the Theatre unattended, and the great diversion of course is the extreme piquancy of the incognito conversations; since, in a limited circle, in which few are unknown to each other, it is of course not difficult to impregnate this slight parley with a sufficient quantity of Venetian salt.

I went to one of these balls, as I thought something amusing might occur. I went in a domino, and was careful not to enter my box, lest I should be discovered. As I was sauntering along one of the rooms near the stage, a female masque saluted me.

'We did not expect you,' she said.

'I only came to meet you,' I replied.

'You are more gallant than we supposed you to be.'

'The world is seldom charitable,' I said.

'They say you are in love.'

'You are the last person to consider that wonderful.'

'Really quite chivalric. Why! they said you are quite a wild man.'

'But you, Signora, have tamed me.'

'But do you know they say you are in love?'

'Well! doubtless with a charming person.'

'Oh! yes, a very charming person. Do you know they say you are Count Narcissus, and in love with yourself?'

'Do they indeed! They seem to say vastly agreeable things, I think. Very witty, upon my honour.'

'Oh! very witty, no doubt of that, and you should be a judge of wit, you know, because you are a poet.'

'You seem to know me well.'

'I think I do. You are the young gentleman, are you not, who have quarrelled with your Papa?'

'That is a very vague description.'

'I can give you some further details.'

'Oh! pray spare me and yourself.'

'Do you know I have written your character?'

'Indeed! It is doubtless as accurate as most others.'

'Oh! it is founded upon the best authorities. There is only one part imperfect. I wish to give an account of your works. Will you give me a list?'

'I must have an equivalent, and something more interesting than my own character.'

'Meet me to-night at the Countess Malbrizzi's.'

'I cannot, I do not know her.'

'Do not you know that, in Carnival time, a mask may enter any house? After the ball, all will be there. Will you meet me? I am now engaged.'

This seemed the opening of an adventure, which youth is not inclined to shun. I assented, and the mask glided away, leaving me in great confusion and amazement, at her evident familiarity with my history.

Pietro Aretino

(1492–1556)

A gambling fever gripped Venice from her early days, sometimes with tragic results, as described here by the irrepressible Pietro Aretino.

In 1527 Aretino took up residence in a house on the Grand Canal and fell violently in love with his adoptive city. In a memorable letter he opined, 'If Eden, where Adam dwelt with Eve, had resembled Venice she would have had a hard time trying to tempt him out of that earthly paradise with her fruit . . . And I would love, just so as not to have to leave Venice, to become one of those little copper coins with which people pay the ferry man. If I were a rat, that feeds in the Venetian treasury, I would feel like one of heaven's cherubim.'

The illegitimate son of a Tuscan nobleman, Aretino was known as 'the scourge of princes' for his irreverent wit. He impressed Pope Leo X but lost favour with him after writing his famous lewd sonnets *Sonetti Lussuriosi*, which were graphically illustrated by the painter Giulio Romano. (Casanova kept a copy constantly about himself.)

Aretino lived in Venice for twenty-two years, keeping a luxurious and disorderly house with a resident harem. Larger than life and generous to all comers, Aretino was greatly beloved in the town. The Venetian painter Titian and the architect-sculptor Jacopo Sansovino were among his close friends. It is said that he died of apoplexy after falling off his stool while laughing at an amusing anecdote. He is buried in the Church of San Luca.

On 3 December 1537, Aretino wrote to Giovanni Manenti, the supervisor of the popular game of *lotto* in Venice. Although the letter is typically florid and jocular, Aretino shows serious compassion for those caught in the net of the lottery, no one was safe from its seductions: priests, friars and bankrupts succumbed helplessly to its lure. He describes in detail how the 'skinflint' who conducted the lottery laid out his cups, rings, chains and coins and drew the crowd with his banter. Some fantasised about what they would win, others dreamt of what they would buy with the proceeds. In the meantime they swarmed deliriously around the master of ceremonies. Aretino, no stranger to crudity, noted that those in the sway of lottery fever used the saltiest, dirtiest and most diabolical words in the world. He concluded that their faces when the tickets were drawn and they had won nothing 'resembled nothing more than an army bereft of its commander after a shameful surrender'. In this extract, he begins his complaint.

Feeling, my dear old friend, raining down on me the maledictions of sixty thousand *thousand* people who have been disembowelled, crucified and bamboozled by speculating in the lottery, I plied a strenuous discourse in your defence, to calm all those who wanted to believe that you were the inventor of lottery gambling. Believe me, to protect you from this tempest of critics, an army of swordsmen could not have fought harder. And of course, this new game is really the invention of that mule Lady Fortune, and of Madam Hope, who's a cow. It's those two who devised this devilish torment in order to make people renounce Christ and hang themselves. Those harlots are just like the two gypsies at the fair of Folingo and Lanciano who make one man look a village idiot and the other a bloody fool. Hope takes those cretins by the hand and leads them on, and Luck, as she pretends to play on their side, thumps them in the back. In the meantime their purses are left flat as a pricked balloon. Luck, eh? Hope, eh? We would all proceed to Hell quite cheerfully if we did not know that we would find those bitches there, carrying on with Satan himself! They are wicked liars, and when they fell a good man, they are out of their heads with joy, just like peasants with their teeth in a slice of bread with something nice on top. Now tell me, is this lottery of yours male or female? For myself, I see it as a hermaphrodite, as it goes by masculine [lotto] and feminine [ventura] names.

Vincenzo Coronelli

(1650–1718)

The city's addiction to gambling is also related by one of her native sons, Vincenzo Coronelli, writer, geographer and draughtsman.

The following is a short passage from his *Guida de' Forestieri* (*Guide for Foreigners*) published in 1700, a tiny book designed to be carried easily by travellers.

La Cavallerizza is played in the morning near San Giovanni e
Paolo on working days. Ballone is played at the appropriate time –
around 10 p.m. – at San Giacomo dell'Orio, at Gesuiti and at
Rialto nuovo. But Racchetta is played at places specifically dedicated to that game, in particular at Santa Caterina, in Birri. The
Ridotto Pubblico is at San Moisè, . . . where more than in any
other City, immense amounts of money are played, with a great
company of every kind of Person joining in, also Outsiders, as
long as they are masked, excepting only the Nobles, who may be
there without a mask. But with extreme quiet and exemplary
modesty, and with due respect towards one another, in the great
heat of the game not even a Word is pronounced aloud, this
expensive entertainment continuing only with silent gestures for
most of the day and also the night.

Giuseppe Tassini

(1827–?)

Since the mid-nineteenth century, Giuseppe Tassini has been invariably cited in almost every book about Venice. His 1863 volume, *Curiosità veneziane*, reveals the secrets behind the names of all the streets and squares, and has never been equalled for its detail. In this extract he describes the very epicentre of play and nightlife in Venice, the Ridotto.

Calle del Ridotto, near S. Moisè.

In this *calle* an antique *palazzo* was built, according to the historian Girolamo Priuli, in the fourteenth century by Marco Dandolo . . . In 1638, [another] Marco Dandolo had allowed the building to be used as a public gathering place (*ridotto*), where gambling was allowed during *Carnevale*. To avoid illegal activities, the government wanted to supervise the operations itself and sent there some noblemen who officially controlled the gambling tables.

In 1708, the King of Denmark, Frederick IV, went to Venice and in a masked outfit went to gamble at Palazzo Dandolo. Playing against a Venetian nobleman, the king won a large amount of gold. When the moment of settlement arrived, Frederick revealed his regal nature and, pretending to slip, knocked the table covered in gold coins over the floor. So all the money went back into the pockets of the nobleman.

In 1768, Maccaruzzi restored the *palazzo*, and built new smaller halls around the main one. Since this refurbishment was financed with money coming from the sale of property belonging to suppressed convents, many satirical epigrams were written on this subject . . .

In the following years, the government realised that some of the games played in the *palazzo* – such as *faraone* and *bassetta* – were devouring fortunes and ruining families. On 27th November 1774 the government issued a law that permanently forbade any gambling activity in the *palazzo*. In the last years of the Republic and under French rule though, the *palazzo* became once more the theatre of gambling activities, which were again outlawed by the Austrians.

Lorenzo da Ponte

(1749–1838)

'Unfortunately, I went to Venice,' wrote Lorenzo da Ponte in his memoirs. 'I was at the boiling point of youthful spirit . . . and, as everyone said, attractive in person. I allowed myself, through the customs and examples about me, as well as by my own inclinations, to be swept way into a life of voluptuousness . . .'

This confession prefaces the anecdote here, in which da Ponte, crazed with love of a woman and love of play, is forced to accept charity from his gondolier.

Da Ponte is best known as Mozart's librettist for *Don Giovanni*, (for which he was helped by his old friend Casanova), *The Marriage of Figaro* and *Così Fan Tutte*.

Born into a family of Jewish converts, he took holy orders after finishing his studies. He arrived in Venice in 1773 where he fell in love with Angiolina Tiepolo and was employed as a tutor in the noble Pisani family. Like Casanova, he travelled to Dresden, and to Vienna where he was made welcome at the court of Joseph II, but on the death of the Emperor he was left penniless. He wandered aimlessly around Europe with his English bride until departing in 1793 for London, where he wrote libretti for the Drury Lane Theatre, and finally in 1805 for New York, where he became a professor of Italian literature at Columbia. He died there at the age of ninety.

~~~

The lady I loved was continually agitated by a passion for gambling. Her brother, an insolent, overbearing, headstrong youth, was, to our fatal misfortune, even more vicious than she. I humored his failings now out of courtesy, and now for lack of better to do. In that way I too gradually became a gambler. No one of us three was rich, and soon we lost all our money. Then we began to borrow, now selling, now pawning, till we had stripped our wardrobes bare. Still flourishing in those days in Venice was the famous gambling house known commonly as the *Pubblico Ridotto* — or 'Resort,' where wealthy noblemen alone enjoyed the privilege of playing to unlimited stakes with their own money, and the poor, for a certain consideration, with the money of others . . . Thither we three repaired every evening, and from thence every evening we returned home, cursing cards and the man who invented them. The establishment was open only during Carnival. The last day of that season had come, and we had no money, nor the means of procuring any. At the urge of vicious habit, and even more of that fallacious hope which ever animates the gambler, we pawned or sold such clothes as were left us, and scraped together ten sequins; then to the *Ridotto* we went and in a twinkling had lost them too. Our state of mind as we quitted that room can be imagined. We walked in sullen silence toward the place where we were accustomed to take a gondola every night. The gondolier knew me — I had treated him to handsome gratuities several times. Remarking our silence and bad-temper, he divined what had happened and asked me whether I were in need of money. Taking the question as a jest, I replied, likewise jesting, that I needed fifty sequins. He looked at me, smiling, and without adding a word, rowed for a few moments, singing, then stopped at the ferry landing at the

Prisons. There he left the gondola, but returned in a few minutes and placed fifty sequins in my hands, muttering between his teeth:

'Go, play your cards, and learn to know Venetian boatmen better!'

My astonishment knew no bounds. At sight of so much money, so overpowering temptation grew that it left me no time for certain reflections which, from a sense of delicacy, I would have made at any other time. We returned forthwith to the *Ridotto*. Entering the first room I picked up a card and approaching one of the banks laid half of the money I possessed on that card. I doubled my money. Then I went on to many other banks, playing for more than half an hour with such constant good luck that I shortly found myself laden with gold. I dragged my companion to the stairs, hurried down with her, ran to the gondola, and, having returned the gondolier's money and given him a fine present, bade him row us home.

Lady Mary Wortley Montagu

(1689–1762)

'I bless my destiny,' declared the formidable Lady Mary, on arriving in Venice in 1739. The English woman of letters rented lodgings in one of the four Mocenigo *palazzi* on the Grand Canal and she relished a colourful social life among the noble families, opining that 'Venice is more agreeable than Florence, as freedom is more eligible than slavery . . .' She declared it the only town in which she could bear to reside, albeit 'infested with English, who torment me as much as the frogs and lice did the palace of the Pharaoh'.

In this letter of May 1740, she describes, with characteristic diligence, the *Regatta* held in honour of the Prince of Saxony.

Apartments in the Mocenigo *palazzi* would one day be the home of Byron; in 1622 the buildings hosted another strong-minded Englishwoman, the Countess of Arundel, who faced down the Council of Ten when her friend Antonio Foscarini was executed for violating the code of secrecy that forbade all noblemen to consort with foreigners. Part of one *palazzo* is said to be haunted by the ghost of the gentle philosopher Giordano Bruno, betrayed by Giovanni Mocenigo in 1592 and burnt at the stake in Rome.

Lady Mary herself was haunted by her unrequited passion for a young Venetian writer, Francesco Algarotti, whom she met in 1736. An attempt to make some kind of progress in that relationship was evidently behind her visit to the city. However, he failed to join her there and she was obliged to put an end to her fantasies of romance. Nevertheless, she did not return to her husband Edward Wortley Montagu (with whom she had eloped in 1712 and whom she had accompanied to Constantinople when he was appointed ambassador). After her sojourn in Venice she settled in rural Italy and did not return to England until her husband died. She spent a further period in Venice in 1757.

The recipient of this letter from Venice was her friend, Lady Pomfret.

You seem to mention the regatta in a manner as if you would be pleased with a description of it. It is a race of boats: they are accompanied by vessels which they call Piotes, and Bichones, that are built at the expense of nobles and strangers that have a mind to display their magnificence; they are a sort of machines adorned with all that sculpture and gliding can do to make a shining appearance . . . It would be too long to describe every one in particular; I shall only name the principal: – the Signora Pisani Mocenigo's represented the Chariot of the Night, drawn by four sea-horses, and showing the rising of the moon, accompanied with stars, the statues on each side representing the hours to the number of twenty-four, rowed by gondoliers in rich liveries, which were changed three times, all of equal richness, and the decorations changed also to the dawn of Aurora and the midday sun, the statues being new dressed every time, the first in green, the second time in red, and the last blue, all equally laced with silver, there being three races. Signor Soranzo represented the Kingdom of Poland, with all the provinces and rivers in that dominion, with a concert of the best instrumental music in rich Polish habits; the painting and gilding were exquisite in their kinds. Signor Contarini's piote showed the Liberal Arts; Apollo was seated on the stern upon Mount Parnassus, Pegasus behind, and the Muses seated round him: opposite was a figure representing Painting, with Fame blowing her trumpet; and on each side Sculpture, and Music in their proper dresses. The procurator Foscarini's was the Chariot of Flora guided by Cupids, and adorned with all sorts of flowers, rose-trees, etc. Signor Julio Contarini's represented the Triumphs of Valour; Victory was on the stern, and all the ornaments warlike trophies of every kind.

Signor Correri's was the Adriatic Sea receiving into her arms the Hope of Saxony. Signor Alvisio Mocenigo's was the Garden of Hesperides; the whole fable was represented by different statues. Signor Querini had the Chariot of Venus drawn by doves, so well done, they seemed ready to fly upon the water; the Loves and Graces attended her.

William Dean Howells

(1837–1920)

Another delightful description from the urbane American consul William Dean Howells, this time of the two different kinds of puppet show that captivated him in Venice. The Marionettes had their own miniature theatre in the Calle del Ridotto, with pit tickets at ten *soldi* each.

The drama of the Marionettes is of a more elevated and ambitious tone than that of the Burattini, which exhibit their vulgar loves and coarse assassinations in Punch-and-Judy shows on the Riva and in the larger squares; but the standard characters are nearly the same with both, and are all descended from the *commedia dell' arte* which flourished on the Italian stage before the time of Goldoni. I am very far from disparaging the Burattini, which have great and peculiar merits, not the least of which is the art of drawing the most delighted, dirty, and picturesque audiences. Like most of the Marionettes, they converse vicariously in the Venetian dialect, and have such a rapidity of utterance that it is difficult to follow them. I only remember to have made out one of their comedies, – a play in which an ingenious lover procured his rich and successful rival to be arrested for lunacy, and married the disputed young person while the other was raging in the mad-house. This play is performed to enthusiastic audiences; but for the most part the favorite drama of the Burattini appears to be a sardonic farce, in which the chief character – a puppet ten inches high, with a fixed and staring expression of Punch-like good-nature and wickedness – deludes other and weaker-minded puppets into trusting him, and then beats them with a club upon the back of the head until they die. The murders of this infamous creature, which are always executed in a spirit of jocose *sangfroid*, and accompanied by humorous remarks, are received with the keenest relish by the spectators . . .

Their audiences, as I said, are always interesting, and comprise: first, boys ragged and dirty in inverse ratio to their size; then frail little girls, supporting immense babies; then Austrian soldiers, with long coats and short pipes; lumbering Dalmatian sailors; a transient Greek or Turk; Venetian loafers, pale-faced, statuesque, with the drapery of their cloaks thrown over their shoulders; young women, with bare heads of thick black hair; old women, all fluff and fangs; wooden-shod peasants, with hooded cloaks of coarse brown; then boys – and boys. They all enjoy the spectacle with approval, and take the drama seriously, uttering none of the gibes which sometimes attend efforts to please in our own country. Even when the hat, or other instrument of extortion, is passed round, and they give nothing, and when the manager, in an excess of fury and disappointment, calls out, 'Ah! sons of dogs! I play no more to you!' and closes the theatre, they quietly and unresentfully disperse. Though, indeed, *fioi de cani* means no great reproach in Venetian parlance; and parents of the lower classes caressingly address their children in these terms; but to call one Figure of a Pig, is to wreak upon him the deadliest insult which can be put into words.

Leslie Poles Hartley

(1895–1972)

This description of Venice's most beloved festival, the *Redentore*, comes from the 1947 novel *Eustace and Hilda*, by L. P. Hartley. Best known for *The Go-Between*, Hartley preferred short stories with macabre twists and psychological novels. Another atmospheric novella set in Venice by the author is *The White Wand* (1954), the tale of a man's obsession with a woman who appears in a *palazzo* window.

The *Redentore*, which takes place in the third week of July, commemorates the end of one of the worst plagues to have ravaged the city. To thank the Redeemer for saving their town, the Venetians commissioned Palladio to build the Church of the Redentore in 1575. Every year since then a bridge of boats has been laid down from Zattere to the stairs of the church on Giudecca. For many years the Italian army dragged an old Bailey bridge from World War II overland to Venice for the weekend, but in 2002 the city finally produced her own sturdy floating structure. There have been suggestions that the bridge may be used for other festivals, perhaps to join Venice to the cemetery island of San Michele for the Day of the Dead; or to use part of it for the festival of Salute in November, when a smaller bridge is laid over the Grand Canal to connect Santa Maria del Giglio with the Church of Santa Maria della Salute, built to commemorate another plague deliverance in 1630, which left the city's population depleted by a third.

For many Venetians the highlight of the *Redentore* is the more secular entertainment. It is traditional for every Venetian to take to the water that evening, in boats gaily decorated with verbena leaves and Chinese lanterns. The boats proceed up the Grand Canal for hour after hour, until the *bacino* in front of San Marco is so crowded that it seems possible to walk across the boats' decks all the way to San Giorgio Maggiore. The revellers picnic on stuffed duck breast and wait in their boats for the dazzling firework display. Each device is applauded as enthusiastically as a goal at a football match. The hardiest revellers spend the entire night afloat and refresh themselves with a dawn swim at the Lido.

Hartley's chapter below shows a Venetian trying to explain the joys of the *Redentore* to his foreign charges, one of whom remains resolutely impervious to the excitement of the night.

They had finished supper, they had eaten the duck, the mulberries and the mandarins, the traditional fare of the feast, and were sitting with their champagne glasses in front of them on the white tablecloth when the first rocket went up. Eustace heard the swish like the hissing intake of a giant breath, and his startled nerves seemed to follow its flight. Then with a soft round plop the knot of tension broke, and the core of fiery green dissolved into single stars which floated down with infinite languor towards the thousands of upturned faces. A ripple of delight went through the argosy of pleasure-seekers. Night rushed back into the heavens; the moon, now low down behind the houses, tried to resume her sway; but Nature's spell was broken, everyone was keyed up for the next ascent. Soon it came, bursting into an umbrella of white and crimson drops that almost reached the water before they died, and were reflected in the tablecloth. For a time, at irregular intervals, single rockets continued to go up; then there was a concerted swish, a round of popping as though scores of corks were being drawn, and arc upon arc of colour blotted out the sky. The infant stars burst from their matrix and, still borne aloft by the impetus of their ascent, touched the summit of their flight, brushed the floor of Heaven and then fell back appeased. The lift and spring in the air all around him was like an intoxication to Eustace, and he glanced at the others to see if they shared it.

'Good show,' said Lord Morecambe. 'A bit old-fashioned, of course, but good considering.'

'Considering what, my dear?' asked Lady Nelly.

'I don't want to hurt your feelings, but I saw some Italian shooting on the Isonzo, and I'm surprised they're so handy with fireworks. Of course, the sky's a big target, and doesn't hit back.'

'I wish you would try not to see things always in terms of bloodshed,' said Lady Nelly. 'Couldn't you stop him, Héloise?'

'I do try to make him think of something else,' said Lady Morecambe.

'Darling Héloise, I think of you all the time,' her husband said, and put his hand on hers.

Eustace was touched by this gesture, which he attributed to the liberating influence of the fireworks, and wondered how Lady Nelly would respond to a caress from him. Perhaps the same impulse was felt in all the hundreds of little boats that gently rocked beneath their lanterns on the windless, unfretted water; perhaps every heart sent up a rocket to its objective in the empyrean of love. The thought pleased Eustace, and he tried to make the symbol more exact. Viewless, perceptible only by the energy, the winged whizz of its flight, desire started up through the formless darkness of being; its goal reached, it burst into flower – a flower of light that transfigured everything around it; having declared and made itself manifest, it dropped back released and fulfilled, and then at a moment that one could never foresee, it died, easily, gently, as unregretted as a match that a man blows out when it has shown him something more precious than itself.

Silvestro and Erminio had finished their supper and were disposed upon the poop – Erminio upright and slender at the back, Silvestro accommodating his bulk horizontally to the curves and planes, the projections and recesses, of which the rear end of the gondola was so bewilderingly composed. Catching Eustace's eye, he pivoted monumentally upon his elbow and said:

'Piace ai signori la mostra pirotecnica?'

'What does he say?' said Lord Morecambe.

'He wants to know if we are pleased with the pyrotechnics,' said Eustace.

'What long words they use,' said Lord Morecambe. 'Why couldn't he have said fireworks? Tell him we're enjoying it very much, but the ladies want to know when it'll be over.'

'Oh, don't say that, Mr. Cherrington,' said Héloise. 'It would hurt his feelings terribly. I've never been so happy in my life. I should like to stay here all night – wouldn't you, Lady Nelly?'

'Perhaps not quite all night,' said Lady Nelly, 'though I'm loving it too. What time is it, Eustace?'

Eustace took out his watch. A burst of ice-blue stars were reflected in the glass, hiding the hands. When they died out he said, 'Just about one.'

'Long past Héloise's bedtime,' said Lord Morecambe. 'Look, even the moon's worn out from sightseeing.'

Eustace noticed for the first time that the moon had set, and this realization made the night suddenly seem much darker.

Silvestro, still holding the acrobatic pose on his elbow, spoke again. 'Sono contenti i signori?'

'Don't keep him waiting for an answer,' said Lord Morecambe. 'It's rude, and besides, you might get knifed. Let's hear you give him a vote of thanks, Cherrington, in your best Italian.'

'Please say it's heavenly, Mr. Cherrington,' said Lady Morecambe.

'I wouldn't, Cherrington; it might sound blasphemous to him. You never know with foreigners. Say it's fair to medium.'

Eustace glanced at Lady Nelly, who was obviously enjoying his embarrassment.

'Say we couldn't be happier, but we remember he has to get up early, and we're ready to go back as soon as he is.'

'Truckling to them,' muttered Lord Morecambe.

Eustace cleared his throat.

'La Contessa dice che siamo contentissimi,' he began. 'Ma ricordando che loro due debbono alzarsi ben presto—'

'Bravo!' cried Lord Morecambe. 'He's a regular Wop.'

'Ma, signore,' protested Silvestro, without giving Eustace time to finish, and swivelling round so as to impend portentously over the heads of Héloise and Lady Nelly, 'loro dovrebbero aspettare la fine della mostra, perchè stasera abbiamo una novità, qualcosa di raro, unica si può dire uno spettacolo veramente tremendo, mai ancora visto alla festa del Redentore mai, mai. Sarebbe un disastro perderlo, sicuro.'

Evidently afraid that Silvestro's appeal might fall on deaf ears, Erminio, pressing forward as far as he dared, translated it.

'He says you ought to await the finish of the show, because to-night we have something most hextraordinary, a novelty, a thing unique, never seen before at the Feast of the Redeemer. Hit would be a disaster to lose hit, sure thing.'

'Yers,' said Silvestro, using the monosyllable to underline everything Erminio had said, and forgetting in his excitement to reprove him for showing off. 'Il professore pirotecnico m'ha detto lui stesso che sarà roba fantastica, indimenticabile.'

'The pyrotechnic professor has told him hit will be fantastic stuff, hunforgettable,' said the interpreter, breathing gustily.

By now both gondoliers were on their feet and the gondola rocked from side to side.

'Well, tell us what it is,' said Lord Morecambe, 'don't kill us with suspense.'

Too tactful to reply directly, Erminio passed the question to Silvestro, who spread out his hands and looked despairing and, so far as in him lay, pathetic.

'Non so, signore, non so neanch' io. Sarà una sorpresa – una sorpresa molto, molto religiosa.'

Hardly were the words out of his mouth when Erminio said, 'He does not know, not heven he. It will be a surprise, a very, very religious surprise.'

'In that case I think we must wait,' said Lady Nelly, and signified as much to the gondoliers, who subsided with deep sighs of thankfulness, as though they had successfully appealed for someone's life.

'What can it be?' said Lord Morecambe. 'Anything religious could surprise me. Let's have a bet. Cherrington, your book, please.'

'Sh!' cried Héloise. 'Look!'

Instinctively their eyes turned to the church. For several minutes there had been a lull in the fireworks and the nip of tension was in the air. Since the moon set the church had receded and grown indistinct: its outlines were lost in its vast bulk. Shadowy but solid, it seemed part of the substance of the night.

Suddenly two lines of fire ran up from the extremities of its base. Systematically they explored the great façade until all its outlines were re-created in light. Floodlit below, dark at the top, the dome still floated free of the golden chains; then from three points at once the creeping fire attacked it, and in a moment the huge bubble was imprisoned in three ropes of light. Broken by the moving shapes of boats, elongated and wavy, the reflection of the fire-girt church spread across the quiet water almost to where they sat.

'Why, that's the most beautiful thing I ever saw in my life,' Héloise exclaimed.

'Ah, but you haven't seen Piccadilly Circus on Boatrace Night,' her husband reminded her. 'White Horse Whisky and Sandeman's Port have this beat, as your compatriots say.'

'Guardi, guardi,' cried Silvestro, urgent with excitement. 'Adesso comincia la vera sorpresa.'

As though traced by an invisible finger, the outline of a face began to appear on the dark wall, a pointed face, drooping in weariness. The features were hardly more than indicated, but it was plain that the eyes were closed. Then, above the face, little runnels of light started in all directions, branching out until they filled and overflowed the architrave, leaving at the edges sharp golden spikes that pierced the darkness. Always when it seemed that the representation was complete another thread of fire would worm its way through the others, to add its sharp point to the bristling circumference. Soon it seemed to Eustace as though the lines of light began to move and the whole emblem was aflame; and at the same moment thin trickles of red, starting from the top, dripped their way downwards on to the forehead of the Redeemer.

'The Crown of Thorns,' murmured Héloise, awestruck.

City of Sights

FOREIGNERS

He who loves foreigners loves the wind.

Italianised Englishman:
The Devil Incarnate.

Seven buttocks, three arseholes and a half.
(Venetian description of a typical land-dweller.)

VENETIAN PROVERBS

An English child in Venice, on seeing the Place St Mark for the first time, is said to have asked, 'Pray, Mamma, are people allowed to see this every day, or only on Sundays?'

. . . being newly from a land where everything, morally and materially, was in good repair, I rioted sentimentally on the picturesque ruin, the pleasant discomfort and the hopelessness of everything about me there.

WILLIAM DEAN HOWELLS

I scarcely wake in the morning but I thank God he has let me spend my days in Venice . . .

RAWDON BROWN

In short, he who doesn't go to Venice is a fool.

ANTON CHEKHOV

The senses are so dazzled and almost bewildered, I think, on arriving here, that we are tempted at first to run (or rather swim) up and down, staring at one thing, peeping at another, and endeavouring to find our way about the strange new world, much as a cat does on arriving at a new abode.

FRANCES TROLLOPE

One dreams again so of some clutched perch of one's own here. But it's the most drivelling of dreams.

HENRY JAMES

Mr. Cook's first trainload has arrived, and two more tours are due.

FREYA STARK

What is worst of all is that these *tourists* wield a terrible power: they bear an image of Venice back out into the rest of the world as a city too-seen, too-visited, too-known to bother with. Venice: been there, done that.

PAOLO BARBARO

If I had been an unconnected man,
I from this moment, should have formed some plan
Never to leave sweet Venice . . .

PERCY BYSSHE SHELLEY

Seat of enchantment! Head-quarters of pleasure, farewell!

HESTER PIOZZI

Niccolò of Poggibonsi

(14th century)

'When the Venetians stroll out in the evening,' Mary McCarthy observed, 'they do not avoid the Piazza San Marco . . . The Venetians go to look at the tourists, and the tourists look back at them.'

An ambivalence tinges the expression of those looks given by the Venetians. On one hand, they see the tourists as not just their livelihood but their entertainment; on the other they see their city consumed by visitors: the only theme park in the world where admission is free.

A non-Venetian is known as a *forestiero*, an outsider. (Though a Venetian from the *sestiere* of Castello has been known to call someone who moves there from Dorsoduro a *forestiero* too.)

One of the first *forestieri* to record his experiences of the city was Niccolò of Poggibonsi, probably born in Tuscany and educated as a priest. In 1346, he decided to undertake a pilgrimage to the Holy Lands of the East. Venice being the starting point for all such journeys, he came first to the city.

On 6 April he embarked for Cyprus, then visited Galilee, Jerusalem, Beirut, Cairo, Alexandria and Sinai, returning to Venice by Christmas 1350. His *Libro di Oltramare*, *Book of Beyond the Seas*, describes his experiences. It seems that he conceived his writings as an early kind of guidebook for other pilgrims, and so practical advice predominates, but his interest took in everything: art, customs, engineering, bizarre tales.

In the sixteenth century, Venice would make a fetish of one of her secular martyrs: in an urn at San Giovanni e Paolo is preserved the skin of Marcantonio Bragadin, Venetian commander at Cyprus, flayed alive by the Turks in 1571.

Poggibonsi observed, as Ruskin did later, how Venice coveted the relics of saints. Another pilgrim noted in 1480 that the following saintly parts, among others, were to be found in the city: the arms of St Luke the Evangelist and St Cecilia, the head of St John the Almsgiver, a leg bone of St Simon the apostle, the thigh bones of St Ursula and St Hadrian, ribs from St Stephen and St Martin and one of the thorns from the crown of thorns worn by Jesus Christ.

~~~

Here I shall tell something of the sanctuaries of Venice, albeit they are not overseas sanctuaries. The city holds many holy bodies, to wit, that of San Marco Evangelista; though indeed it is not to be seen. But I saw entire the complete body of Santa Lucia and that of San Zaccheria, the father of San Giovanni Battista, wholly entire, and those of the Santi Cosma and Damiano, and the foot of Santa Maria of Egypt: and I saw the thigh-bone of San Cristoforo and measured it; which was from the hip-joint to that of the knee four very large spans and the measurement of the thickness of the said bone was also four spans: and many other bodies of saints I visited.

Herman Melville

(1819–91)

The American author of *Moby Dick* arrived in Venice in April
1857 on a train: a 4000-yard bridge had joined the city to the
mainland for the first time just twelve years before. Residing at
the Hotel Luna, Melville spent five memorable days in the city,
sketching every experience in his journal. He particularly enjoyed
the atmospheric Armenian convent where Byron had studied.
Among other places he noted was the Ca' d'Oro, then in the possession of the dancer Maria Taglioni, who was rousing the ire of
John Ruskin with her ruinous modernisations.

Melville seems to have spent most of his time afloat in a gondola. The writer, born in New York, had begun his long
love-affair with the sea in 1839, when he took his first job as
cabin boy on a boat. He went on to work on a whaler. After
many adventures at sea, including capture by cannibals, he settled
down to writing sea sagas instead of living them.

The observations in his journal are jotted in note-form –
'Numbers of beautiful women. The rich brown complexions of
Titian's women drawn from nature, after all' – which makes
them seem very fresh and modern, but also has the effect of
making his itinerary exhausting merely to read.

Dinner. Walk in St. Mark's. To bed. – No place like the St. M.s Square for enjoyment. Public ball room – no hours. Lights. Ladies taking refreshments outside. (In morning they breakfast on sunny side). Musicians. singers. soldiers &c &c &c. Perfect decorum. Fine architecture. – In the evening met in Ducal Palace (the court) affable young man (Antonio) engaged him to meet me for guide tom(orrow).

April 3rd Friday. To Glass bead manufactury. Drawing the rods like twine-making. cutting, rounding, polishing, coloring a secret. To Gold chain manufactury. Old Venetian gold . . .

On the canals of Venice all vehicles are represented. Omnibus, private coach, light gig, or sulky, pedler's cart, hearse. – [You, at first, think it a freshet, it will subside, not permanent, – only a temporary condition of things. – St: Mark's at sunset. gilt mosaics, pinnacles, looks like holyday affair. As if the Grand Turk had pitched his pavilion here for a summers day. 800 years! Inside the precious marbles, from extreme age, look like a mural of rare old soaps. – have an unctuous look. Fairly steamed with old devotions as refectories with old dinners. – In Venice nothing to see for the Venetian. – Rather be in Venice on rainy day, than in other capital on fine one. – My Guide. How I met him, & where. Lost his money in 1848 Revolution & by travelling. – To day in one city, tomorrow in next. Fine thing to travel: When rich, plenty compliment.

How do you do, Antonio – hope you very well, Antonio – Now Antonio no money, Antonio no compliment. Get out of de way Antonio. Go to the devil, Antonio. Antonio you go shake yourself. You know dat Sir, dat to de rich man, de poor man habe always de bad smell? You know dat Sir? (For Con. Man)

Yes, Antonio, I am not unaware of that. Charitably disposed. Old blind man, give something & God will bless you [Will give, but doubt the blessing]. [Antonio good character for Con. Man] Did not want to die. Heaven. You believe dat? I go dere, see how I like it first. – His rich anecdote. Byron swimming over by (secrecy) to wake a lady in palace opposite.

Elizabeth Barrett Browning

(1806–61)

Venice, as we have observed, seldom goes begging for praise, but one of her most enthusiastic visitors was the English poet Elizabeth Barrett Browning, who spent a month there in 1851 with her husband, the poet Robert Browning, and their son, known as Pen.

The couple had eloped in 1846 to Italy where they lived in great happiness, chiefly at the Casa Guidi in Florence.

The 'gloriously fatter' toddler of this letter would one day, make his home in Venice. Pen Browning, condemned to mediocrity by the length of his parents' shadows, sculpted and painted, a little. In 1888, with the fortune of his American wife at his disposal, he bought the handsome Ca' Rezzonico on the Grand Canal.

Robert Browning, a frequent visitor to the city, had tried to buy the Contarini del Zaffo palazzo without success, and stayed as a guest of the wealthy American hostess Katharine de Kay Bronson. He died at the Rezzonico in 1889. Several of his famous poems have Venetian settings. The ageing poet and his sister Sarianna were a well-known sight in the town. They particularly enjoyed feeding the elephant and a large baboon in the zoo at the Giardini.

The 1851 trip to Venice was Robert Browning's second, but his wife's first. She had expected to find the city immersed in squalid desolation, but instead found it tranquil and restful, and discovered that it suited her perfectly, emotionally and physically.

The doting mother attributed a great love of the Venetian pigeons to the infant Pen. Her faithful maidservant Wilson, who had collaborated in the elopement and lived with them in Italy, was clearly less impressed with Venice and apparently declared that another month there would kill her.

In this letter to her friend Mary Russell Mitford, Elizabeth Barrett Browning describes the joy she found in the city. In another letter to her cousin, written on her journey home, she confessed that she would have been happy to live and die there without ever leaving it.

I have been between heaven and earth since our arrival at Venice. The heaven of it is ineffable. Never had I touched the skirts of so celestial a place. The beauty of the architecture, the silver trails of water up between all that gorgeous colour and carving, the enchanting silence, the moonlight, the music, the gondolas – I mix it all up together, and maintain that nothing is like it, nothing equal to it, not a second Venice in the world. Do you know, when I came first I felt as if I never could go away. But now comes the earth side. Robert, after sharing the ecstasy, grows uncomfortable, and nervous, and unable to eat or sleep; and poor Wilson, still worse, in a miserable condition of continual sickness and headache. Alas for these mortal Venices – so exquisite and so bilious! Therefore I am constrained away from my joys by sympathy, and am forced to be glad that we are going off on Friday. For myself, it does not affect me at all. I like these moist, soft, relaxing climates; even the scirocco doesn't touch me much. And the baby grows gloriously fatter in spite of everything.

George Sand (Amandine Aurore Dudevant)

(1804–76)

Venice made an ideal backdrop for the melodramatic love-life of the eccentric French writer, who not only took a male name but adopted masculine attire and *mores*. In 1834 she staged there the finale of her affair with the febrile young writer Alfred de Musset: while he lay ill in the Danieli Hotel, Sand, under the pretence of writing a poem, composed ardent love letters to Pietro Pagello, the handsome young Venetian doctor.

'Born under different skies we have neither the same thoughts nor the same language – have we, perhaps, hearts that resemble one another?' she scribbled . . . 'The ardour of your glances, the violent clasp of your arms, the fervour of your desire, tempt me and frighten me. I do not know whether to combat your passion or to share it. One does not love like this in my country; beside you I am no more than a pale statue that regards you with desire, with trouble, with astonishment . . . Shall I be your companion or your slave?'

Sand's Italian was poor and Pagello's French non-existent. She chose to see this as an advantage: 'What I have sought for in vain in others, I shall not, perhaps, find in you, but I can always believe that you possess it. Those looks, those caresses of love that have always lied to me in others, you will allow me to interpret as I wish, without adding deceitful words to them. I shall be able to interpret your reveries and fill your silences with eloquence . . . Let us remain thus, do not learn my language, and I shall not look for, in yours, words to express my doubts and fears. I want to be ignorant of what you do with your life and what part you play among your fellow-men. I do not even want to know your name. Hide your soul from me that I may always believe it to be beautiful.'

And so the imperious, impulsive Sand peremptorily abandoned the whining and drunken de Musset for Pagello. A lengthy and, in some ways, grotesquely funny emotional blackmailing by de Musset ensued. Each of the two writers created their own thinly disguised fictional accounts of their frenzied love-affair, which quite possibly generated more purple prose than real passion.

Sand took up with Pagello for some time, even living for a period *en famille* at his home in the Corte Minelli near the Ponte Barcaroli. As ever, her ardour for the man soon palled, but her adoration of his city was for ever. Venice stars in her novels *L'Uscoque*, about the pirates of the Adriatic, *Consuelo*, *Les Maîtres Mosaïstes*, and *Leone Leoni*. She also waxes lyrical in her *Lettres d'un Voyageur*, from which comes this extract on the delectations of Venetian nights, a subject on which she was an undoubted expert.

No one has ever said enough of the beauty of the heavens, and the delights of the night at Venice. The lagoon is so calm, that in fine evenings, the stars do not even tremble on its surface. When you are in the midst, it is so blue, so quiet that the outline of the horizon cannot be distinguished, and the waves and the heavens form an azure veil, where reverie loses itself and sleeps. The atmosphere is so transparent, so pure that thousands more stars may be seen, than in our North of France. I have seen here, nights, when the silvery lustre of the stars occupied more space in the firmament than the blue of the atmosphere. It was a galaxy of diamonds giving almost as good a light as the moon at Paris . . . Here Nature, more powerful in her influence, perhaps, imposes too much silence on the mind; she sends all thought to sleep, but agitates the heart, and dominates the senses. One must not even dream, unless one is a man of genius, of writing poems during these voluptuous nights: one must love or sleep.

Constance Fenimore Woolson

(1840–94)

Life bleakly imitated art for this vulnerable American writer. On 24 January 1894 she fell – or jumped – from the third floor window of her Grand Canal apartment onto the pavement below. Woolson's death ironically reflects a scene in her book *Dorothy*, published just two years earlier. The eponymous character considers suicide under the influence of depression.

Born in New Hampshire, Woolson led a life punctuated with tragedy. Her husband died in a train accident in 1871; she was shattered by the deaths of her father and brother. When her mother died in 1879, Woolson left for Europe, drifting through Egypt, North Africa and England before arriving in Venice for the last year of her life. Apart from melancholy, she suffered from hearing problems, financial difficulties and the pressure of deadlines. Her meticulous work, including six novels and many short stories, often reflected her own sense of dislocation.

She first lived in the Casa Biondetti near the Accademia and then moved to the Casa Simitecolo, opposite the Europa Hotel. She enjoyed the friendship of the thriving American community in Venice, at whose heart were Henry James and his hosts the Curtis family, who had bought and restored the Palazzo Barbaro on the Grand Canal. But Woolson's sense of alienation proved stronger than the kindness they offered. It is also possible that she nursed an unrequited attraction to James.

James was devastated by her death, which he attributed to a

'violent cerebral derangement'. Appointed her executor, he found the role almost unbearable, and it seems that he eventually destroyed all her letters, unfinished manuscripts and even some of her clothes by drowning them in the Venetian lagoon.

'In Venice', extracted here, comes from *In the Front Yard and Other Italian Stories*, published posthumously in 1895. Other stories in the book describe incidents and real characters the writer had encountered, such as James' great friend in Venice, the wealthy and cultured Bostonian Katharine de Kay Bronson, who kept court at the Ca' Alvisi opposite the Salute.

In this story, as elsewhere, Woolson shows a maliciously acute ear for that other kind of American visitor to Venice – the kind that gives the tribe a bad name: her Mrs Marcy, speaking below, expresses sentiments the writer must have heard many times.

〜

'Yes, we came over again in February, and have been here in Venice since the last of March. For some reasons I was sorry to come back – one *is* so much more comfortable at home! What I have suffered in these wretchedly cold houses over here words, Mr. Blake, can never express. For in England, you know, they consider fifty-eight Fahrenheit quite warm enough for their drawing-rooms, while here in Italy – well, one never *is* so cold, I think, as in a warm climate. Yes, we should have been more comfortable, as far as *that* goes, in my own house in New York, reading all those delightful books on Art in a properly warmed atmosphere (and I must say a properly warmed spirit too), and looking at photographs of the pictures (you can have them as large as you like, you know), instead of freezing our feet over the originals, which half the time the eyes of a lynx could not see. But it is not always winter, of course. And then I have lived over here so long that I have, it seems, acquired foreign ways that are very unpopular at home. You may smile, and it *is* too ridiculous; but it is so. For instance, last summer we went to Carley Ledge (you know Carley; pretty little place), and we found out afterwards that the people came near mobbing us! Not exactly that, of course, but they took the most violent dislike to us . . .'

George Augustus Sala
(1828—95)

Another writer to arch an eyebrow over Venice was the irrepressible Englishman George Augustus Sala, social satirist, travel writer, novelist and journalist.

In 1851, Charles Dickens accepted one of his articles for his journal *Household Words* and later sent him to Russia as special correspondent. In 1857 Sala was writing up to ten articles a week for the *Daily Telegraph*, although thanks to his avid collecting of rare books and expensive china, he was never out of debt.

As the *Telegraph*'s foreign correspondent, he reported on wars and uprisings all over Europe. During the Franco-Prussian War he was arrested in Paris as a spy but was eventually released. The author of *The Strange Adventures of Captain Dangerous* (1863) found himself in Italy just at its moment of liberation.

But in Venice, as Sala explains, the joy was mixed: 'national vanity was intensely mortified . . . by the contemptuous cession of Venetia by the Austrians, not directly to the Italians, but through the intermediary of France: a scornful flinging away, as though the Kaiser were saying, "here, give this dog his bone; and let your General Leboeuf hand it to him; for I will not."'

With enormous relish, Sala describes the astonishing transformation of the Piazza San Marco, sullen and silent under the yoke of the Austrians, but exploding with patriotic joy once the hated oppressors, their toadies and the symbols of their dominance had been sent packing. Sala finds himself carried away with the fervour.

The plebiscite to which he refers, joining Venice to the Kingdom of Victor Emmanuel, was won by 674,426 votes to 69.

Now yesterday I looked through the great entrance-portal, and all was changed. The vast expanse was full of human movement. It was as though a whole federation of ant-hills had spumed forth their teeming commonwealths upon one vast marble slab. I emerged into the Place, and I strove to look upon the strange and unaccustomed spectacle, first from the enthusiastic, next from the morose point of view. Regarding it from the first, the sight was glorious. It made one's heart leap for joy. Gone, for ever, were the Austrian sentries from before the Zecca and the royal palace. Gone were the detestable patrols, whose bayonets were continually, morally speaking, prying over your shoulders, or poking into your loins. There were no more gray-coated, bandy-legged Croats, sulking or grinning behind the hideous bars of the Cancellate, like hyaenas in their dens. That aggressive standard of black and yellow was furled for ever. Those two murderous field-pieces had ceased to point menacingly across the Piazzetta. They had been unlimbered for good, and packed, with other rubbishing marine-stores, on board an Austrian Lloyd's bound for Trieste. The two monstrous gilt eagles that used to flap their domineering wings from twin pedestals in the palace-garden had taken away their four ugly heads to other eyries. The Austrian military band had uttered their last toot, and migrated to more congenial orchestras. There were no more white-tunicked or sky-blue-coated Tedeschi to loll over the tables at Quadri's, or promenade up and down the Piazza with their much-bedizened *Frauen*, eyeing the Venetians, half with a scowl of hatred, half with a sneer of supercilious contempt. There were no more skulking gendarmes, with murderous-looking cutlasses stuck in their rusty belts, like those of the *bravi* in the *Promessi Sposi*.

In their place I saw, for the first time in Venice, the real Italian people, enjoying themselves to their heart's content. Soldiers walking arm-in-arm with gondoliers; Garibaldini in their red shirts, followed by cheering and applauding groups; National Guards, belonging mostly to the club and shopkeeping class, and who, a fortnight since, would have no more presumed to handle a musket and bayonet than to climb the three tall masts under the nose of an Austrian patrol, and hoist the Italian tricolor there. In their place I saw dozens of organ-grinders playing Garibaldi's Hymn; booksellers' shops full of the portraits of the King, the Princes, and Garibaldi; legions of ballad-singers, yelling patriotic lyrics; and from every window a kaleidoscopic display of the national colours. Among the people nine out of every ten men you met had the tricolor arranged as a cockade for their caps or a rosette for their button-holes; the women had scarves and neckbows of the three hues; the children wore frocks and petti-coats of red, white, and green; and almost every adult, gentle or simple, wore in his hat, or pinned to his breast, a little piece of white cardboard, bearing the monosyllable 'SI,' and signifying that his electoral mind was firmly made up, and that on Sunday next, when the solemn vote or *plebiscitum* will be taken, he intended to return to the elaborate question, 'Are you desirous that Venetia should be united to the kingdom of Italy under the rule of Victor Emmanuel the Second?' one conclusive and sonorous 'YES.'

So much for the enthusiastic side of the picture. Remembering, as I did, that I had known Venice as an old curios-ity-shop, as a museum of antiquities, as a barrack-yard governed only by the bayonet and the stick, as a city in a state of siege, as a dungeon, as a tomb, I felt very much inclined to fling up *my* cap and burst forth in a series of ecstatic *evvivas* for Victor Emmanuel, for United Italy, for Giuseppe Garibaldi, for *la bella famiglia*, which is an Italian equivalent for 'our noble selves,' for the Lion of St. Mark, St. Theodore, St. Zuliano, San Moïsè, and all our Venetian Saints. The aspect of so many newspapers, where once newspapers were all but entirely prohibited, filled me, in particular, with feelings of the liveliest gratification. It was a sight for sore eyes to see the ragged little newsboys running about barefoot, their wallet of intelligence, damp from the press, under their arms, and screeching out the names of the hundred and one newspapers which, in a deluge of typography, have fallen on Venice. There is *Daniele Manin* number one, and a rival *Daniele Manin* number two. There is the *Conte Cavour*, the *Pungolo*, the *Perseveranza*, the *Opinione*, the *Sole*, the *Sciolo*, the *Gazzetta del Popolo*, and the *Unione*; and in particular there is the *Gazzetta di Venezia*, once the terrible *Gazzetta Ufficiale*, but which is now bereft of the effigy of the double-headed eagle, and which the little newsboys, who are arch wags, cry about as *senza gallina* – without the cock-a-doodle-doo – or as *La Paolona Pentita*, la Paolona being the traditional Scarlet Woman whose repentance once equally amused and scandalised Venice.

It was as well that I did not fling up my cap, and that I did not break forth into *evvivas*. I recollected that it was no affair at all of mine . . .

Douglas Goldring

(1887–1961)

Foreigners arriving in Venice for the first time are to be envied. The excitement conjured by a virgin approach is well described by the London novelist Douglas Goldring in a letter from his *Dream Cities*, *Notes of an Autumn Tour in Italy and Dalmatia*, published in 1913.

Goldring had previously worked on *Country Life* and the *English Review*. In 1910 he founded and edited *The Tramp*, famous for its verse contributors, of which he was one, as he somewhat ruefully observes below.

In Venice he stays on the Riva degli Schiavoni and in San Marco finds himself jostled by all kinds of foreigner. This leads him to muse on the procession of visitors who enlivened the history of the city with their indefatigable curiosity and histrionics. He concludes that the best kind of tourism in Venice is of another variety entirely . . .

~~~

Venice, September 7th

My dear, – It is hard, in any case, to write in an Italian train, but excitement is making my hand shake almost more than the speed at which we are going. That, alas! is not very great. It is dark now. It seems years since we left Milan and at every station I get up and peer out of the window to see if we're at Venice, and we never are. I suppose my agitation is due partly to having written so many inferior verses about Venice, and I tremble now like a lover preparing to meet, for the first time, a lady of whom he has conducted a frenzied wooing by letter!

I hadn't the least idea that Italy could take so long to cross; on the map it looked such a slim country; yet here we are at seven o'clock, and no Venice. The series of hideous anti-climaxes I have been through has left me emotionally bankrupt. But now the train is drawing up once more; we *must* be there at last . . . No, it was only Mestre! I leaped on to the permanent way, twisted my ankle, and have had to crawl back again . . . Venice, though, I have just discovered, is really the next station; and now that the people are bustling about getting down suit-cases and walking-sticks, I feel unnaturally calm – no doubt from nervous exhaustion. The night outside has the peculiar velvet quality of darkness over water: we must be on the causeway which joins Venice to the mainland, with the lagoon on either hand. Yes, it is water right enough. The darkness has just been made tangible by a distant splash of gold light, which grows nearer and larger, and seems now like a giant firefly scudding over the waveless surface. It is a little brightly-lighted steamer, evidently one of those *vaporetti* of which one hears so often, and I can distinguish the br-r-r of its engine through the roar of the train. I can't write any more now because the fat woman opposite me is standing on my toe . . .

*

The human interest of Venice, one guesses, is almost as much concerned with its foreign visitors as with the wonderful race of whom it is the memorial. As the tide passes swiftly up the Grand Canal, one has a vision of Byron plunging into the water, from the steps of the Palazzo Mocenigo, to swim to the Lido. Then one can see Musset and Georges Sand – *elle et lui* – arriving gracefully at the steps of the Teatro Goldoni (the Teatro Malibran, presumably, would not then have been built). She, I think, would be wearing a *visite* and a bustle, flounces, or possibly a crinoline, with a flimsy veil floating from her straw bonnet: while he would be adorned in a surprising waistcoat and frilled shirt, trousers strapped over his boots, and a shaggy top-hat, while his tie would be scrupulously *à la* Byron. Then Shelley, Meredith, Turgenev, Whistler, Théophile Gautier, and a hundred others, whom one can't remember at the moment, have they not all endowed Venice with the glamour of their genius? Of Browning one is reminded with rather too much insistence by the great pile of the Palazzo Rezzonico, and thousands of eyes are raised daily from little red books, to hunt out the window of the third-floor room in which he died. And then there is Ruskin, who tells you precisely what you must admire, and what you must not admire, who has appraised, with wearying finality, each separate 'stone.'

For myself, My Dear, I can't bow the neck to Ruskin, and this thirst for detail makes me obstinate and languid. I like just to sit motionless, lapped round by the wonderful air that is so charged with immemorial, haunting whispers, and drink in the place in large gulps. I like the effect of a mile of great palaces, one following another, but I have no curiosity as to which palace is which. I like to watch the great domes, of a dazzling white, standing out against a faery sky, with campaniles, thin almost as minarets, tapering upwards by the side of them. I like to get an impression of a congeries of noble buildings filled with treasures that are the world's wonder, and to have it crowded by a vision of the Duomo or of some other culminating point, like the Rialto. To pull my idea of a complete Venice into little, distinct pieces, each with a label attached, is in a sense grievous, as grievous as it would be to dismantle some wonderful piece of jewellery made up of precious stones, each separately of value, but of far greater significance as part of a designed whole. To examine a jewel in detail under the microscope, to remove it from its setting, is to ask for disappointments.

Clarence Major

(1936–)

In his book *Surfaces and Masks* the American poet and novelist
Clarence Major conjures a modern Venice still arrayed in all her
faded glory. The poem included here pinpoints the subtle ways in
which an outsider who lives in Venice can never really feel himself an insider.

Alone, I went into that special
           little windowless bar
near Rialto market,
      said to be the oldest
            of its kind
in Venice; ordered,
        with exaggerated ease,
(like an exhibitionistic
            bullfighter
waving his *muleta* unnecessarily,)
       a tocai and began
to eat the sausages
      from the tray,
  just like the regulars do,
attempting to feel
         Venetian.
It didn't work.
      The fish at the end
of the line finishes himself
       by pulling
against it. The bartender
     overcharged me
as though I were a tourist.
        Had I not lived here
a long, long time?

Then I returned
            a week later,
      quite by chance,
                  with A.,
         who's very, very Venetian,
                  classy and quick,
We had our tocai
            and sausage together.
Two fishermen in the alley
                        outside
      were laughing happily.
The bartender gave me,
                  like a present,
his biggest smile.
            I felt the Great Blue
River running through my veins.
            I was a way
      I had never been before.
A. and I had our tocai again,
                  and the bartender
insisted we have thirds
            on him.
      With a light head,
            and happy at noon,
I walked home the busy way,
      and found P.
            making lunch.

City of Forgotten Voices

THE VENETIANS' VENETIANS

The just man sins seven times a day.

Conscience is like tickling: there are those who feel it and those who don't . . .

You know a man by his work, his marriage and his will . . .

The tongue doesn't have bones, but it breaks bones.

I've read lots of epitaphs, I've looked everywhere, but I have never found written: 'Here Lies a Scoundrel'.

VENETIAN PROVERBS

Venice is extremely singular for . . . the liveliness of its minds, wonderfully quick and skilled in all activities, particularly in commanding; for its decorum that is worn without ambition and without luxury; for its grandness, which shines without flattery . . .

DOMENICO MARTINELLI

Let Virtue be esteem'd, in whatever Person it is found; and altho' the Person that it endowed with it be not Noble, yet let him be highly valued, and encouraged to live among us, for his own Merit makes him Noble sufficiently . . .

FRA PAOLO SARPI

It was reserved for our times of arrogance and ignorance, to represent the Venetian Patricians as a set of petty tyrants, haughty and imperious, whom no law could bind. You know, my dear Countrymen, how false is this representation . . . This Nobility, invidiously represented as preying on the vitals of the country, served the public . . . without any emolument; nay more, the wealthy among us spent a great part of their fortunes in the public service. As to the accusation of haughtiness, nothing can be more false. Did you find anywhere the nobility so affable as in Venice?

COUNT ZENOBIO

Venetian intelligence was directed solely to the acquisition of that most difficult of all knowledge, knowledge of one's self.

POMPEO MOLMENTI

Venice is not something one can explain. You need to see it, feel it, and experience it from the right point of view . . .

MASSIMO CACCIARI (FORMER MAYOR)

Marino Faliero

(1274–1355)

In a city where few personalities outshine the architecture, one angry old man casts a long shadow: the traitor Doge Marino Faliero.

Faliero was a son of one of the original noble families, which had already given Venice two Doges. A soldier and merchant, as well as an ambassador to Rome, he was elected Doge in 1354.

The hot-tempered octogenarian was outraged when an insult against his wife, perpetrated by a minor noble, went lightly punished, and he embroiled himself in a conspiracy to transform the Republic into a dictatorship. But the plot was betrayed, his accomplices put to torture, and Faliero himself was dragged before a tribunal of the Council of Ten and the Grand Council. Found guilty, he was executed on the first steps of the Giant's Staircase inside the courtyard of the Doge's Palace, the very place where he had received his ducal robe and coronet. His portrait in the frieze of Doges in the great Council Chamber still shows just an empty frame with a scroll that reads: 'This is the place of Marino Faliero, decapitated for his crimes.' Four hundred of his co-conspirators were hunted down and killed or exiled.

Faliero's ghost is said to haunt a *campo* behind San Giovanni e Paolo. With his hands tied behind his back, he stalks the street looking for his head, not realising that it has been buried between his own legs. On his trail is the phantom of the blind Doge Enrico Dandolo, who massacred civilians when he took Constantinople in the Fourth Crusade. Dandolo carries a sword with which he slashes his own hands: his punishment for the innocent blood he spilt. He now chases Faliero to avenge the honour of the city, but never finds him, for neither of them can see. Dandolo has burning brands instead of eyes, and Faliero, of course, has no head at all.

Many writers, including Byron, have seized on the dark tale of Faliero with delight. This portrayal of the Doge comes from the Sicilian writer and actor Giovanni Emmanuele Bidera, who interpreted the story as a lyric tragedy in three acts. His *Marino Faliero* was set to music by Donizetti and, with a libretto translated into English by Federico Doca, performed at the King's Theatre in London's Haymarket in May 1835.

In this emotional scene (act III, scene 10) the Doge faces his accusers, led by Leoni, in the Council of Ten and tramples on the famous *corno*, the Doge's hat, cursing his own city. To those hearing these words, the fall of the Republic in 1797 would have been a recent historical event, seeming to fulfil Faliero's curse; the effect must have been electric.

~~~

Leoni: Why, Doge (for such you are as long as the royal diadem adorns your (brows), why have you turned traitor?

Faliero: He who is vanquished is a traitor, and such am I; both the people and prince groaned under your oppression, I looked tyranny in its face and dared to challenge it.

Leoni: You shall receive a punishment adequate to your crime. (*He reads the sentence*). We condemn Faliero, Doge of Venice and Count of Val Marino, to death for felony. Within the noble walls where glorious portraits of the Doges are hung, his portrait shall be covered with a black veil, and infamous words inscribed in its place.

Faliero: Cowards! You dare insult the dead? And who? Faliero! But for him would you be here? I burn with anger! You, the slaves of the Turks, you would have been kept chained at the oars. To me words of infamy! But on the enemy's towers, and on the fields of battle, where I have spread the victorious banner, not my infamy, but your own will be written.

Leoni: It is too much! Lay down the ducal diadem at the foot of the throne!

Faliero: Down to the ground, detestable badge of infamy! I trample it under feet! Perfidious and cruel City, do not rejoice at the fate of this old man! The hours are now silently rolling on to thy last day! Obscure shall be thy death! You shall be a vile mercenary, and an infamous slave, a disgrace to all Italy.

Marino Sanudo

(c. 1466–1536)

'It is impossible,' wrote Thomas Okey in 1907, 'to turn over their worm-eaten covers and venerable pages without a feeling of admiration and almost amazement, at the imperturbable industry and long-suffering patriotism of this author . . .'

The writer described was Marino Sanudo, a Venetian nobleman descended from one of the original ruling families, who bequeathed modern scholarship a remarkable insight into early sixteenth-century Venetian life and European politics in his detailed diaries, which he kept from 1 January 1496 until 30 September 1533.

As a nobleman, Sanudo played his part in the government in the Privy Council, the Senate and the Great Council, but he would also spend time talking to the merchants at Rialto and listening to the local gossip and rumours on the streets. He had access to ambassadors' reports and other official documents; all this gave him an unparalleled bird's-eye view of Venetian life at every level.

His diaries, now kept in the library of St Mark in Venice, are written in Venetian. The early volumes are in a neat upright script with hardly a blot or erasure. However, the later volumes reveal Sanudo's growing disillusionment and advancing old age: they are less scrupulously written and scrap paper was sometimes used. The writer complains that he has to go without the necessities of life in order to buy paper and bindings. He did not receive payment for his efforts until he had completed the fifty-fourth volume in 1531. The Council of Ten then offered to pay him a yearly salary of 150 ducats to continue his patriotic task. Two more volumes were completed before he died in 1536.

He bequeathed the diaries to the Council of Ten, who stored them in such a safe place that they were not rediscovered until 1784, since which time they have provided the essential nourishment for any researcher into sixteenth-century Venice. The Austrians appropriated these precious documents and took them back to Vienna, leaving only copies which were not exchanged for the originals until 1866. Rawdon Brown, the English scholar, was among the first to study them and alert the world to their importance.

This extract describes the earthquake that struck Venice in 1511 and its aftermath. Sanudo's good-humoured cynicism flavours his account with characteristic irony.

On 26 March, a Wednesday, at the hour of 20¾ . . . the weather being somewhat unsettled, a mighty earthquake came suddenly upon this city of Venice. It seemed as though the houses were collapsing, the chimneys swaying, the walls bursting open, the bell-towers bending, objects in high places falling, water boiling, even in the Grand Canal, as though it had been put on a fire. They say that, although it was high tide, when the earthquake came some canals dried up as though there had been a tremendous drought. The earthquake lasted as long as a *Miserere*; all felt the sheer horror of it, in view of the great danger to the people of Venice, who are not used to such earthquakes and have suffered none for many years. The bells in their towers rang by themselves in many places, especially at St Mark's, a terrifying thing to happen. It chanced that the Senate had just assembled to deal with affairs of state, and they had scarcely entered and begun to have a letter read when they heard the noise and felt the trembling of the chamber; then everyone jumped up, the doors were flung wide, and they descended as best they could by the wooden staircase, so quickly that some were carried from top to bottom, their feet touching none of the steps, so fierce was the stampede.

Notable things happened in the midst of all this, and the first was that at St Mark's the marble statues of four kings fell. They were on the façade, in front of which they stood upright, and no other damage occurred, except to certain columns in the church. On the San Basso side, however, there fell the marble statue of a woman, the figure of Prudence, who stood up straight in the midst of other Virtues . . .

Then our Patriarch, Don Antonio Contarini, came . . . saying
that the earthquake is a sign from God, and that misfortunes
occur on account of sins. Venice is full of these, especially of
sodomy, which is recklessly practised everywhere. The female
whores sent to him to say that they cannot make a living because
no one now goes to them, so rampant is sodomy: even the old
men are getting down to it. He has heard from confessors that
fathers are interfering with daughters, brothers with sisters, and
so forth. And the city is becoming irreligious . . . We are now
halfway through lent. In other years the confessors would have
heard the confessions of half the Venetians by this time; but now
they have heard no one but the female tertiaries and a tiny
number of others. The Patriarch then said that he wished to order
processions at St Mark's for three days, and processions in the
parishes in the evenings, and three days fasting on bread and
water to appease the wrath of God. And he said other things too.
The Doge and other members of the Collegio supported him;
they were taking measures against blasphemy, and making sure to
dispense justice, etc. Today, in the Council of Ten, they would
take action against sodomy.

Hence all the preachers appointed to the churches were
ordered to preach, with effect from tomorrow morning, and the
Patriarch ordered a three-day fast on bread and water and a procession around the public squares in the evenings, singing the
litanies, with one at St Mark's in the mornings. I applaud these
things as an aid to piety and good conduct; but as a remedy for
earthquakes, which are a natural phenomenon, this was no good
at all . . .

Aldus Manutius

(c. 1450–1515)

Another name inextricably associated with Venice and still known worldwide is that of the man who brought the art of printing to a peak of perfection never since surpassed.

Aldus Manutius was the founder of the Aldine Press, which produced first editions of many Greek and Roman classics and of Italian writers. The beauty of his Greek and Latin types is still cited as the ideal, and numerous modern computer fonts seek to imitate their graceful subtleties. Among many innovations, Manutius was the first printer to make use of italics in a significant way.

Every Aldine refinement was organic to the text it carried. The incomparable beauty of his printing was informed by a scholarly nature: Aldus was a lover of words in every way and gathered around him a network of scholars, writers, editors, senators, students and priests, who came to be known as the *Neaccademia* of Aldo.

Originally from Bassiano, Manutius settled in Venice around 1488. He married the daughter of the printer Andrea Torresani, who had acquired the press of the famed French typographer Nicholas Jenson.

Printing had arrived in Venice twenty years before Manutius, started by the Germans Johann and Wendelin von Speyer. But the industry had suffered from persecution, plague and an overcrowded market. It was Manutius who transformed Venice into the printing capital of the world. After his death, his son carried on his business.

Manutius is thought to have lived in Rio Terra Secondo, in the parish of San Agostino, or in the nearby Calle del Pistor. He transferred his works around 1506 to Campo San Paternian, now named Campo Manin and sadly blighted by the ugliest structure in Venice, a modern bank, built on the very site of the Aldine Press. How such a piece of Venetian history came to be erased in so brutal a way is a mystery perhaps best left to the American writer Donna Leon, whose gently charismatic Commissario Brunetti, protagonist of her excellent Venetian novels, sadly and philosophically strips bare the corruptions of the city.

In this 1514 book dedication, addressed to his friend Andrea Navagero, Manutius (affectionately known as 'Aldo') makes a humorous complaint about his popularity with the Venetians. He is beset by so many correspondents that merely to answer them would occupy him night and day. So many people come to consult him, embrace him or look on him with curiosity, he explains – quoting Horace's description of leeches that will not yield a piece of skin till it is drained of blood – that it is hard to get any work done and he has been obliged to erect a warning outside his door.

Some from friendship, some from interest, the greater part because they have nothing to do – for then 'Let us go,' they say, 'to Aldo's.' They come in crowds and sit gaping –

'Non missura cutem, nisi plena cruoris hirudo.'

I do not speak of those who come to read to me either poems or prose, generally rough and unpolished, for publication, for I defend myself from these by giving no answer or else a very brief one, which I hope nobody will take in ill part, since it is done, not from pride or scorn, but because all my leisure is taken up in printing books of established fame. As for those who come for no reason, we make bold to admonish them in classical words in a sort of edict placed over our door – 'WHOEVER YOU ARE, Aldo requests you, if you want anything, ask it in few words and depart, unless, like Hercules, you come to lend the aid of your shoulders to the weary Atlas. Here will always be found in that case something for you to do, however many you may be.'

Luigi Cornaro

(1464–1566)

Alvise (known as Luigi) occupied a minor branch of the illustrious Cornaro family tree and was therefore not in line for the usual public offices and honours. Humiliated, he withdrew from Venice and made his home in nearby Padua. He suffered a choleric temperament and an infirm constitution until the age of forty, by which time he had nearly destroyed himself with intemperate habits. At this point he changed the manner of his life completely and recovered to a perfect state of physical and mental equilibrium. He married, and a daughter was born when the couple were both surprisingly advanced in years.

Cornaro was in his eighties when he published his book, *La Vita Sobria (The Temperate Life)*, which takes the form of four discourses. It is suffused with disarming smugness. As he wrote, 'I never knew the world was beautiful until I reached old age.'

He preached an abstemious existence, simple foods in sparing amounts, though wine was allowed, as was a certain flexibility since each person, Cornaro argued, has his own level of excess and moderation to balance. The book received a rapturous welcome and has remained a classic in Italy.

Its doctrines seem to have served the author well. In an age when life expectancy was much shorter than today, Cornaro died peacefully in his hundred and third year.

He was also the author of a treatise on the preservation of the Venetian lagoons, *Trattato delle Acque*, published in 1560, showing him ahead of his time in thoughts of saving the town from the waters. He believed that the problems caused by a dramatic increase in Venice's population (from 110,000 to 175,000 between 1509 and 1563) could be solved only by increased self-sufficiency.

This extract comes from *La Vita Sobria*.

Oh, how glorious will have been this life of mine! so full of all the happiness that can be enjoyed in this world, and so free – as it truly is – from the tyranny of sensuality, which, thanks to my many years, has been driven out by reason! For, where reason reigns, no place is left for sensuality, nor for its bitter fruits, the passions and anxieties of the mind accompanied by a well-nigh endless train of afflicting and sorrowful thoughts.

As for the thought of death, it can have no place in my mind; for there is nothing sensual in me. Even the death of any of my grandchildren, or of any other relatives or friends, could never cause me trouble except the first instinctive motion of the soul, which, however, soon passes away. How much less could I lose my serenity through any loss of worldly wealth! Many of my friends have witnessed this to their great astonishment. However, this is the privilege of those only who attain extreme age by means of the temperate life and not merely through the aid of a strong constitution; it is the former, not the latter, who enjoy every moment of life, as I do, amid continual consolations and pleasures.

And who would not enjoy life at an age when, as I have already shown, it is free from the innumerable miseries by which we all know the younger ages are afflicted! How wholly mine, in its happiness, is free from these miseries, I shall now set forth.

To begin, the first of joys is to be of service to one's beloved country. Oh, what a glorious enjoyment it is, what a source of infinite pleasure to me, that I am able to show Venice the manner in which she may preserve her valuable lagoon and harbor so that they will not alter for thousands of years to come! . . .

There is another thing which affords me much contentment; it is, that I have shown this Virgin and Queen how she may be abundantly supplied with food, by preparing for cultivation – with returns much above the expense – large tracts of land, marshes as well as dry plains, all hitherto useless and waste.

Another sweet and unalloyed satisfaction I experience is, that I have pointed out to Venice how she may be made stronger, although she is now so strong as to be almost impregnable; how her loveliness may be increased, although she is now so beautiful; how she may be made richer, although now exceedingly wealthy; and how her air, which is now so good, may be made perfect.

These three pleasures afford me the greatest possible satisfaction, because based wholly upon my desire to be useful to others. And who could find a drawback to them, since in reality none exists!

Veronica Franco

(1546–91)

In a city famed for its courtesans, none was more celebrated than Veronica Franco, a poetess, free spirit, and a protector of women of her own condition.

Franco was that sought-after commodity, a high-class prostitute who pandered not just to the physical but the intellectual needs of her clients.

Alliances with powerful Venetian men enabled her to publish her work. Her audience was assured by her chief patrons, Marco and Domenico Venier, who held informal literary meetings on a regular basis. She lived a public life, mingling with the highest society. Henry III of France was said to have been enraptured by Franco, and the writer Montaigne was introduced to her.

Whilst most female writers of her time took much care not to tread on the male ego, Franco wrote whatever she wanted, and between 1570 and 1580 she published a large collection of letters from the female viewpoint and gathered material for anthologies. These works made her wealthy and she quit her original profession. However, she never forgot her origins, and set up a halfway house at Santa Maria del Soccorso for courtesans and their children.

In 1575 Veronica Franco fled the plague in Venice. Her self-imposed exile lasted for two years during which she wrote prolifically but, in her absence, her home in San Moisè was ransacked and her possessions stolen. To make matters worse, in

1580 she was charged with witchcraft and although found innocent was publicly humiliated by the Inquisitors. Domenico Venier
died in 1582 leaving her financially and politically vulnerable.
She published nothing more before her death at the age of forty-
five. One of her two wills left a bequest to be used to help
prostitutes give up their 'wicked lives' and take the veil, or as
dowries to enable young women to marry.

In this letter Franco reproaches the mother of a girl who wants
to become a courtesan.

Although the main concern here is the interest of your daughter, I am also talking about you, since her ruin cannot be separated from yours, because you are her mother and because if she were to become a woman of the world you would become her ambassador in the world's eyes and would be the one to be severely punished, while her wrongs would be allowed some excuse as provoked by your faults. You know how many times I have begged you and warned you to take care of her virginity; and since the world is so dangerous and so weak and mothers' houses are not entirely safe from amorous dangers and lustful youth, I showed you the way to free her from dangers and how to help her, giving her a good knowledge of life and how to honestly marry her and I offered you any possible means to make sure she would be accepted in the House of the Maidens, and also to help you, when you would take her there, with my own means . . .

Now, finally, I wanted you to have these lines, exhorting you once again and warning you on your own situation, not to kill with one stroke your soul and your honour together with that of your daughter, who — to consider the situation from a physical point of view — has so little beauty, not to say worse, because my eyes do not fail me, and has so little grace and spirit in conversation, that you are breaking her neck in trying to please her in making her a courtesan, a profession in which it is very hard to succeed for those who are very beautiful and have manners and judgement and knowledge of many virtues; and even harder for a young woman lacking in many of these characteristics and who would only exceed mediocrity in a few of them. And since you, persisting in your error, could tell me that this is all a matter of fortune, I would first answer that one could not do worse in this life than submit oneself to the will of fortune, which can so easily administer evil or good; but those who have good sense, in order not to find themselves eventually cheated, build their hopes on the real characters they have in themselves and on what they can realistically achieve. But then I also add that, even if fortune were favourable and benign to you, this is a kind of life that is eventually miserable in all respects. It is a deeply unhappy thing and too contrary to human nature to force one's body and behaviour to such a slavery which is frightening only to think about. To give oneself as a prey to many, with the risk of being deprived, robbed, and killed, of being able to lose in only one day what you had earned over a long time, with so many dangers of injuring yourself, of catching contagious and terrifying diseases; to eat with someone else's mouth, to sleep with someone else's eyes, to move according to someone else's desires, clearly running towards the wreckage of your faculties and your life; what misery could be worse? What riches, what comforts, what luxuries can acquire so much weight? Believe me: among all possible mundane calamities this is the extreme one; but then if we add to the worldly considerations also those relating to the soul, what a perdition and certainty of damnation is this one? Listen to what people say and do not follow other people's example in matters that concern life and the salvation of the soul: do not allow the flesh of your poor daughter to be slaughtered and sold, or even to become yourself her own butcher . . .

Count Carlo Gozzi

(1720–1806)

Literary life in eighteenth-century Venice was dominated by this redoubtable figure, whose trenchant *Memorie Inutile della vita di Carlo Gozzi, scritte da lui medesimo e pubblicate per umilità (Useless Memoirs of the life of Carlo Gozzi, written by himself and published out of humility)* appeared in three volumes in 1797 when he was seventy-seven years old.

Gozzi was a controversial figure: known not only as a writer of dramas, tales and poems, but also for the war of words he had waged on two other playwrights, Pietro Chiari and Carlo Goldoni, between 1756 and 1762. He was also involved in a dispute with a member of the Contarini family, Pier Antonio Gratarol, in 1777, and the aspersions cast on Gozzi's character by his adversary were probably among his reasons for writing his self-vindicatory autobiography.

Unlike his more famous contemporaries, Casanova and Goldoni, Gozzi never left the Veneto except to serve as a soldier for three years in Dalmatia. Perhaps this insularity partly explains the fervour of his territorial bickerings in the small literary world of Venice.

I ought to render a candid account here of the impression made upon me by those two deluges of ink, Goldoni and Chiari. To begin with Goldoni, I recognised in him an abundance of comic motives, truth, and naturalness. Yet I detected a poverty and meanness of intrigue; nature copied from the fact, not imitated; virtues and vices ill-adjusted, vice too frequently triumphant . . . surcharged characters; scraps and tags of erudition, stolen Heaven knows where, and clumsily brought in to impose upon the crowd of ignoramuses . . .

In spite of all the praises showered upon Goldoni, paid for or gratis . . . [he] was never able to fabricate a single play which does not swarm with faults . . .

Proceeding next to Abbé Chiari. In him I found a brain inflamed, disordered, bold to rashness, and pedantic; plots dark as astrological predictions; leaps and jumps demanding seven-league boots; scenes isolated, disconnected from the action, foisted in for the display of sententious philosophical verbiage; some good theatrical surprises, some descriptions felicitous in their blunt *naiveté*; pernicious ethics; and, as for the writer, I found him one of the most turgid, most inflated, nay, the most turgid, the most inflated, of this century.

Lady Dorothy Nevill

(1826–1913)

Lord Walpole of Orford was not the easiest of companions in Italy, as his daughter Lady Dorothy Nevill recalls: 'My father during our travels would become very irascible at times, particularly when coming in contact with pompous foreign officials. He knew little Italian, but what he did know he used in earnest. For instance, whenever they attempted to stop us at any barrier, he would shout out "Il vostro Re è un scroccone" (Your King is a swindler!), which somewhat trenchant assertion, owing to the tones of thunder in which it was delivered, as a rule paralysed opposition . . .'

Despite such problems, Nevill and her sister enjoyed the most privileged of insights into Venice when the family came there in the 1840s. Their guide was none other than Rawdon Lubbock Brown (1803–83). Among other highlights, he introduced the English visitors to the last tattered remnants of the once-dominant Foscari family.

We had a very kind friend at Venice, Mr. Rawdon Browne, a literary man, who was said to be the greatest living authority upon the history of the city. He possessed a most interesting collection of Venetian antiquities, including some illuminated books once belonging to the Doges . . .

Mr. Browne's rooms were well arranged with old carved chairs, antique writing-tables, and ancient tapestry – everywhere was something to be admired and everything had a story. These charming rooms were in the Palazzo Ferro, looking upon the Grand Canal and the glorious *ex voto* of grateful Venice – Santa Maria della Salute.

Mr. Browne was most kind to us during our stay, and consenting to act as our cicerone, we saw much which would otherwise have been closed to us. With him we went to pay a visit to two old maiden ladies of the great family of Foscari, the last of their race, who lived in the Palazzo Foscari, in a sad state of squalor. We found them in what had been the State bedchamber of the unhappy Doge who fell dead on hearing the bell of the Campanile ringing to celebrate the election of his successor. The room retained little of its ancient splendour, but the figures which formerly supported the bed canopy were in existence, and their fine carving, though terribly worm-eaten, still visible. There were a few broken miserable chairs, table, and a bare old settle, on which we were requested to sit as a seat of ceremony; the bed was of very poor appearance, but large and scrupulously clean. It was a most desolate apartment. One of the old ladies seemed gloomy and cold, whilst the other was very lively and gay, though complaining of being disabled by age. I told her that her happy disposition was a compensation. Poor thing, she had lost all her teeth, and was quite crooked and bowed down. Both of these old ladies wore dresses of the poorest make and quality, but they were always addressed as Contessas and had nothing common in their manners. They had had a little annuity of two zwanzigers a day (about three shillings, I think) arranged for them through a Jew who cheated them out of half of it, which caused the poor old things to lament that, 'whereas on one zwanziger they could hardly exist, on two they could have been perfectly happy.' By a lucky chance, however, their last years were passed in comfort, for the story of their vicissitudes chancing to reach the ears of Lord Alvanley (the well-known wit) when he was staying at Venice, the sad tale touched him, and to the honour of this gay man of fashion be it recorded that, moved by pity for these forlorn old maids, he settled on them the sum which they had desired, and so enabled the last of the Foscari to end their days in complete contentment and peace.

Arnaldo Fusinato

(1817–88)

Arnaldo Fusinato, author of many patriotic and satirical poems, was very much involved in the battle for the independence and unity of Italy. The Venetian revolution of 1848, part of a chain of rebellions from Paris to Milan, was led by Daniele Manin; it provides the backdrop for Fusinato's searing poem.

Manin was the last great political name in the history of Venice. A lawyer by training, he was deeply resentful of the Austrian occupation and conceived a plan of rebellion, printing a call to arms for his fellow citizens. He rallied them together, orchestrating a demonstration where the poet Niccolò Tommaseo openly attacked the suppression of the free press. The two of them were arrested in January 1848 and the Venetians soon rose up in a general strike. Manin raised a civic guard of four thousand and challenged the Austrians, who eventually capitulated. Manin was acclaimed President, a post he held for just eleven months. The Austrians regrouped and encircled the lagoon with 30,000 troops. A pitiless siege and bombardment ensued, and cholera soon spread through the starving streets. On 24 August 1849, Manin was forced to surrender and was sent into exile.

'Addio a Venezia' ('Farewell to Venice') was written at the height of the penultimate drama, on a vigil on the island of the Lazzaretto Vecchio where the author was garrisoned. It is dated 19 August 1849, just days before the defeat, and is among the most beloved of all Venetian poems. It describes the city's emotional desolation in the time of the Austrian sieges.

Gloomy the air
And muted the sky
And in silence, on the terrace,
There sit I.
Melancholy, solitary,
I behold you and sigh,
And I let loose my tears
For Venezia mine.

Through a break in the clouds
Hanging west of the moon,
The last living ray
Of the dying sun swoons
And it whispers in falling
Through the burnished air's gloom
The very last groan
Of our own dear Lagoon.

There passes a gondola
That comes from the streets.
From that black boat
Fresh news we beseech —
'There rages a plague,
There's no bread to eat,
And from the bridge waves
The white flag of defeat.'

No, no, Sun, shine not
Though such pitch-black gloom,
No, sun of Italia, our fortune's
Extinguished, no more shall it bloom.

Never shine you at all
On Venezia's doom,
So draws out the groan
O'er our own sweet Lagoon.

Venezia! This moment
Your last hour greet;
Illustrious martyr,
You must face your defeat.
There rages a plague,
There's no bread to eat,
And from the bridge waves
The white flag of defeat.

But you'll not be consumed
By the cannon's fiery breath
And a thousand explosions
Will not cut the thread
Of your days as a city
Of liberty yet.
Long live Venezia!
Starving to death.

On the pages of history
Let them always be read,
Those foul deeds that murdered
Your glory now fled
And three times deride him
His infamy spread
He who wants Venezia
Starved until dead.

Long live Venezia!
For when a rage thrives

Against such an enemy
Old virtues revive . . .
Yet, there rages a plague,
There's no bread to eat,
And from the bridge waves
The white flag of defeat.

Comes a time I'll dash down
My lyre on these stones
But as long as a freedom
In Venezia glows
On my city
My lyre's last song shall be spent:
My last hymn, my last kiss,
And my last lament.

If exile should claim me,
Venezia mine,
My thoughts shall stay yours
In that foreign clime,
You will live in the shrine
Of my heart and my mind
Like the face of the very first love
That was mine.

But there whistles the wind
O'er the waves of the deep,
And Nature herself seems
Darkly asleep
The voiceless lyre-strings
Discordantly bleat,
And from the bridge waves
The white flag of defeat.

Francis Hopkinson Smith

(1838–1915)

Quite the opposite of the soul-weary Venetian depicted in
Fusinato's poem is the carefree beggar described by Francis
Hopkinson Smith, in his *Gondola Days* (1897). The book recalls a
long period the author spent enjoying himself in Venice. His
affectionate nature soon embraces his gondolier, Espero, and an
eccentric French professor. Hopkinson Smith becomes
acquainted with all the lowlife characters of the town, past and
present, including the layabout Luigi, who is lovingly and vividly
extolled in the following passage.

He is a happy-hearted, devil-may-care young fellow, who haunts this particular vicinity, and who has his bed and board wherever, at the moment, he may happen to be. The bed problem never troubles him; a bit of sail-cloth under the shadow of the hand-rail will do, or a straw mat behind the angle of a wall, or even what shade I can spare from my own white umbrella, with the hard marble flags for feathers. The item of board is a trifle, yet only a trifle, more serious. It may be a fragment of polenta, or a couple of figs, or only a drink from the copper bucket of some passing girl. Quantity, quality, and time of serving are immaterial to him. There will be something to eat before night, and it always comes. One of the pleasures of the neighborhood is to share with him a bite.

This beggar, tramp, *lasagnone* – ragged, barefooted, and sun-browned, would send a flutter through the hearts of a matinée full of pretty girls, could he step to the footlights just as he is, and with his superb baritone voice ring out one of his own native songs. Lying as he does now under my umbrella, his broad chest burnt almost black, the curls glistening about his forehead, his well-trimmed mustache curving around a mouth half open, shading a row of teeth white as milk, his Leporello hat thrown aside, a broad red sash girding his waist, the fine muscles of his thighs filling his overalls, these same pretty girls might perhaps only draw their skirts aside as they passed: environment plays such curious tricks.

This friend of mine, this royal pauper, Luigi, never in the recollection of any mortal man or woman was known to do a stroke of work . . . And yet one cannot call him a burden on society. On the contrary, Luigi has especial duties which he never neglects. Every morning at sunrise he is out on the bridge watching the Chioggia boats as they beat up past the Garden trying to make the red buoy in the channel behind San Giorgio, and enlarging on their seagoing qualities to an admiring group of bystanders. At noon he is plumped down in the midst of a bevy of wives and girls, flat on the pavement, his back against a doorway in some courtyard. The wives mend and patch, the girls string beads, and the children play around on the marble flagging, Luigi monopolizing all the talk and conducting all the gayety, the whole coterie listening. He makes love, and chaffs, and sings, and weaves romances, until the inquisitive sun peeps into the *patio*; then he is up and out on the bridge again, and so down the Riva, with the grace of an Apollo and the air of a thoroughbred.

When I think of all the sour tempers in the world, all the people with weak backs and chests and limbs, all the dyspeptics, all the bad livers and worse hearts, all the mean people and the sordid, all those who pose as philanthropists, professing to ooze sunshine and happiness from their very pores; all the down-trodden and the economical ones; all those on half pay and no work, and those on full pay and too little – and then look at this magnificent condensation of bone, muscle, and sinew; this Greek god of a tramp, unselfish, good-tempered, sunny-hearted, wanting nothing, having everything, envying nobody, happy as a lark, one continuous song all the day long; ready to catch a line, to mind a child, to carry a pail of water for any old woman, from the fountain in the Campo near by to the top of any house, no matter how high – when, I say, I think of this prince of good fellows leading his Adam-before-the-fall sort of existence, I seriously consider the advisability of my pensioning him for the remainder of his life on one *lira* a day, a fabulous sum to him, merely to be sure that nothing in the future will ever spoil his temper and so rob me of the ecstasy of knowing and of being always able to find one supremely happy human creature on this earth.

Riccardo Calimani

(1946–)

Venice bears few visible signs of the wars that ravaged Europe in the twentieth century. The Austrian bombardment in the 1840s probably did more damage than the few bombs that fell during World War I. More people died then from drowning after falling into the canals during the blackout.

But World War II saw the near extinction of Venice's Jewish community. One of its members here explains what happened.

Riccardo Calimani was born in Venice and studied at the University of Padua, developing an interest in Jewish history and identity. Still resident in Venice, he has worked as a teacher and lecturer and written poetry, essays, novels and children's books as well as reviews and translations.

Calimani's account of the fate of the Venetian Jews during World War II makes distressing reading.

Venice was by chance the place where Benito Mussolini and Adolf Hitler staged their first meeting, in June 1934. Hitler was apparently very impressed by the Doge's Palace.

The dangers of the German-Italian pact were not immediately apparent; events moved subtly and quickly, and Mussolini's Fascists copied their Nazi colleagues in promulgating racial laws. By the summer of 1943, discrimination against the twelve hundred and sixty Venetian Jews was institutionalised and they were forbidden to swim at the Lido. Mussolini's government fell in July 1943 and German troops arrived in Italy the following September.

A week later, as Calimani explains below, Giuseppe Jona, president of Venice's Jewish community, committed suicide, and that single death was the beginning of the Holocaust in Venice.

Slowly, during those months, the awareness of danger grew. Some Jewish families fled early to far-off lands, to South America or the United States, driven by the progressive worsening of the situation and their realization of increasing, imminent danger. On the other hand, some who could have gone chose to remain, either for family or other personal reasons, or even out of optimism. The Jews in Venice were not a homogeneous group. On the contrary, they were highly differentiated. Many families also had ties and relationships with Catholics, which strengthened their resistance to flight or an underground existence and encouraged the feeling that, all things considered, they were better off staying: the storm would pass. The refugees who had passed through Venice in the early forties were no longer coming; in any case, their tales had failed to reawaken an ancient, ancestral fear in the face of a more powerful feeling of disbelief. There was another factor, too, that contributed to keeping many Jews in Venice, although it now seems ironic, and that was their scrupulous compliance with Italian law and their desire, to the very last and even in the face of undeniable factual evidence, to avoid going underground and being hunted for the sole crime of being Jews.

On the night of December 5, the Fascist guard of the Republic of Salò and the police organized a huge roundup in Venice, Chioggia, and Trieste, on the islands of the lagoon and on the Lido. Over a hundred people were arrested, including children aged three to fourteen. A news article, based on eyewitness reports, said that 'all those torn from their homes and those captured in the Rest Home were first taken to the Marco Foscarini school, which became an improvised prison with no beds.'

According to the police reports of December 31, 1943, they were all transported to Fossoli . . .

The camp at Fossoli fell into German hands in mid-February, 1944. Until the first trainloads of people left for Germany, life in the camp still fell short of tragedy. It had been possible to send letters and care packages, and families had not been divided. A Venetian Jewish child of thirteen wrote from Fossoli on February 1, 1944, to a Christian friend in Venice: 'Dear Mario, I haven't written you since the day they separated us in Venice, and I know you'll forgive me, because of the confusion here for the first few days after we arrived in camp. But we're better organized now, and I've found this free moment to write. We're in good company in our room, with my parents, Aunt Ida, cousin Bruno, and aunt Pina. During the day we live in a corridor, well heated by two huge stoves that send heat to the room, so it's not too bad, we sing and play, and even have some fun . . . Yours T.A.'

But on February 21, on the eve of their departure for Germany, two sisters interned at Fossoli sent a short message in a different tone: 'We're leaving. Pray God to protect us. Say good-bye to everyone. It is useless to send money or food. Now as never before we think of those who are distant. Our future is a question mark, and we hope for good health.'

Throughout 1944, while war raged on all fronts, Venice was the scene of a manhunt, with continuous persecutions and deportations.

In the summer of 1944 a group of SS soldiers, returning from Treblinka, was especially active in hunting out and deporting Jews, on the orders of Franz Stangl. In their first roundup the SS deported about ninety people, including twenty-two inmates of the rest home, twenty-nine hospital patients, and the community's chief rabbi, Adolfo Ottolenghi, who was old and nearly blind. Early in October, the SS took some mental patients from the psychiatric hospitals on the islands of San Servolo and San Clemente. All these sick people, along with others now taken from the rest homes who had been judged untransportable at the time of the first roundup, were concentrated in the guard-room of the San Giovanni e Paolo hospital and deported on October 11. Some were eliminated at the extermination camp of Risiera di San Sabba at Trieste and others were sent to Auschwitz.

Despite their awareness of approaching defeat and the effect of the partisan resistance movement, felt especially strongly during the final months, the SS and its Italian collaborators continued hunting down Jews in Venetia, arresting them and deporting them to Germany.

Between September 8, 1943, and the final, longed-for liberation from Nazi Fascism on April 25, 1945, two hundred Venetian Jews had been killed. Entire families had been annihilated.

One by one, the survivors returned to Venice from the German camps. There were barely four or five, and while some talked about their terrible experiences, others preferred silence. Venetian Jews who had sought refuge in foreign lands returned. Others emerged from their hiding places in Venetian attics, or came back from the countryside or mountains of Venetia where they had been hidden, some by mere acquaintances, others by the parish priests of tiny villages. The alleys of Venice, freed from the Nazi-Fascist nightmare, breathed the exhilarating air of Liberation at the end of the long tunnel of war. Once again, life prevailed.

Dark Side of the City

CRIMES AND PUNISHMENTS

The world doesn't point a finger at you,
if you haven't done something wrong.

Guilt is a gorgeous girl but nobody wants her.

God wants us hurt but not dead.

In hell, there are no fans.

VENETIAN PROVERBS

. . . Putrefying city, magnificent sore from the past . . .

FILIPPO TOMMASO MARINETTI

I had my foot upon the spot, where, at the same dread hour, the shriven prisoner was strangled; and struck my hand upon the guilty door – low-browed and stealthy – through which the lumpish sack was carried out into a boat, and rowed away, and drowned where it was death to cast a net.

CHARLES DICKENS

. . . a city where traditions of treachery and secret murder were interwoven with all her splendour and her beauty.

MARY BRADDON

Whatever the Venetian can or cannot do, he can certainly hate, and that well.

DOROTHY MENPES

If a Woman has any Mind to be wicked, *Venice* seems to be the last Place in the World to give her better Sentiments.

'MISS N' to the actor Thomas Hull, 1765/6

Pompeo Molmenti

(1852–1928)

Venice's reputation for dark deeds and subtle crimes is here conceded by her great chronicler Pompeo Molmenti.

But in this extract from his illustrated volume *Venice* (1926), the historian asserts that the Venetians themselves were happily ignorant of these charges against them, and that scholars have now deconstructed the unjust myths . . .

If a certain literature has thrown a veil of terror and mystery over the city of St. Mark, the Venetians themselves knew nothing of it. No government was less despotic. No people knew such serenity and happiness. The surprising aspect of the city, intersected by its dark little alleys and canals, its picturesque customs, the singularity of its political constitution, — such are the elements which have impressed themselves on the exaggerated imagination of visionary historians and poets. Abductions, homicides, spies, poisonings, assassins, bravos, torturers — a whole terrifying phantasmagoria is inseparable from the Venice of convention. Of what horrible injustices has the government of Venice not been accused, that formidable Council of Ten, whose very name caused one to shudder! And what can one say of the tribunal of State Inquisitors, who, according to the accepted legend, gave summary judgment on the evidence of anonymous spies? Imagination calls up dark chambers dimly lit by the yellow, flickering light of torches, secret stairs leading down to the prisons of the *Pozzi* — funereal barges disappearing into the darkness of the canals in which the victims were drowned. Critical historians have reduced these legends to nought.

Giambattista Giraldi Cinthio

(1504–73)

Of all tales of passion and murder, that of Othello is the one most closely identified with Venice.

In Cinthio's version of the story, the ending is somewhat different from Shakespeare's: Desdemona is struck three savage blows by 'the ensign' (Iago) and then a part of the ceiling is brought down on her head to disguise her death as accidental. The Cassio character (known as 'the lieutenant') has had one leg cut off in a previous encounter with Othello.

Born in Ferrara, Cinthio was a professor of natural philosophy at Florence, then of fine arts. His *Ecatommiti*, published in 1565, consisting of one hundred and thirty moral tales, is probably the source of Shakespeare's plot for *Othello*, while his *Epitia* of 1583 may be the inspiration for *Measure for Measure*.

A beautiful *palazzo* opposite the Salute has acquired the notoriety of being Othello's house in Venice. It is easy to identify: the owners have thoughtfully named their motor-launch 'Desdemona' and painted her title in clear letters on the stern.

This extract is from a translation by Wolstenholme Parr, dated 1795.

. . . Afterwards they placed her in the bed; and after breaking her skull, they drew down, as they had determined beforehand, a part of the ceiling. The Moor then called out for help as the house was falling. The neighbours on this alarm ran thither, and found Desdemona dead under the beams. Her life had been so virtuous that every one lamented her fate; and the following day she was buried, to the great sorrow of the whole island.

But God, who is a just Observer of the hearts of men, suffered not so great a crime to pass without the punishment that was due to it. So that the Moor, who had loved Desdemona more than his eyes, finding himself deprived of her, began to regret her so extremely, that he almost lost his senses, and went about the house looking for her in every room. Reflecting besides that the ensign had been the cause of his losing along with her all the enjoyments of life, and even his own faculties, that villain became so insupportable to him that he could not bear the sight of him; and had he not feared the strict and impartial justice of the Venetians, he would have put him openly to death. But not being able to do this with safety to himself, he degraded him from his commission, and permitted him no longer to remain in the company.

Hence arose between them the most bitter enmity that can be conceived; and the ensign, the greatest of all villains, studied only how he might be revenged on the Moor. He went to the lieutenant, who was cured and walked about with his wooden leg, and said to him, 'The time is now come when you may be revenged for the loss of your leg; and if you will come with me to Venice, I will tell you who the assassin was. Here I dare not inform you for many reasons; but there I will be your witness in a court of justice.'

The lieutenant, who felt himself violently exasperated against the person though unknown to him, thanked the ensign, and came away with him to Venice. When they were arrived, the ensign told him that the Moor was the person who had cut off his leg, because he suspected him of adultery with his wife, and that for the same reason he had murdered her, and afterward given out that she had been killed by the ceiling's falling in upon her.

The lieutenant on hearing this, immediately accused the Moor before the Council of the injury done to himself and the murder of Desdemona; and the ensign, being called as a witness, asserted the truth of both these accusations, and added that the Moor had communicated to him the whole project, with a view of persuading him to execute both these crimes; and when he had murdered his wife from the impulse of a furious jealousy, he had related to him the manner in which he had put her to death. The Venetian magistrates, hearing that one of their fellow citizens had been treated with so much cruelty by a barbarian, had the Moor arrested in Cyprus and brought to Venice, where, by means of torture, they endeavoured to find out the truth.

But the Moor possessed force and constancy of mind sufficient to undergo the torture without confessing any thing; and though by his firmness he escaped death at this time, he was after a long imprisonment condemned to perpetual exile, in which he was afterwards killed, as he deserved to be, by his wife's relations.

Matteo Bandello

(1480–1562)

This prime tale of crime and punishment comes from Matteo Bandello, one of the most celebrated novelists of the Renaissance.

In this classic Bandello story the wicked gambler Pietro turns serial killer to subsidise his addiction to games of chance. Having disposed of his aunt, her two children and the serving maid, he is condemned to the slow and public death the Venetian state reserved for murderers. But he attempts to cheat justice – as the son of an apothecary, there are ways and means at his disposal. His accomplice, Nasone, is not so lucky.

The apothecaries plied a profitable trade in Venice, selling pigments to painters as well as medicines for the sick. Their most famous concoction, a picturesque placebo that contained amber and oriental spices, was known as *triaca*, and the Venetians swore by it for all ills. Poison was also to be obtained from the apothecaries. It was believed that Murano glass was sensitive to poison, and that it would begin to tremble if any was poured into it.

~~~

. . . The sentence pronounced, the wretched Pietro's father and mother and brother went to the prison to see him and comfort him, and abode with him a good while. Now his brother had spoken with him on the foregoing day and had been besought of him to give him some poison that should kill him immediately, so he might not die that ignominious death in the sight of the people, and had accordingly prepared a terrible and instantaneous poison; then, placing it in a little phial, he hid the latter in a pantable and, telling Pietro what he had done, changed pantables with him, unobserved of any ...

. . . the drug, which was exceedingly violent of its nature, began to work its effects, so that, Pietro's eyes rolling and his face swelling an extraordinary wise, he became so horrible to look upon that he resembled anything rather than a man. His eyes and nose ran, and there issued from his mouth slaver of various colours, fetid beyond measure . . . the wretched man chose to die a surpassing villain than a repentant Christian. He altogether refused to confess or to repent him of his many misdeeds; nay, in the very agony of death, the poison having usurped the vital arteries, so that he could no more speak, he scrupled not, at his last moments (having already done so many wrongs to God, his neighbour and himself), to persist in evil-doing; for that, dumb as he was become, he sought yet to add iron to the cruzet and studied to compass the death of one of his keepers . . . striving as most he might with signs and gestures (for that he was unable to speak) to inculpate the warder aforesaid and making signs that it was he had given him the poison; wherefore the poor wretch was taken and cruelly tortured, but suffered the torments with constancy and confessed nothing; for what indeed should he confess, being innocent?

. . . Meanwhile Pietro died and, dead as he was, was embarked with Nasone aboard a barge and carried throughout all Venice, what while both were tanacled sore with red-hot pincers, albeit Pietro, being already dead, felt nothing; after which they were, as they deserved, hewn into four pieces and hanged on the gibbets in the Lagoons for food to the corbies and other birds of prey. Such, then, was the end of the wicked gambler Pietro, who had eke another very great default, in that, by what I hear of him, he was the foulest blasphemer and denier of God and the Saints in those parts; but it is no marvel that he should have blasphemed, that heinous vice being as proper and peculiar unto gamblers as heat to fire and light to the sun.

William Lithgow

(c. 1582–1645?)

This early traveller to Venice rejoiced in the nickname 'Lugless Will', on account of a rumour that his ears had been cut off by the four vengeful brothers of a girl caught in a compromising position with him.

Whatever the state of his ears, Lithgow's eyes were forced wide open on his arrival in Venice, where the first thing he saw was a friar being burnt at the stake.

Born in Lanark, Lithgow started travelling in his twenties. In 1632 he published the first collected edition of his writings under the title *The Totall Discourse of the Rare Adventures and Painful Peregrinations of Long Nineteene Yeares Travayles*. This extract comes from the beginning of his account of Venice, which he describes as 'a Garden of riches, and worldly pleasures'.

Mine associate and I, were no sooner landed, and perceiving a great throng of people, and in the midst of them a great smoake; but we begun to demaund a Venetian what the matter was? who replied, there was a gray Frier burning quicke at S. Markes pillar, of the reformed order of S. Francis, for begetting fifteene young Noble Nunnes with child, and all within one yeare; he being also their Father confessor. Whereat, I sprung forward through the throng, and my friend followed me, and came just to the pillar as the halfe of his body and right arme fell flatlings in the fire; The Frier was forty sixe yeares old, and had bene Confessor of that Nunnery of Sancta Lucia five yeares: Most of these young Nunnes were Senators daughters; and two of them were onely come in to learne vertue, and yet fell in the midst of vice.

These fifteene with child, were all re-cald home to their fathers Pallaces; the Lady Prioresse, and the rest of her voluptuous crew, were banished for ever from the precincts of Venice. The Monastery was razed to the ground, their rents were allowed to be bestowed upon poore families, and distressed age, and their Church to be converted to an Hospitall. Most part of all which M. Arthur and I saw, before ever we either eate, drunke, or tooke our lodging in Venice: And I cannot forget, how after all this, we being inhungred, and also overjoyed tumbled in by chance, Alla capello Ruosso, the greatest ordinary in all Venice, neare to which the Friars: bones were yet a burning: And calling for a Chamber, we were nobly & richly served: After dinner they layd up our budgets and our burdons, and abroad went we to see the Citie: Night come, we supd, and supd alone: The next morne, I begun to remarke the grandeur of the Inne, and saw it was time that we were gone: I demanded our dependant, what was to pay?

he answered, Un scudo all huomo par ciascun ripasto, A Crowne the dyet for each of us, being ten Julets or five shillings starling: Mr. Arthur lookd upon me, and I laughd upon him: In a word our dinner and supper cost us 40. Juletts twenty shillings English; being foure Crownes, whereat my companion being discontented, bad the divell be in the Friars ballocks, for we had payd soundly for his Leachery: many like deaths, for like causes, and worser, have I seene in all my three voyages, if time could permit me to particularize them.

Thomas Coryate (or Coryatt)
(1577–1617)

Thomas Coryate was born at Odcombe in Somerset, where his father was the rector. He was educated at Westminster and Oxford, although he left the university in 1603 without finishing his degree and worked as a jester at the court of King James I.

In 1608 this bearded comedian set out on a walking tour of Europe, through France, Italy and Germany, a journey of over 2000 miles which he completed with just one pair of shoes. (These were later displayed at Odcombe Church as the 'thousand mile shoes'.)

He had difficulties finding a publisher for *Coryate's Crudities: Hastily Gobbled up in Five Moneth's Travels* (1611) and only succeeded after persuading eminent men of the day to write 'Panegyrick Verses' of support, duly printed along with his own words. (Ben Jonson, in his 'character of the author', sturdily vouched for Coryate's enthusiasm as a travel writer: 'at seeing the word Frankfort or Venice, though but on the title of a Booke, he is readie to break doublet, cracke elbowes, and overflowe the room with his murmure.')

Coryate followed up the *Crudities* with *Coryate's Crambe or Colewort Twice Sodden* (1612). For many years these facetious and quirky books were the only handbooks for continental travel. In 1612 he set off again, travelling through Greece, Egypt, India, Afghanistan, Palestine and Persia, but he died in Surat in 1617 before being able to finish a third volume.

Coryate's descriptions of Venice are among the most amusing to be found. Alternately curmudgeonly and *faux*-innocent, he no doubt set out to make his readers chortle. Venice met him more than halfway, providing all the eccentric and colourful material he could wish for. He sincerely adored the city, declaring with touching candour at the end of his account 'of this incomparable city, this most beautiful queene, this untainted virgin, this paradise, this temple, this rich diadem and the most flourishing garland of Christendom' that 'had there been an offer made unto me before I took my journey to Venice, either that four of the richest manors of Somersetshire (wherein I was born) should be gratis bestowed upon me if I never saw Venice or none of them if I should see it; although certainly those manors would do me much more good in respect of a state of livelihood in the world than the sight of Venice, yet notwithstanding I will ever say, while I live, that the sight of Venice and her resplendent beauty, antiquities, and monuments, hath by many degrees more contented my mind and satisfied my desires, than those four lordships could possibly have done.'

In this brief extract from his *Crudities* he talks of the dread Venetian gangsters known as Bravoes. Armed with their slender daggers, known as stilettos, these men roamed the dark and narrow streets looking for victims . . . And almost as vicious, in Coryate's eyes, were the Venetian boatmen who preyed on innocent tourists.

There are certaine dreadful and desperate villaines in Venice called Braves, who at some unlawfull times do commit great villainy. They wander abroad very late in the night to and fro for their prey like hungry Lyons, being armed with a privy coate of maile, a gauntlet upon their right hand and a little sharpe dagger called a stiletto. They lurke commonly by the water side, and if, at their time of night . . . they happen to meete any man that is worth the rifling, they will presently stabbe him and take away all about him that is of worth, and when they have thoroughly pulled his plumes they will throw him in one of the channels . . .

There are in Venice thirteen ferries or passages, which they commonly call Traghetti, where passengers may be transported in a Gondola to what place of the City they will. Of which thirteene, one is under this Rialto bridge. But the boatmen that attend at this ferry are the most vicious and licentious varlets about all the City. For if a stranger entereth into one of their Gondolas, and doth not presently tell them whither he will goe, they will incontinently carry him of their owne accord to a religious house forsooth, where his plumes shall be well pulled before he commeth forth againe . . . Besides they shall finde the iniquity of them to be such, that if the passenger commandeth them to carry him to any place where his serious and urgent businesse lies, which he cannot but follow without some prejudice unto him, these impious miscreants will either strive to carry him away, maugre his hart, to some irreligious place whether he would not goe, or at the least tempt him with their diabolicall perswasions.

Fra Paolo Sarpi

(1552–1622)

In 1607 Venice was convulsed by a vicious attack on one of her leading citizens, the visionary priest Fra Paolo Sarpi.

The son of a merchant, he was educated for the Church and entered a monastic order at the age of nineteen. He lectured on canon law, and wrote on philosophy, natural science and optics, working with Galileo on the first telescope. He was interested in anatomy and appears to have discovered the valves that aid in circulation of the blood.

When Venice and Pope Paul V were in serious dispute on legal and property issues, Sarpi, as State Theologian and adviser to the Venetian Senate, opposed Rome's threat of excommunication, brilliantly exposing the chicanery of the Church. Pope Paul was forced to withdraw, but Sarpi had put himself at risk. He was attacked by five would-be assassins at the bridge of Santa Fosca, near his monastery of the Servites. The men were later seen escaping in a gondola to the palace of the papal nuncio.

Sarpi was carried to his cell, badly wounded, and it is reported that he asked to be shown the dagger which Ridolfo Poma, his attacker, had embedded in his cheek. He recovered from his wounds and survived another fifteen years. He continued to serve Venice as an invaluable counsellor in matters ranging from law to art and public morality, and was given unique free access to all the state archives for his researches.

The following is a contemporary English translation of a notice exhibited on 10 October 1607 on the stairs of San Marco and the Rialto Bridge, by Vincenzo d'Antonio, the public crier, after the attempted murder.

The Sentence of the High Councell of Ten against Ridolfo Pomo, Michael Viti Priest, Alessandro Parrasio, John of Florence the son of Paul, and Pasquall of Bitonto.

Forasmuch as *Ridolfo Pomo*, *Michael Viti* Priest, accustomed to serve in the Church of H. Trinitie, *Alexander Parrassio* of Ancona, *John* of Florence the sonne of *Paul*, a man of common stature with grayish eyes, and a red bearde, inrolled heeretofore in the Company of Governor *Bartolamio Nieno* of Vincenza, appointed over the ships for Syria and Alexandria, and being runaway from the sayd Company, *Pasquall* of Bitonto of the age of thirty-two or thereabout, of ordinarie stature, a fat man, with a black beard, black haire, and wont heeretofore to serve in the company of Captaine *John I Roglioni* of Ancona in Padoa.

Having been proclaimed according to the deliberation of this Councell, and not appearing, but resting wilfully absent, the which that is to say *Ridolfo*, Priest *Michael*, and *Alexander*, having beene made the Ministers of a most enormous conspiracy, after they had woven and managed a long and trayterous treaty, used divers awaytes, and espials, for the consummate effectuating of Murther above all other most odious and impious, against a religious Person . . .

Wherefore, Be the foresayde *Ridolfo*, Priest *Michael*, and *Alexander* banished from this Citie of *Venice*, the confines thereof, and from all other Cities, Villages, and places of our Dominion, all shippings armed and unarmed for ever.

And breaking the confine, and being taken whichsoever of them hee bee, Let him bee conducted into this Citie, and set in a broad boate upon an high scaffolde, with a Cryer who shall continually publishe his fault, as well by land as by water, and brought to the bridge of Saint *Fosca*; where, by the Minister of Justice, Be his abler hand cut off, so as it bee severed from his arme: with which tyed to his necke, let him be drawen at a horse tayle by land to the middest of the two pillars of Saint *Marke*: where upon an highe scaffolde, Be his head cuttee off, so as it bee severed from his body and he die, and his body divided into foure quarters to be fastened upo (sic) the Gibbets in the places accustomed.

Henri de Régnier

(1864–1936)

The French poet and writer Henri Régnier lived in Ca' Dario, reputed to be the most haunted house in Venice. Gabriele D'Annunzio, looking at Ca' Dario from his own home at the Casetta Rossa across the Grand Canal, saw the house as 'a decrepit courtesan, bowed beneath the pomp of her baubles'.

Régnier is still honoured there with a plaque on the leaf-shadowed wall of the house, which tells that he '*veneziamente visse e scrisse*' (lived and wrote as a Venetian). It was as an aristocratic Venetian that he wrote, in his novel *L'Altana*, describing a life of reclusive luxury.

The extraordinary house, built in 1486 by the diplomat Giovanni Dario, shows the influence of the East where he spent so much time in intricate negotiations on behalf of the Venetian government. On his death it went to his daughter, Marietta, married to a member of the noble Barbaro family, who retained it for many years. Other owners included Abdollo, an Armenian diamond merchant, and Rawdon Brown, the English scholar who researched the state papers of Venice, a great friend of John Ruskin and a guide to many English visitors. Brown, who bought the house for less than £500 in 1838, could not afford to maintain it, so just four years later it was taken over by Count Zigismund Zichy, an official of the Austrian administration, and then by a Countess Kolowrat, Lieutenant Marshall Nugent, and his daughters Princess Strozzi and Princess Pallavicini. It was a *pensione* at the end of the nineteenth century and then came into the hands of the Countess de la Baume-Pluvinel, who restored the plumbing and fountains. She was Régnier's hostess when he lived there at the turn of the twentieth century.

The Short Life of Baldassarre Aldramin, Venetian, shows that the mystical influences of the house were perhaps at work on Régnier, a genial man at the centre of a group of effete French intellectuals clustered in Venice at the time. This eerie story was published in the *Revue de Paris*, and is here translated from the Italian version that appeared in Alberto Lumbroso's *Pagine Veneziane* in 1905.

~~~

It is Baldassare Aldramin in person who is speaking through my mouth. Of course, he will never more drink the wine of Genzano, or bite again into one of the figs of Pienza; he is resting under the marble in the church of Santo Stefano, with his hands folded over his chest, on the deep red wound that put an end to his short life, on the third day of March, in the year of Our Lord 1779.

He was almost thirty years old, and his *palazzo* was next door to mine, and we would see each other two or three times a day; we were companions in the pursuit of pleasure, but among all of those, for him love held the first sway.

We would never miss a single one of the thousands of voluptuous pleasures offered by the city. In this way passed the years of our adolescence.

It seems to me that I could have continued to live like this forever, without ever wishing anything more for myself.

But Aldramin did not think that way, and he went away. He was absent three years, and returned as suddenly as he had departed. And our previous existence was resumed, only to be interrupted by the bloody drama of which I have already recounted the outcome.

And this is why, today, he borrows my mouth to tell you, through me, Lorenzo Vimani, that which can paint a picture to explain his demise: and it seems to me that he himself told me those things, one evening, in a wood of red pines, he himself, my friend, Baldassarre Aldramin, Venetian.

'One day, Lorenzo, I was on the Riva degli Schiavoni with my delicious mistress, la Signora Balbi, when I saw a seagull which was breaking the air with its blade-like wings. That seemed to me a salutary example, which I followed the very next day.

'My plan was to see the world and to search for my pleasure in diverse and changing realms.

'I took ample funds, and left. The gondola, sweet and light, set me down on dry land.

'I made a stop at the luxurious villa of an old relative, the senator Andrea Baldipiero, five hours or less from Mestre, to say my farewells.

'He knows none of the many infirmities of old age; and he's still handsome to look at. He welcomed me most kindly, but his expression disquieted me.

'He left me to write some letters of introduction for my journey to Rome and to Paris.

'I looked at myself in the mirror; it seemed to me that my face was good, attractive.

'I went to walk in the garden, and reached a little rock grotto whose sweet and murmuring waters gave a pleasing freshness to the air.

'As I turned towards the villa, it came to my attention that one of the windows was being closed. In the meantime, my uncle caught up with me and suggested that, instead of going to Noletta to spend the night, I should stay in the villa. I was astonished, since I was sure that he was involved in one of his usual "adventures" and *"fully occupied in completely different matters"*'.

'Dinner arrived, very sumptuous, and the wine did not fail to intoxicate me so deliciously that I would have jumped to any enterprise whatever.

'Observing my host the senator, I became convinced that he was tired. I could not account for it. But little by little, in the conversation, he came to confess to me what I had already supposed, that he appreciated my felicity and contrasted it with what a miserable thing it is to grow old.

'In the meantime, I was drinking the Genzano and biting into the fruit.

'And he was feeling sorry for me as I was the one who would shortly be going to bed alone between two sheets – which is not the right way of the world, he added, for a young man, and even less for a young man who loves women.

'At the word "women" I looked at the senator . . . The fumes of the wine were leaping into my brain, and it seemed to me that my uncle was telling me that I just had to leave the table to find, in the famous room with the shutters well closed, on a bed, a sleeping woman. But I had to take a solemn oath, on my honour, not to try to find out who she was nor where she came from.

'Guided by the senator, I reached the room, and I found myself – finally – alone in the middle of a deep silence. I listened. I tensed my ears. It seemed to me that I could hear a light, regular breathing.

'The darkness was warm and perfumed. I found my way with my fingertips. At each step I was getting closer to an invisible sleeper. I was closer and closer to her. I stretched out my hand, I touched naked, sweet skin that shivered at my contact; my other hand sought about and I felt the features of a face and of a warm, half-opened mouth . . .

'It was an extraordinary and strange night; a terrible and silent struggle.

'I found myself at the door after a hard battle, convincing myself to keep faith with the word I had given, not to find out anything more about this love of a few hours.

'I forgot about her. I had other women, other caresses, other kisses.

'In Paris, I received a letter in which my uncle told me that he had made me his heir; he foresaw an imminent death for himself, having realised that his lover – and mine – was every night pouring poison into his cup. But he was dying happy, because he was dying in the throes of love.

'And he begged me to go to him.

'I found everything unchanged, but the senator dead. I was the only one who knew that I had a sword hanging over my head. That woman I had never seen, that lover whom I had adored for a short hour, was longing for my death, wanted to administer it with her own beautiful hands.

'I returned to Venice, and took up again, with you, Lorenzo, our crazy life.

'The carnival of that year, 1779, particularly in Venice was madly gay and spirited.

'I was the friend of you and a certain Leonello, who claimed to be from Sicily and had beautiful hands and very small feet.

'Together we went to the villa of my uncle Baldipiero. I was arm-in-arm with Leonello. In one room – the banquet room – I had the lights turned off to be able to obtain complete darkness . . .

'I shouted to the servants to come quickly and turn the lights on, when, – exactly then – I felt something cold and sharp penetrating my breast, pushing up to the centre of my life . . .

'My mouth filled up with a surge of blood . . .'

When we laid our poor friend Baldassarre Aldramin on the bed, we found a blade in his heart.

Those present were Ludovico Barbarigo, Nicolò Voredan, Antonio Pirmiani, Giulio Bottarol, Ottavio Vernuzzi, Leonello and myself.

We thought he had killed himself. Then we suspected one of us had killed him.

Our suspicions reached such a peak that fights broke out,

duels; and in one of those, between Bottarol and Barbarigo, the former was killed.

I became wretched, and sadder each day. Seeing that, Leonello suggested that I took a trip.

We left.

Robbers attacked us, stripped us of our clothes, blindfolded us, and tied us to a tree. I couldn't see anything, but I could hear that after having stripped my companion, all the robbers started to laugh.

Lifting a little the blindfold that was blackening my vision, from the corner of my eye, I managed to obtain a glimpse of Leonello . . . who, tied to a tree, showed himself to be of a feminine outline.

The torches were extinguished, and the following day Leonello had disappeared.

In the morning, a forester freed me, cutting my bonds. I came back to my senses, lying on the ground, and I remembered. My eyes flew to the tree where I had seen naked the most beautiful woman; the place was empty. Without any doubt, the unknown woman had managed to free herself and run away.

I went back to Venice with no more painful adventures. The bells of Santo Stefano were ringing in the red air, the old façade of the palazzo of the Aldramin was reflecting in the clear water of the canal its discs of blood-red marble.

City of Love

AFFAIRS OF THE HEART AND
THE BUSINESS OF LOVE

Love makes your stockings floppy.

Hunger makes you jump, but love makes you jump higher.

Bed is the heaven of the poor.

Marriage comes from love
the way vinegar comes from wine.

Marriage and macaroni —
if they are not hot, they are not good.

Venice is Paradise for priests and prostitutes.

VENETIAN PROVERBS

Cultivating whatever gave pleasure to my senses was always the chief business of my life . . .

GIACOMO GIROLAMO CASANOVA

. . . a great many ladies negligently dressed, their hair falling very freely about, and innumerable adventures written in their eyes . . .

WILLIAM BECKFORD

She lay back, thrilling with smiles, in the twilight shed
By the gondola bent like darkness over her head;
I saw her eyes shine subtly, then close awhile:
I remember her silence, and, in the night, her smile.

ARTHUR SYMONS

. . . the women *kiss* better than those of any other nation, which is notorious, and is attributed to the worship of images and the early habit of osculation induced thereby.

GEORGE GORDON, LORD BYRON

Beautiful girls in Venice, however odd it may seem in a city filled with painters, consent much more readily to be your mistress than to be your model; they understand love better than art, and believe themselves pretty enough for one to drop crayons and palettes as soon as one sees them.

THÉOPHILE GAUTIER

To all public Places, they constantly go in Pairs, with their *Cavalier Serventes*, and put me much in Mind of the *clean* and *unclean* Beasts going into the Ark . . .

'MISS N' to the actor Thomas Hull, 1765/6

When we cried out, 'Let's murder the moonshine!' we were thinking of you, old Venice soiled with romanticism! . . . Nevertheless, O Venice, I used to love the sumptuous shade of your Grand Canal steeped in exotic lewdnesses . . .

FILIPPO TOMMASO MARINETTI

And you be not fitted in Venice, 'tis strange, for 'tis counted as the best flesh-shambles in Italy.

JOHN DAY

The place whither he brought us was a pernicious curtizans house named *Tabitha* the Temptress, a wench that could set as civill a face on it as chastities first martyr *Lucrecia* . . . I warrant you should not see one set of her neckercher perverted or turned awrie, not a piece of a haire displast. On her beds there was not a wrinkle of any wallowing to be found, her pillows bare out as smooth as a groning wives belly, and yet she was a Turke and an infidel, and more doings then all her neighbours besides.

THOMAS NASHE, 1594

. . . the sum of five thousand pounds sterling is no great deal, particularly when I tell you that more than half was laid out in the Sex; – to be sure I have had plenty for the money . . .

GEORGE GORDON, LORD BYRON

Mario Equicola

(c. 1470–1525)

Books of this period often omit mention of the author's name but it is certain that this guide to lovers (sometimes attributed to Mario Equicola) was published by the Venetian printer Johannus Tacuinus, also known as Johannes de Cereto de Tridino, working in the mid-sixteenth century.

Il Novo Cortigiano de vita cauta e morale (*The New Courtier, on Prudent and Moral Living*, 1530) is typical of its time. It preaches strict moderation in all things, suggesting that no one should be too passionate in their friendships or curiosities. The New Courtier, according to the writer, should not inquire into the sciences too deeply, or try to wrestle with mathematics. He should choose his friends from his own class. The book reflects a common theory of the time that overly passionate love led inevitably to disaster. (In this vein, during the sixteenth and seventeenth centuries there were countless Venetian productions of that ultimate love-disaster story, *Antony and Cleopatra*. In the Palazzo Labia, Tiepolo painted a room of frescos featuring a blonde, blue-eyed Cleopatra, identifying her with the typical high-born Venetian woman.)

If human nature could allow such a strength, I would suggest that you should flee extreme Love. Because a soul disordered in its affections is an incurable disease from which derives oblivion of God, and of yourself, forgetfulness of time, diminution of honour, infamy on your house, the indignation of your relatives, disregard for property, and ever arguments, fights, exiles, homicides, poisonings and finally death . . . the souls of the Lovers have the time-honoured privileges of raging, arguing, frequent battles and declarations of peace, of rare pleasures and frequent miseries, and hardly ever a brief moment of stability . . . according to many unvarying testimonies from those who, with irreparable damage to themselves, have essayed excessive Love, there comes a rabid turbulence and an inevitable (even to the wiser minds) blinding passion, which, as well as transforming a man from humble to insufferable, from shy to insolent, also obscures intelligence, confounds the Memory, dissolves conscience, and cancels out mercy, dissipates all earthly faculties, corrupts the strength of the body, exterminates freedom and brings old age before its time.

Thomas Coryate (or Coryatt)

(1577–1617)

This detailed description of the sex industry in Venice comes
from that conscientious tourist Thomas Coryate. In this section of
his *Crudities*, he has already given minute accounts of every tiny
feminine detail, including the 'foolishe' towering shoes of the
Venetian noblewomen and the custom of dyeing their hair blonde
('every Saturday in the afternoone') by anointing it with oils and
spreading the strands around the wheel of a large crownless hat in
direct sunlight. So it is only logical at this point, Coryate insists,
to move on to an explanation of the Venetian courtesans,
'famoused over all Christendome' and yet, he notes, significantly
absent from the accounts of other travellers.

The woman that professeth this trade is called in the Italian tongue Cortezana, which word is derived from the Italian word cortesia that signifieth courtesie. Because these kinde of women are said to receive courtesies of their favourites. Which word hath some kinde of affinitie with the Greeke word ἑταῖρα which signifieth properly a sociable woman, and is by Demosthenes, Athenæus, and divers other prose writers often taken for a woman of a dissolute conversation. As for the number of these Venetian Cortezans it is very great. For it is thought there are of them in the whole City and other adjacent places, as Murano, Malomocco, &c. at the least twenty thousand, whereof many are esteemed so loose, that they are said to open their quivers to every arrow. A most ungodly thing without doubt that there should be a tolleration of such licentious wantons in so glorious, so potent, so renowned a city. For me thinks that the Venetians should be daylie affraid least their winking at such uncleannesse should be an occasion to draw down upon them God's curses and vengeance from heaven, and to consume their city with fire and brimstone, as in times past he did Sodome and Gomorrha . . .

For so infinite are the allurements of these amorous Calypsoes, that the fame of them hath drawen many to Venice from some of the remotest parts of Christendome, to contemplate their beauties, and enjoy their pleasing dalliances. And indeede such is the variety of the delicious objects they minister to their lovers, that they want nothing tending to delight. For when you comme into one of their Palaces (as indeed some few of the principallest of them live in very magnificent and portly buildings fit for the entertainement of a great Prince) you seeme to enter into the Paradise of Venus. For their fairest roomes are most glorious and glittering to behold. The walles round about being adorned with most sumptuous tapistry and gilt leather, such as I have spoken of in my Treatise of Padua. Besides you may see the picture of the noble Cortezan most exquisitely drawen. As for her selfe shee comes to thee decked like the Queene and Goddesse of love, in so much that thou wilt thinke she made a late transmigration from Paphos, Cnidos, or Cythera, the auncient habitations of Dame Venus. For her face is adorned with the quintessence of beauty. In her cheekes thou shalt see the Lilly and the Rose strive for the supremacy, and the silver tramels of her haire displayed in that curious manner besides her two frisled peakes standing up like prety Pyramides, that they give thee the true Cos amoris. But if thou hast an exact judgement, thou maist easily discerne the effects of those famous apothecary drugs heretofore used amongst the Noble Ladies of Rome, even stibium, cerussa, and pur-purissum. For few of the Cortezans are so much beholding to nature, but that they adulterate their faces and supply her defect with one of these three . . . Also the ornaments of her body are so rich, that except thou dost even geld thy affections (a thing hardly to be done) or carry with thee Ulysses hearbe called Moly which is mentioned by Homer, that is, some antidote against those Venereous titillations, shee wil very neare benumme and captivate thy senses, and make reason vale bonnet to affection. For thou shalt see her decked with many chaines of gold and orient pearls like a second Cleopatra, (but they are very litle) divers gold rings beautified with diamonds and other costly stones, jewels in both her eares of great worth. A gowne of damaske (I speake this of the nobler Cortizans) either decked with a deep gold fringe (according as I have expressed it in the picture of the Cortizan that I have placed about the beginning of this discourse) or laced with five or sixe gold laces each two inches broade. Her petticoate of red chamlet edged with rich gold fringe, stockings of carnasion silke, her breath and her whole body, the more to enamour thee, most fragrantly perfumed. Though these things will at the first sight seeme unto thee most delectable allurements, yet if thou shalt rightly weigh them in the scales of a mature judgement, thou wilt say with the wise man, and that very truely, that they are like a golden ring in a swines snowt. Moreover shee will endevour to enchaunt thee partly with her melodious notes that she warbles out upon her lute, which shee fingers with as laudable a stroake as many men that are excellent professors in the noble science of Musicke; and partly with that heart-tempting harmony of her voice. Also thou wilt finde the Venetian Cortezan (if she be a selected woman indeede) a good Rhetorician, and a most elegant discourser, so that if she cannot move thee with all these foresaid delights, shee will assay thy constancy with her Rhetoricall tongue. And to the end shee may minister unto thee the stronger temptations to come to her lure, shee will shew thee her chamber of recreation, where thou shalt see all manner of pleasing objects, as many faire painted coffers where-with it is garnished round about, a curious milke-white canopy of needle worke, a silke quilt embrodered with gold: and generally all her bedding sweetly perfumed. And amongst other amiable orna-ments shee will shew thee one thing only in her chamber tending to mortification, a matter strange amongst so many irritamenta malorum; even the picture of our Lady by her bedde side, with Christ in her armes, placed within a cristall glasse . . .

Moreover I will tell thee this newes which is most true, that if thou shouldest wantonly converse with her, and not give her that salarium iniquitatis, which thou hast promised her, but perhaps cunningly escape from her company, shee will either cause thy throate to be cut by her Ruffiano, if he can after catch thee in the

City, or procure thee to be arrested (if thou are to be found) and clapped up in the prison, where thou shalt remaine till thou hast paid her all thou didst promise her . . .

Amongst other things that I heard of these kinde of women in Venice, one is this, that when their Cos amoris beginneth to decay, when their youthfull vigor is spent, then they consecrate the dregs of their olde age to God by going into a Nunnery, having before dedicated the flower of their youth to the divell; some of them also having scraped together so much pelfe by their sordid facultie as doth maintaine them well in their old age: For many of them are as rich as ever was Rhodope in Egypt, Flora in Rome, or Lais in Corinth. One example whereof I have before mentioned in Margarita Æmiliana that built a faire Monastery of Augustinian Monkes. There is one most notable thing more to be mentioned concerning these Venetian Cortezans, with the relation whereof I will end this discourse of them. If any of them happen to have any children (as indeede they have but few, for according to the old proverbe the best carpenters make the fewest chips) they are brought up either at their own charge, or in a certaine house of the citie appointed for no other use but onely for the bringing up of the Cortezans bastards, which I saw Eastward above Saint Markes streete neare to the sea side. In the south wall of which building that looketh towards the sea, I observed a certain yron grate inserted into a hollow peece of the wall, betwixt which grate and a plaine stone beneath it, there is a convenient little space to put in an infant. Hither doth the mother or some body for her bring the child shortly after it is borne into the world; and if the body of it be no greater, but that it may conveniently without any hurt to the infant bee conveighed in at the foresaid space, they put it in there without speaking at all to any body that is in the house to take charge thereof. And from thenceforth the mother is absolutely discharged of her child.

Carlo Goldoni

(1707–93)

Carlo Goldoni was Venice's Shakespeare and Alan Ayckbourn rolled into one. He left not only a repertoire of comedies that still play the world over but also a vivid set of memoirs, as full of anecdote and eccentric characters as many of his theatrical pieces.

Goldoni started dictating his memoirs at the age of seventy-five. He had left Venice for ever thirty years earlier, in despair at the libels of his rival Carlo Gozzi and his own failure to emancipate theatre scripts in Venice from the old conventions. Actors had become little more than acrobats, improvising the expected lines while always portraying the expression on their masks in situations that were endlessly repeated. Goldoni tried to freshen up the formulaic dialogues and introduce character development and plots.

Goldoni claims to have written his first comedy at the age of eight – 150 more were to follow, as well as comic operas set to music by Galuppi. He is at his best depicting the humble classes of Venice: gondoliers, fisherfolk, servants and waiters. This extract, a kind of manual on how to flirt in a mask, comes from one of his most famous comedies, *The Liar*.

Two key characters from the *commedia dell'arte* inhabit the scene: Arlecchino, the greedy Bergamese servant whose costume is traditionally a colourful confection of rags, and Colombina, the flirtatious sharp-tongued maid.

(*Enter* ROSAURA *and* COLOMBINA *from the house, both masked.*)

LELIO: I say, look at those two masks, Arlecchino.

ARLE: Carnival seemingly.

LELIO: Here on the first day of the fair they always wear masks in the morning.

ARLE: Who can they be?

LELIO: Oh, those two girls I spoke to last night.

ARLE: I dön't like these covered mugs.

LELIO: Ladies, 'tis useless to veil your faces to conceal your beauty while the transcendent beams from your eyes suffice to betray you.

ROSAURA (*indicating* COLOMBINA): Do you mean her, too?

LELIO: I am pledged for the moment not to distinguish between one sister and another.

ROSAURA: But this is my maid.

ARLE: My bit o' goods, mäster.

LELIO: Is it a great matter that I should mistake a mask?

ROSAURA (*dryly*): But I noticed that the beams from Colombina's eyes created the same impression as those from mine.

LELIO: Madam, now that I can speak freely to you, I will tell you that you only are the one who inspires all my admiration, that you entirely occupy my heart, and that if I spoke in equal terms of her whom I believed to be your sister, I did so without admiring her.

ROSAURA: And so you can distinguish me from my sister though I am masked?

LELIO: Of course. I should love you little indeed if I could not tell you apart.

ROSAURA: And how do you know me?

LELIO: By your voice, your figure, your noble and majestic air, the spirit in your eyes, and by my heart which is ignorant of the art of lying.

ROSAURA: For pity's sake, tell me who am I?

LELIO: You are my idol.

ROSAURA: Yes, I know. But what is my name?

LELIO (*aside*): Here's for it. (*Aloud.*) Rosaura.

ROSAURA (*unmasking*): Bravo! Now I see you really know me.

LELIO (*aside to* ARLECCHINO): Luck was with me that time. Look, Arlecchino, what an amiable countenance!

ARLE (*to himself*): Wauns! I'd gie summat for a peep at t'other!

ROSAURA: Then you really love me?

LELIO: I, Asdrubale, cannot lie. I love you, I adore you. When you are from me I can do nothing but repeat your name. (*To* ARLECCHINO.) Isn't that true?

ARLE (*to himself*): One peep ahind that mask!

Angelo Maria Labia

(1709–75)

No one has written in the Venetian vernacular with more power and wit than Labia, able to make wicked fun of both the small weaknesses of society and also the larger issues of the Republic, such as corruption. The son of aristocratic parents, Labia preferred a pious and studious life. It was typical of him not to scruple to marry a woman from a lower class than his own.

Labia's observations on wanton fashions, reflected in the poem 'The Current Fashions' included here, recall the reproving tone of the Milanese Canon Pietro Casola nearly three hundred years earlier. 'Venetian women,' Casola wrote, 'have pleasure in being seen and looked at; they are not afraid of the flies biting them, and therefore they are in no great hurry to cover themselves if a man comes upon them unexpectedly.'

Both writers refer to the voluminous veil, known as the *nizioleto* or *zendaleto*, which women wrapped around their heads and bodies – but which might be made of a light or diaphanous fabric, and therefore had more an effect of 'giftwrapping' than modesty.

Women had recourse to other means of attracting their suitors: an eighteenth-century fashion had developed for fake moles, and the positioning of these tiny patches had a language all its own. A little brown mole by the nose meant *irresistible* (or more probably insatiable). A patch in the cleft of the chin suggested a *donna galante*, an adventuress. One should beware of the one who wore her mole in the corner of her mouth: she was an *assassina*, a murderess.

~~~

Headdresses like the Furies – wild and rampant spirits,
Hair hanging all over your face, and scintillating with spangles
Necks quite nude, you could not be *more* décolletées,
Your breasts flung out in either direction;
      A cut in the bodice to let them loll loose,
Buttocks thrust out like shop canopies against the rain
Skirts and dresses – cut short, really abbreviated,
The package barely giftwrapped in a flame of veil,
      White stockings, pink jewelled slippers, ribbons,
Leaning languidly on your lovers,
And walking like the lady-lice of Buranella
(With a soft, lilting roll);
      A lascivious glance restlessly revolving,
Provoking of speech, be you ugly or lovely
This is the current fashion for women!

Giorgio Baffo

(1694–1768)

Despite a patrician background, the notoriously salacious poet Baffo wrote his verses in Venetian dialect, unceremoniously wrenching the veil from the discreet vices of his city. He also scourged the clerics for their corruptions. Although he was amazingly prolific, none of his work was published until three years after he died.

A great connoisseur of women, Baffo never married, preferring to practise love in the light-hearted, light-fingered style of his own poetry. His work is full of *joie de vivre*, with a tendency to preach *carpe diem*.

Baffo was a close friend of the parents of one Giacomo Girolamo Casanova, who recalls Baffo fondly in his memoirs, describing him as 'a sublime genius, a poet in the most lascivious of all genres, but great and unrivalled'.

Casanova also credits the poet with saving his life: it was Baffo who suggested that the young Casanova be sent to study at Padua because the air there, less dense than in Venice, would cure the child's dangerously voluminous nose bleeds. It was Baffo too who alerted Casanova's adoring but illiterate grandmother to save him when his Slavonian landlady was starving him to death in a rat-infested attic.

This cheerfully amoral poem is perhaps most shocking for the poet's unshockability. He notes everything and criticises nothing. Among Baffo's *oeuvre*, it is one of the cleanest.

There is in Venice such a cheerfulness,
And such a happy way of going about things,
That I do not believe there is
Anything like it in the whole world.

There are thousands of pleasures;
There are sweet and tender manners,
And so many beauties
That the city looks like Venus.

There are no longer, as once upon a time,
Those rustic manners,
Today one can listen to anything
And can go anywhere.

A woman goes out alone with her male friend,
And unlike in the old times,
Today that fool of her husband
Does not follow his wife.

One can go with freedom
To find a woman even in her bed,
While her husband knows nothing,
Or if he does, he keeps quiet.

All women are as gracious as can be,
And dressed in utter elegance,
And, all gussied up, they go
Even to church with their fancy-men.

Once upon a time, noblewomen ,
Would not go to certain *houses*,
Which were attended only
By salacious sluts.

But today one can find there
Respectable women, ladies, merchants,
And all the poor whores
Are now starving to death.

Everybody in the evenings
Leaves their homes to go to the Piazza
Where there are bitches of all breeds
Who go there to wag their tails.

Full of airs, and full of cheek
These women parade around in such a manner
That one cannot help, by God,
Wanting to give them a pinch . . .

There is such a great flirtation
And there are thousands of invitations,
That one wonders if the Sybarites
Could do any better for themselves.

In happiness, playing and singing
One can spend all night awake,
And at those times the housewives
Are making love with their lovers . . .

A problem in this city is
That there are few enough whores,
But married women
Compensate for them very well.

The professional whore
Is an over-used item,
But someone else's wife
Is a private resource.

It's a most particular pleasure
To go where not too many other men are going
And to have fun,
Without handing out cash,

To enjoy a woman without
Having to keep her;
And leaving her husband to take care
Of those children who might come,

To go to the theatre, to the casino,
To go out with her,
And satisfy all her whims
From her husband's pockets.

I believe that when, every so often,
One gets bored with a woman,
One can just put her down,
And take up with another one . . .

These changes are very healthy
So all women can have some pleasure,

And one can give one's sweets
To sweeten more than one mouth.

There are also those talented women
Ballerinas and musicians
Cheerful young mares
That can be mounted for free . . .

They have a way with them that seduces you,
There's nothing wrong with them;
If they are clean upstairs
They are even cleaner down below.

Myself, I have already decided
That I greatly enjoy being with them;
If it weren't for the love-diseases
It would be love on earth as it's done in Heaven.

Oh! What a pleasant life
Oh! What an amiable contentment,
To listen to a virtuoso lady singing
While you are inside her.

Equally enjoyable,
If one has to tell the truth,
Is to feel your darling
Dancing under your prick.

I do not know what France is like
Or what they do in Germany,
But I know that here's the land of plenty
For screwing to the extreme.

The great luxury, and the great fashion
Of so many brothels
Encourages everybody to enjoy oneself
And to spend a lot of money.

The more the money goes around the city,
The more the city becomes beautiful;
But it is really the vice that
Takes the money out of people's pockets.

Should the city be free
from the vice,
All artists would be banned
And it would come to ruin.

If there were not so many affairs,
And such gluttony, and ambition,
All those treasures would end up
Like stones in a corner.

Long life, then, to this city
Which is the centre of all pleasures,
Since anybody living here has a great time
And even more those who come from abroad.

Giacomo Girolamo Casanova de Seingalt

(1725–98)

'It is not beauty, but something more valuable, which I possessed but which I cannot define.' So Giacomo Girolamo Casanova describes his own attractions.

Although Venice's most famous son was born in the city, he spent most of his life in exile from it as a result of one misdemeanour or another. Possibly too big a character for a small town, he was a charismatic and versatile adventurer addicted to novelty and endlessly curious about absolutely everything, be it the mechanism of a corset or the formulas of geometry. This handsome son of an actress travelled and worked all over Europe as a secretary to a cardinal, a soldier, a gambler, a violinist and an alchemist.

His fortunes changed dramatically when as a young man he scammed his way into the heart of the Venetian nobleman Bragadin, but he always pushed his luck just a little too far. A life of lustful luxury as Bragadin's adopted son was brought to an abrupt end in 1755 when he was imprisoned in the Piombi, the famous lead-clad prisons in the roof of the Doge's Palace.

In one of the more colourful escapades of his long life, he broke out of the jail and fled Venice. He spent the next twenty years mingling with high society, indulging in one hundred and thirty-two romances (his own scrupulous tally), and becoming involved with numerous political intrigues all over Europe. When he could, he combined his interest in the occult with money-making, promising, for example, to reincarnate the elderly

Madame d'Urfé in a series of picturesque and highly expensive ceremonies.

He returned briefly to Venice in 1774, but within a few years he had again offended too many people and was forced to flee.

In 1788, when Casanova was on his uppers, Count von Waldstein offered him a position as a librarian in his castle at Dux in Bohemia. Reluctantly, he stayed there until he died, his demise poetically coinciding with that of La Serenissima, to whose reputation for decadence he had personally added such a shine.

He had never married, knowing he would make a bad husband. Yet he had arranged the advantageous and happy marriages of many of his former lovers, who were always pleased to see him again.

He spent his final secluded years reliving his earlier wild pleasures by writing them down. His scandalously candid memoirs, written in French, were first published in Germany thirty years after his death.

In 1998, Venice allowed Casanova out of exile again. He was dusted down, cleaned up and presented to the world in an exhibition at the Ca' Rezzonico.

Respectability was thrust upon him. The city that had exiled him twice, starved him, mocked him, pretended that he did not exist, and then forgotten him, had finally recognised him. But not for the one thing that made him really famous. Only one room of many in the exhibition was devoted to the sexual accoutrements of the original Latin Lover and the women he loved. Instead the exhibits celebrated Casanova as an alchemist, a freemason, a mathematician, a gourmand and spy, but above all as a traveller and a friend of the famous: a Venetian in Europe, who rubbed shoulders with the luminaries of every major city.

This extract, painfully chosen from some 3600 pages of memoirs, reflects a surprisingly analytical view for the eponymous hero of seduction. Casanova's attitude to women was far more modern than he is frequently given credit for. As he observed: 'the visible pleasure which I gave always made up four fifths of mine'.

The question is put which of the two sexes has more reason to be interested in the work of the flesh in respect to the pleasure obtained from performing it. The answer has always been the female sex . . . A summary judgment has led practical minds to declare that the woman's pleasure must be greater because the feast is celebrated in her own house, and this reason is very plausible, for she has only to let the thing be done, without exerting herself; but what makes the truth palpable to the mind of a physiologist is that if the woman did not have more pleasure than the man, nature would not have her play a greater part in the thing than he; she would not have more to do than he, and more organs . . .

Now it is well to reflect that this creature the womb, which has only one issue, which connects it with the vagina, becomes furious when it finds that it is not occupied by the matter for which nature has made it and placed it in the most crucial of all the regions of the female body. It has an instinct which does not listen to reason; . . . if the woman does not give it the food it demands through the channel which she alone controls, it often becomes furious and so gains an ascendancy over her which no strength can resist . . .

I ask if it is to be presumed that Nature _semper sibi, consona_ ('always in conformity with herself'), never in error in her reactions and her compensations, has not given the female sex a pleasure equal in intensity to the vexatious evils which are attached to it. What I can affirm is this: the pleasure which I have felt when the woman I loved made me happy was certainly great, but I know that I should not have wanted it if, to procure it, I had had to run the risk of becoming pregnant. The woman takes that risk even after she has experienced pregnancy several times; so she finds that the pleasure is worth the pain. After all this examination I ask myself if I would consent to be born again as a woman, and, curiosity aside, I answer no. I have enough other pleasures as a man which I could not have as a woman, and which make me prefer my sex to the other. However, I admit that, to have the great privilege of being reborn, I would be satisfied, and I would bind myself in writing, especially today, to be born again not only as a woman but as an animal of any species; provided, of course, that I should be reborn with my memory, for without that it would no longer be I.

Giovanni Boccaccio

(1313–75)

'Clothes more for nymphs than nuns!' sniffed one disapproving visitor at the convent of San Zaccaria in 1664.

The sensual atmosphere of the Venetian streets blew through the open doors of the convents. Much more social than spiritual institutions, they served as repositories for middle- and high-born girls whose families could not afford the dowries necessary to marry them off. These brides of Christ did not invariably adopt the chaste ways of their enforced calling.

Men, often noblemen, frequented the nunneries, where they were able to converse freely with the girls through metal grilles in the *parlatorio*. Foreigners were brought there as a matter of course to admire the beautiful noblewomen they might not meet in the streets, to hear them sing and play, and perhaps more.

Nor did the convent walls confine the nuns. Some 'escaped' and went abroad about the town with more liberty than their married sisters, fulfilling the promises of the glances and words exchanged through the *parlatorio* grilles. The French ambassador De Froullay met the sixteen-year-old nun Maria Da Riva in this way in 1740 and an infamous affair blossomed between them.

The nuns at San Zaccaria and Sant'Angelo di Contorta were particularly wanton. Casanova enjoyed threesomes with two noble nuns from Murano, and the lover of one of them, the future Cardinal de Bernis, was permitted to watch their frolics through a peephole. Such frolics often bore fruit, but the nunnery's normal activities of raising foundlings made useful cover.

All things considered, this story would not have caused as much surprise to a contemporary reader as it would to a modern one. It comes in a mannered translation, 'The Inquisitive Nuns', from *The Decameron*, in a 1737 volume entitled *Venetian Tales, Or, A Curious Collection of Entertaining Novels and Diverting Tales, Designed for the Amusement of the Fair Sex.*

Those who are of the Opinion, that as soon as a young Girl has put on the Veil, she has neither Passion nor Desires, and breathes forth nothing but Piety and Devotion, are very much mistaken; which the following Story will evince: It being impossible to change the Heart as easily as the Habit. On the contrary, a Monastical and secluded Life often produces worse Effects in a Cloister than in the wide World . . . It is a very ill way of arguing; because my Daughter is a Nun, therefore she must be a Saint.

There was formerly in *Venice*, a Convent of young Women, very much celebrated for their Piety, who for their Reputation sake I forbear to name. The Number of them was eight, besides the Abbess. They had an old Gardener, who not being satisfied with his Wages, would not serve them any longer . . . and retired to a neighbouring Village, of which Place he was. All his Neighbours welcomed him home, and amongst them, one *Maffeto*, an unlucky, sturdy young Fellow, and well made for Country Labour . . .

The Monastery being at a good distance from the Village where he lived, and not being known to any Person thereabouts, he resolved to offer himself to them, and pretend to be dumb . . .

Altho' these Sisters were not all very handsome, yet they were young and good-natured, and went often into the Garden to see *Maffeto* work, and took Delight to play unlucky Tricks with him.

The Abbess believing every thing about him to be like his Tongue, was never concerned at it.

One Day when he had been hard at Work, and was laid down to rest himself, two young Nuns, who were walking, seeing him in that Posture, stood still to view him, upon which one of them said, Sister, what a Thought think you comes into my Head? To carry this foolish Fellow into the Arbor and see –

What wicked Thing is this you talk of, said the other: Have you forgot your Vow of Chastity? We make a great many other Vows, replied the first, that we never keep. But, said the other, what if you should be pregnant?

Pray, says the other, trouble not yourself about that, if it should be so, we shall have Time enough to contrive how to conceal it. Let us not lose the present Opportunity.

We have to do with a Man that must keep Counsel whether he will or not, and upon that Account we need not fear a Discovery.

Every body in the Convent was asleep at that Time; the Arbour was thick and shady, but, to prevent surprise, they thought it convenient for one to stand Centinel, while the other kept *Maffeto* company. So one of them went to wake him, who impatiently expected her, where without much Intreaty he endeavoured to please her.

The other succeeded her immediately after, and the dumb Man pleased them both so well, that they never missed visiting the Arbour every Day.

Some of the other Sisters perceiving their Intrigue, resolved presently to acquaint the Abbess with it; but upon second Thoughts were willing rather to taste of the same Dish.

In a little Time *Maffeto* had obliged the whole Convent; the Lady Abbess was the last who participated of his Benevolence: For she perceiving the Care this dumb Man took of her Nuns, was desirous to have her own share, having as much Occasion as any of the rest; she took him to her own Chamber, and kept him there so long, that all the Nuns made great Complaints their Gardener did not come to work as usual . . .

At last *Maffeto* grew weary of so much Business, and began to think he had acted the dumb Man long enough. Being one day with the Abbess who would have had him do more than he was able, he breaks out of a sudden, saying, Madam, one Cock may serve ten Hens, but ten Men can hardly satisfy one Woman. What a hard Task then have I, who have nine to please? Pray Madam, either abate of my Labour, or give me Leave to go Home. The Abbess hearing him speak, whom she supposed to be dumb, cried out, A Miracle! A Miracle! and assembled the whole Convent, who, instead of dismissing him, gave out, that by the Power of their Fastings and Prayers, they had recovered a dumb Man to his speech.

Angelo Maria Barbaro

(1726–79)

Barbaro, born in Portogruaro near Venice, was a patrician, and an eccentric free spirit. He trained as a priest, but more than churches he loved café life, where he could gather the scandals of the city and read aloud his biting satires.

His popular play in Venetian dialect, *Anna Erizzo in Costantinopoli*, points a finger at the beautiful lady-sinners of Venice and their *cavalieri serventi*. He also aimed his wit at the authorities and the shamed husbands of the city.

The poem here, 'The Bride's Mass', deals with the traditional mass said for brides, in the name of the Virgin Mary, before their weddings.

It was sometimes said that all Venetians had two wedding anniversaries, their own and the one they all shared: 31 January, which marks the day in 944 when two Trieste pirate ships swooped in on Venice and kidnapped all the women and their dowries while they were in church. The Venetians gave chase, killed all the pirates and brought the women back in triumph two days later.

—

A young lady went one day to her priest,
A bride-to-be, very nearly
She went there for him to say
The mass of the Virgin Mary.
The priest said to her: 'Not so fast, wait a moment;
We need to talk this through as truthfully
As if you were talking to your confessor.

If you are still a maiden,
The Virgin Mary will help you;
But if you're no maiden
You'll be dead within a year.
To forefend this kind of tragedy
We have a remedy in the form of
A mass for the Mary *Maddalena*
So speak the simple truth . . .'
The girl uttered a deep sigh;
And presently said, 'Mr Priest, you can say . . .
You can say the mass . . .
The mass . . . of the Virgin Mary . . . Oh God, this hurts!
But with a little bit of Maddalena in it too, please.'

Samuel Sharp

(1700–c. 1778)

Another English traveller who discovered that chastity was a scarce commodity in Venice was Samuel Sharp, whose *Letters from Italy* include an outraged account of marriage, Venetian-style: 'The Bride's Mass'. Sharp, a surgeon from Guy's Hospital in London, found fault not just with the moral hygiene of Venice but also with the cleanliness of his accommodations and food, not to mention the absence of such modern amenities as curtains and privies.

Gallantry is so epidemical in this city, that few of the Ladies escape the contagion. No woman can go into a public place, but in the company of a Gentleman, called here, a *Cavaliére Servente*, and in other parts of *Italy*, a *Cicesbeo*. This Cavaliere is always the same person; and she not only is attached to him, but to him singly; for frequently no other woman joins the company, but it is usual for them to sit alone in the box at the opera or playhouse, where they must be, in a manner, by themselves, as the theatres are so very dark that the spectators can hardly be said to be in company with one another. After the Opera, the Lady, and her *Cavaliére Servente* retire to her *Casine*, where they have a *Tete-a-Tete* for an hour or two, and then her visitors join them for the rest of the evening, or night; for on some festival and jolly days, they spend the whole night, and take Mass in their way home. You must know a Casine is nothing more than a small room, generally at or near *St. Mark's-Place*, hired for the most part by the year, and sacred to the Lady and her Cavaliere, for the husband never approaches it. On the other hand, the husband has his revenge; for he never fails to be the *Cavaliére Servente* of some other woman; and, I am told, it would be so ridiculous for a husband to appear in public with his wife, that there is no instance of such a phaenomenon; and, therefore, it is impossible for a woman to bear up against the torrent of this fashion . . .

So many opportunities must, therefore, render this Republick a second *Cyprus*, where all are votaries to *Venus*, unless it please Heaven to pour down more grace amongst them, than falls to the share of other nations in this degenerate age; but the calumniators deny that the husbands believe in this partial favour, and assert, they have very little fondness for their children, compared with the parents of other kingdoms: They are the children of the Republick, they say, but not so certainly the children of their reputed fathers . . .

Some of these Cavalieri according to the nature of the parties, are said to be very abject and servile, doing the meanest offices, and submitting to the grossest tyranny: Others have an ascendant over their mistresses, and there is often as much jealousy betwixt the Ladies here, on the subject of their Cavalieri, as in other countries on account of their husbands; and it happens now and then that the Ladies and Cavalieri separate in favours of others; but this seems to be a delicate point, and to be avoided as much as divorces are with us . . .

This is the picture of *Venetian amours*, in the present age.

Lady Sydney Morgan

(1776–1859)

The Irish writer Lady Sydney Morgan published an account of
Florence, Naples, Milan, Genoa, Rome and Venice during a
residence in Italy in the years 1819–20.

Venice is often said to have the effect of maddening her visitors: her beauty and the sadness of her dilapidations can drive the
susceptible into depression. In this case, though, Lady Morgan
describes a local madwoman, locked up on one of the islands of
the lagoon. From the description, it is probably San Clemente,
where the female lunatics of the town were kept from Napoleonic
times. Sometimes, as a warning, they were suspended in cages
hanging over the water.

As we neared the island for the benefit of shade (for the heat was intense), we came close under a dreary-looking wing of the building of the *lazaretto* – so close, that we distinctly heard a young silvery-toned voice frequently repeating, '*Venite per me? Venite per me, cari amici?*' Directed by the sound, we perceived a pale face pressed against the iron bars of a sashless window, in an elevated part of the building: one hand, that looked like snow in the sunshine, had forced itself through the grating, and accompanied, by its impatient motion, the anxious oft-repeated question of '*Venite per me?*' As we rowed on, the voice lost its cheeriness, its tones seemed suffocated by disappointment, and the wind that bore them died not on the waters with a more melancholy murmur, than the last sobbing sound which we caught of '*Venite per me?*'

'*Poverina!*' said the gondoliere in a tone of compassion – '*Poverina!* If we passed twenty times a day, she would ask if it was for her we were coming.'

We inquired who the *Poverina* was. He said he did not know; she was some young maniac – mad for love, he had heard: she had been for many months confined in that apartment in the wing of the *lazaretto* dedicated to insane patients; but in winter or summer, the plashing of the oar of a gondola was sure to bring her to the iron bars of her cell, and elicited that question, repeated in tones so various and affecting, as hope faded into disappointment – '*Venite per me?*'

George Gordon, Lord Byron

(1788–1824)

All Byron's best-known conquests in Venice were married women: the draper's wife Marianna Segati, the baker's wife Margherita Cogni and the count's wife Teresa Guiccioli. In the letter extracted here, to his publisher, John Murray, Byron describes the blossoming relationship with Segati.

Apart from these recorded loves, Byron patronised a *casino* at Santa Maria Zobenigo. These *casini*, also described by Casanova, were discreet and often luxurious 'safe houses' for lovers. Exquisite meals were served by means of turn-tables set in the walls so that not even servants were permitted sight of the sinners.

Venice, November 25, 1816.

. . . Talking of the 'heart' reminds me that I have fallen in love, which, except falling into the Canal (and that would be useless as I can swim), is the best (or worst) thing I could do. I am therefore in love – fathomless love; but lest you should make some splendid mistake, and envy me the possession of some of those princesses or countesses with those affections your English voyagers are apt to invest themselves, I beg leave to tell you, that my goddess is only the wife of a 'Merchant of Venice;' but then she is pretty as an Antelope, is but two-and-twenty years old, has the large, black, Oriental eyes, with the Italian countenance, and dark glossy hair, of the curl and colour of Lady Jersey's. Then she has the voice of a lute, and the song of a Seraph (though not quite so sacred), besides a long postscript of graces, virtues, and accomplishments, enough to furnish out a new chapter for Solomon's Song. But her great merit is finding out mine – there is nothing so amiable as discernment. Our little arrangement is completed; the usual oaths having been taken, and everything fulfilled according to the 'understood relations' of such liaisons.

Francis Marion Crawford

(1854–1909)

The city's Byzantine ways of love and marriage have also inspired some stirring fiction, including *Marietta, A Maid of Venice* (1901). Its author was the cosmopolitan and multilingual American writer Francis Marion Crawford, who produced forty-four novels and also *Salve Venetia: Gleanings from Venetian History* (1905).

Marietta is a swashbuckling tale of passion and deceit, innocence and corruption. The eponymous Marietta, the daughter of the famous glassmaker Beroviero, falls in love with the humble but talented Dalmatian apprentice Zorzi. Her father, however, wants to marry her off to the nobleman Contarini, whose vicious, voluptuous mistress Arisa has plans of her own . . . In this scene Beroviero contrives an 'accidental' meeting of his daughter with her supposed future husband in the basilica of San Marco.

(Angelo Beroviero was the real head of a dynasty of glassmakers and had the most famous furnace on Murano in the first half of the fifteenth century. He kept a much-coveted manual of secret formulas for brilliantly coloured glass.)

~~~

Just as they were within sight of the great doors of the church, Beroviero saw a very tall man in a purple silk mantle just going in alone. It was Contarini, and Beroviero drew a little sigh of relief. The intended bridegroom was punctual, but Beroviero thought that he might have shown such anxiety to see his bride as should have brought him to the door a few minutes before the time.

Marietta had drawn her veil across her face, leaving only her eyes uncovered, according to custom.

'It is hot,' she complained.

'It will be cool in the church,' answered her father. 'Throw your veil back, my dear – there is no one to see you.'

'There is the sun,' she said, for she had been taught that one of a Venetian lady's chief beauties is her complexion.

'Well, well – there will be no sun in the church.'

. . . They entered the great church, and the servant went before them, dipped his fingers in the basin and offered them holy water. They crossed themselves, and Marietta bent one knee, looking towards the high altar. A score of people were scattered about, kneeling and standing in the nave.

Contarini was leaning against the second pillar on the left, and had been watching the door when Marietta and her father entered. Beroviero saw him at once, but led his daughter up the opposite side of the nave, knelt down beside her a moment at the screen, then crossed and came down the aisle, and at last turned into the nave again by the second pillar, so as to come upon Contarini as it were unawares. This all seemed necessary to him in order that Marietta should receive a very strong and sudden impression, which should leave no doubt in her mind. Contarini himself was too thoroughly Venetian not to understand what

Beroviero was doing, and when the two came upon him, he was drawn up to his full height, one gloved hand holding his cap and resting on his hip, the other, gloveless, and white as a woman's, was twisting his silky moustache. Beroviero had manoeuvred so cleverly that Marietta almost jostled the young patrician as she turned the pillar.

Contarini drew back with quick grace and a slight inclination of his body, and then pretended the utmost surprise on seeing his valued friend Messer Angelo Beroviero.

'My most dear sir!' he exclaimed. 'This is indeed good fortune!'

'Mine, Messer Jacopo!' returned Beroviero with equally well-feigned astonishment.

Marietta had looked Contarini full in the face before she had time to draw her veil across her own. She stepped back and placed herself behind her father, protected as it were by their serving-man, who stood beside her with his staff. She understood instantly that the magnificent patrician was the man of whom her father had spoken as her future husband. Seen, as she had seen him, in the glowing church, in the most splendid surroundings that could be imagined, he was certainly a man at whom any woman would look twice, even out of curiosity, and through her veil Marietta looked again, till she saw his soft brown eyes scrutinising her appearance; then she turned quickly away, for she had looked long enough. She saw that a woman in black was kneeling by the next pillar, watching her intently with a sort of cold stare that almost made her shudder. Yet the woman was exceedingly beautiful. It was easy to see that, though the dark veil hid half her face and its folds concealed most of her figure. The mysterious, almond-shaped eyes were those of another race, the marble cheek was more perfectly modelled and turned than an

Italian's, the curling golden hair was more glorious than any Venetian's. Arisa had come to see her master's bride, and he knew that she was there looking on. Why should he care? It was a bargain, and he was not going to give up Arisa and the house of the Agnus Dei because he meant to marry the rich glass-blower's daughter.

Marietta imagined no connection between the woman and the man, who thus insolently came to the same place to look at her, pretending not to know one another; and when she looked back at Contarini she felt a miserable little thrill of vanity as she noticed that he was looking fixedly at her, and that his eyes did not wander to the face of that other woman, who was so much more beautiful than herself . . .

It all happened in a few seconds. The two men exchanged a few words, to which she paid no attention, and took leave of each other with great ceremony and much bowing on both sides. When her father turned at last, Marietta was already walking towards the door, the servant by her left side. Beroviero had scarcely joined her when she started a little, and laid her hand upon his arm.

'The Greek merchant!' she whispered.

Beroviero looked where she was looking. By the first pillar, gazing intently at Arisa's kneeling figure, stood Aristarchi, his arms folded over his broad chest, his shaggy head bent forward, his sturdy legs a little apart. He, too, had come to see the promised bride, and to be a witness of the bargain whereby he also was to be enriched.

As Marietta came out of the church, she covered her face closely and drew her silk mantle quite round her, bending her head a little. The servant walked a few paces in front.

'You have seen your future husband, my child,' said Beroviero.

Horatio F. Brown

(1854–1926)

The complicated rituals of a Venetian wedding are here described
by that expert on all things folkloric – the historian, Horatio F.
Brown. The festivities here are, of course, for brides and grooms
from the lower or middle classes. Weddings of the nobles were
far grander affairs. Casanova played the violin at an alliance of the
Cornaro and Soranzo families in 1746. Those extravagant entertainments went on for three days. The spectacle of another
wedding cost Venice one of its original wooden bridges, the
Rialto (the current stone structure was completed only in 1591).
So many people crowded onto the bridge to watch the nuptial
procession of the Marchesa di Ferrara in 1444 that the entire edi-
fice collapsed.

The bridegroom has to find among his friends his best man, or *compare* — not always an easy task, for the *compare*'s duties are onerous, and will not cost him less than one hundred lire if he wishes to escape criticism. The ceremony for securing a *compare* is this: The bridegroom will go to the *traghetto* or to his favourite wine-shop, where he is sure to meet his friends; to one of these he will hold out his hand, and say 'Pare là;' if his friend takes his hand, and replies 'Pare paròn,' then the bargain is struck; if not, the groom must look for another. If the *compare* wishes to make a *bona fegura* and be a *compare cortesan*, this at least he must do: the day before the wedding he must send, not take, to the house of the bride a large box lined with silk and filled with bon-bons, on the top of which must lie a baby in sugar; along with the box a bouquet of sham flowers and a bouquet of real, and his present to the bride, which should be a brooch or earrings, but not a ring. He must also send six bottles of Marsala, Cyprus, and *liqueur* for the wedding supper and four large candles for the wedding mass. Besides this he has to provide four gondolas for the guests who come to supper, to fee the *nonzolo* of the church, and to provide largess for all the poor who crowd about the doors.

This accumulation of duties renders a *compare* not so easy to find. But when he has been secured the day for the marriage is fixed. It is, almost invariably, a Sunday. The other days of the week are unlucky or unsuitable for various reasons: on Monday you go mad; on Tuesday you suffer; Thursday is the day the witches comb themselves and are loose, and so on. Saturday alone is a good day, and that is reserved for the wedding of widows. The ceremony takes place at the earliest Mass to avoid a crowd and the inevitable *critica*, of which all concerned have such a lively dread. The bride wears a black veil, and the second of her two wedding dresses; the better is kept for the supper and the dance. The groom is dressed in black; he, too, keeps his best and newest for the evening. The *compare* takes the bride; the *sposo* takes the *compare*'s nearest female relative, who is called the *comare*; the parents and relations follow; and so they walk to church in the early morning air. The bride, bridegroom, and groomsman kneel at a crimson-covered faldstool before the altar; the rest of the guests range themselves on either side of the chancel. The Mass is galloped through; the *compare* places the wedding ring on the bride's middle finger; the sacristan gives them the pax to kiss; the register is signed; the priest and *nonzolo* duly feed; the doors are flung open, and the beggar boys shout, 'E viva la sposa!' and the *compare* scatters his copper coins. So, in the same order that they came, the procession returns to the house of the bride.

From the moment that the marriage ceremony is performed the bride is under the immediate charge of the *compare*; he is responsible for her during the day; he must never lose sight of her unless he has consigned her to her mother's care. So the bride returns on the groomsman's arm to her father's house; and all the guests partake of the *rinfresco* – lemonade, coffee, Cyprus, Marsala, and cakes. Then they separate till four o'clock, the hour of the supper . . .

The supper is a serious and long-drawn affair, occupying at least four hours. Like everything else in the wedding ceremony, the dishes are prescribed by *costume*; and they are, *Risi*; *lesso, manzo e pollo*; *rosto*, *pollo co la salata*; *frittura, de figà e de cervele indorae*. When dessert comes, a huge pyramid of hardbake is placed before the bride; she breaks it open, and out flies a little bird, and all the company cry. 'E viva la sposa!'

Eugenio Montale

(1896–1981)

'I always felt in total disharmony with reality,' explained the Italian poet Eugenio Montale – a condition that surely predisposed him to adore Venice.

Montale was born in Genoa. His father wanted him to join the family firm, but Montale's interest was in literature and he left home to live in Florence, where he worked as a librarian. He was sacked from his job just before World War II for refusing to support Mussolini's regime. After the war he settled in Milan where he worked as a literary editor and music critic for the *Corriere della Sera*.

There is often an element of pessimism, even despair, in his works, evident in this evocative fragment from his 'Two Venetian Pieces'.

But then we were there strolling among the pigeons
and photographers in the bestial heat,
carrying the heavy catalogue of the
     Biennial Exhibition,
which was never consulted, and which
wasn't easy to get rid of. We came back
by the boat, stepping over birdseed,
buying souvenirs, post cards and sunglasses
at the stalls. I think it was in '34
and we were too young or too strange
for a city that demands tourists and old lovers.

Jack Clemo

(1916–94)

In this poem, entitled 'Ring and Pen', the Cornish writer Jack Clemo ingeniously links two significant objects: the pen that was a gift from his lover and the golden ring with which the Doge used to marry the sea.

This extraordinary writer received only a village school education, but devoted himself entirely to writing in his adolescent years. After his father's death, he lived in poverty with his widowed mother. He lost both his sight and his hearing before the age of forty.

He won an Atlantic Award in Literature from Birmingham University in 1948 for his first novel, *Wilding Graft*. A second novel, *The Shadowed Bed*, was written soon afterwards, but not published until 1986. He also wrote two volumes of autobiography, *Confession of a Rebel* (1949) and *Marriage of a Rebel* (1980), and several volumes of poetry, including *The Map of Clay* (1961), *Broad Autumn* (1975) and *Approach to Murano* (1993) from which the following poem is taken.

A Murano goblet, church wine for the Doge
After the sea-wedding. No signature
Marked the fluid bond, but centuries later
A betrothal pen struck an echo.
My partner gave me that pen
In the clay-waste of the sixties,
And it caught rich clues from Italy.

I confirmed those insights there
In the Doges' city of doves, bell-tongues
And holy running branches. The liquid criss-cross
Linked with Christ's cross in a safe ardour,
Chimes caressing the screened flow.

On balconies and water-buses,
In a stately gondola treading the Grand Canal,
Amid glass-factory heat, at café tables,
In Browning's death-room and by St Lucy's shrine,
I fingered the slim hard bulge
In my holiday coat. My faith's ripe outline,
Taking Venetian colour as she pressed me,
Made my heart swell, made the pen dearer,
Its labours vindicated.

Then a tremor of chill dismay
Struck our apartment on the first floor,
Tranquil scenes beyond the hotel window
Unheeded as we rummaged
Even under the bed, for my pocket was empty.

Tides bore the Doge's dropped ring
To the fish's mouth or the cliff crack —
A city's emblem, never cast astray.
But my recorder, our engagement trophy . . .

The tension ebbed. In a crevice
Near the window-frame, gold glinted suddenly.
My pen had lodged there, forced by thud and roll
None noticed amid the chatter, the glow
Of Rialto shopping. The lovers' pledge
Was usable again, and our voyaging joy
Relaxed in a whim of weather.

October rain had just pricked down
Where the Doge landed, at Porto di Lido,
And she had tripped through a Cornish deluge,
Bearing the pen, on our betrothal day.

Paolo Barbaro (Ennio Gallo)

(1922–)

Paolo Barbaro's *Venice Revealed* is an essential 'insider' source. Here he presents Venetians debating the nature of their women and the love they inspire, making sly comparison with the visiting English. Until recently, he has observed elsewhere, the Venetians thought that English women came to Venice to harvest lovers before being stranded in a northern winter. 'A minute after getting together, they're ready for anything, all the more so since they hardly have any clothes on to begin with . . .'

~~~

'There are three or four types of them, *le venexiane*,' Venetian women, according to my friends Alvise and Gianni, one of whom is younger and one of whom is older than me. Alvise is a painter and Gianni, although he works at the Generali, is taking courses in creative writing. 'The ancient ethnic groups,' they assure me, 'are still recognizable if you pay a little attention.'

I'm paying attention. This is what they teach me:

1. '*Tipo levantine*' – Levantine. These women have dark or olive-skinned faces, but everywhere else they're a smooth, delicate white. Black hair: smooth beneath the sirocco, flying every which way with the bora, always *tormentati* (the hair, never the women). Huge golden-brown eyes, or else golden-green, or something between nut-brown and bronze – with or without their knowledge, the eyes of a medium, of a fortune-teller. Slight and small-boned, yet sturdy in the hips . . . and those eyes without end. More persuasive than docile in manners and character, with their 'winning ways.' Ready enough with the men, when they *want* to be. Tenacity to burn, often obstinate. Indifferent at times; yet at others, clinging and vibrant with passion (this from Gianni).

'The picture I'm getting,' I say to my teachers, 'is the iron fist in the velvet glove.'

'Right! But with a great, natural sense of humor, always ready to do something crazy.'

'They exude an appeal,' explains Alvise the artist, 'that is truly sensual. It's more than sexuality,' he clarifies further, 'it's *complete attraction*, emanating from every pore, every glance, every word they speak in that hoarse, tuneful, lilting voice. It's hard to describe, hard to capture.'

Add to that the fact that they speak '*soft*' – never trampling their syllables like their southern cousins – and never moving their hands. They move only what counts the most, in or out of their clothes. Naturally, they know all this, but they appear (with just the right touch of Venetian nonchalance) not to know it, and to care even less.

'And then they appear,' says Gianni, in the grip of a poetic-creative moment, 'in their composite nature: something between human and who knows? prehuman, marine.'

(At this point all three of us gaze out to sea. The beach is deserted; not even a dog in sight.)

'A local variation,' I hazard, 'of the Mediterranean type?'

'Probably.' But they're on a roll: sometimes these women are focused (they say) and at other times scattered; but they're always fairly spontaneous, improvisational, ready for the *comico*, the *maschera*, the *scena*.

'Faced with any question that counts,' say both my friends very seriously, 'they have a distinct tendency to debunk . . . whatever: the subject, you, what you're saying, your relationship, everything.'

End of subject, for the moment. A brief, relaxed silence; sighs all around. It's cold on the beach.

2. 'Blondes in general, *tipo cadorine* and such.'* Tall, slender, wiry, with a kind of *démodé* distinction all their own – not a bad change from Type One. Sensitive, even spiritual – in Italy! It's hard to say if they're more intelligent or more spiritual. Or more hysterical. The ones we've known have been constantly anguished and ambivalent, with a tendency to fall into states of ecstasy (over sunsets, lagoon, islands, and such). But those colors of theirs that you never forget! Blond, strawberry-blond, straw-blond;

*From the Cadore region of the Veneto. – TRANS.

even lemon, canary, and orange. Splendid clear skin – pale blue
and rose, like a tender evening sky in the foothills of the Alps.

'They'll follow you all of your life, these ones – good luck!'

3. 'Intermediates,' somewhere between Type One and Type
Two. But it's important to make the distinction between the
Slavic blondes and the black-haired beauties from Friuli. Both
are solid and generous, big wonderful women. Only sometimes
they're kind of like *wardrobes*: It's hard to embrace them – *they*
embrace *you*. They have a certain way of opening and throwing
back their legs like wings . . . If you've ever been with one, you'll
never forget her again.

'But watch out! Once they've got you, they turn the key in the
lock,' warns Alvise, not laughing, 'and you won't ever come out
again.'

Now they laugh.

'The truth is that they hold, they enclose in themselves – how
can I say it – so many beings,' tries Gianni, in another creative
leap, 'so many *persons*, even though they don't seem to.' He
explains: 'Friends, lovers, companions – everything: they can
become anything, even that comfortable presence-beside-you
that's natural at times in a manfriend – if he's a true friend (which
is rare).'

A pause ensues. We understand that Gianni, in his own way –
not because of the creative writing courses – will become a
writer.

4. '*Tipo marrone-italiota*,' according to Alvise: the brown-
Italiote type. 'Our own ethnic group,' he says, looking at me,
'yours and mine – there's no need to say anything else.' At this
point we could mix them all up and start over again. Whatever.

There's no doubt – I admit to myself, going home, watching
the islands and the women on the boat – that Venice has always

filtered men and women, as America does now, from a great number of reservoirs: from the Levant, from the North, from the Germans, Hungarians, Croatians, Istrians, Dalmatians, Friulians, from the Greeks, the Hebrews and Arabs . . . What mixtures are whipped up in this richest and maddest of cities! And who knows what it will be like from here on in, in the near future?

Alvise and I, for the moment, are most attracted by the representatives of Types Two and Three. However, for some time – we mull this over with Gianni – it seems like there are more Types One and Four around; whether there are just more of them or they're more on the scene, or what, we don't know. The truth is, we're attracted by all of them; we hardly know where to turn.

Maybe Venice has always been what she is – strange, feminine, changeable, surprising, utterly beautiful – because of all those streams of women, those galaxies, those constellations, those beings wrought out of stardust. (It's night by now; could it be affecting my thoughts?)

As a final result we know nothing, neither of Venice, nor of women, nor of the world.

The constellations, or galaxies, go on, but here at the Caffè Rionale they're a whole other thing. It's late at night and still hot, so all the tables are out in the campo or rioterrà, crowded with groups of young girls – gangs of young girls, in this city without even a discotheque. In the houses and apartments upstairs the windows are shuttered and dark; it's already way too late for the people behind them. We look around: all we see are the opposites of Type One, Two, Three, and Four . . . or at least nothing recognizable among all this green, purple, yellow, red, and blue hair. We must have invented 'our' types, then; or maybe they're extinct. We feel lost, can't seem to manage to talk to each other.

'Once upon a time,' I falter, finally, 'there were more blondes, real blondes, weren't there? Or am I wrong?'

'What blondes?' retorts Gianni. 'There were more women with black or chestnut-colored hair — I mean, *real* black and chestnut . . . *Everything* was more real.' He's a little older than I am.

So: Eyes change, hair changes, everything changes in the course of a few years; while we continue to consider the women each of us knows (or thinks he knows) and sees (or thinks he sees) as the only real ones. The others seem like poor imitations. Or maybe it's simply that 'ours' are the individual human beings whom each of us, by the grace of God, has brushed against once in a lifetime.

And for them, for the women — we wonder, eyeing all these different faces around us — who knows how it is or how it will be. At bottom, maybe *way* down at bottom, not much different. All we know for sure is that among the young these days everything changes very swiftly, perhaps from one hour to the next. There's a big turnover, a lot of shuffling of partners, swapping and switching. There's a lot more experience-that-isn't-experience; everyone goes with everyone else; no grace of God. The new 'Slavs' are the vague and powerful Americans, or the Australians you see wherever you look, whole squadrons of them. Once we would have said they were enticingly 'provocative' — today they just make us laugh, except for their bouts of ingenuous imagination, which are more likely to make us cry. For the Australian women who come here everything rides the wave of a precise and prefabricated symbolic fantasy, which leads them immediately to encounter the symbols and marry the allegories of Venice: gondoliers, waiters, nobles, and so forth.

In my opinion, however, as far as I've been able to touch on the subject (not enough, never enough), no one can compare to the English. It must be the story of the double island: they come down from theirs – populated, perhaps by very few males – and are, how shall I put it? ready and willing. Can it be that only the most eager and lusty of women from Britain make it this far? They come here and find the Venice-island, the place of their dreams: Carnevale, boats, sea, beauty, classical characters, Romantics, postmoderns . . . Who will ever write the infinite story, which continues generation after generation, of the *inglesine* on the lagoon? Even today the journey to Venice, the islands, the Lido, becomes for these British women a voyage beyond the confines of the common, transcending the ordinary human world and sailing wildly into the mythic. (This, too, I've experienced firsthand – 'on my own skin,' as we say; it wasn't easy.) It's a little like that for us in the British Isles, as well, in the Shetlands and Hebrides. It's as if there were a dark nucleus crying out from island to island, subconscious, and language were no barrier at all.

But how many there are – or seem to be! All these women brushing by you, only a breath or a touch away: in the *caffè*, in the calli, in the dark, solitary *sottoportici*, on the bridges and canal banks, on the little outside staircases of the houses, on the huge inner stairwells of the palazzi . . . All the different voices, languages, and scents wafting around you envelop you in fantasies. These clouds of perfumes-voices-signals become very concentrated when women walk alongside or pass by you in the longest and narrowest calli (San Barnaba and Santa Maria Formosa, for instance). They wheel, return, and then vanish like smoke between the canals and the campi. And you: you either swiften or slow down your pace, or duck down a side street, depending on whether you want to follow them or just save yourself; but it's no use, they're imprinted on your retina (or on something) – salvation is not a possibility. Is it the way they're dressed, or does it take no more than a particular color, some little nothing? All of the above, I guess, depending on the time, the place, the occasion. In the great observatories of Campo Santo Stefano, the Rialto, and Stradanova, you can mistake one face or one dress with another; but on the small, nameless bridge it is *she* who comes toward you: the unknown woman you will never see again, who has nonetheless entered and become part of you forever. Radiant marvels in blossom, dressed in gossamer and set afire by each smallest gleam of the sun: beauty lighting up beauty. Later on in life all this may fade; but not always, it isn't a given. I think it's this way everywhere, more or less. But we may *see* it more here, since we continue to find them beside us, our wonderful women. They keep walking with us, brushing lightly against us, touching us, spilling their scents on the air, spying on us and each other. They *want* to be looked at, listened to, noticed, observed, remembered. Venetian calli are brief, briefer still the apparition we call life. And *le venexiane*, oh my God, are evermore rare.

Raymond Carver

(1939–88)

This wistful little vignette, entitled 'Venice', comes from the American writer Raymond Carver, renowned for his short stories but also the author of much fine poetry.

Venice clearly inspired the poet with insecurity, even when grasping at 'a little light' from a high-up shutter.

The gondolier handed you a rose.
Took us up one canal
and then another. We glided
past Casanova's palace, the palace of
the Rossi family, palaces belonging
to the Baglioni, the Pisani, and Sangallo.
Flooded. Stinking. What's left
left to rats. Blackness.
The silence total, or nearly.
The man's breath coming and going
behind my ear. The drip of the oar.
We gliding silently on, and on.
Who would blame me if I fall
to thinking about death?
A shutter opened above our heads.
A little light showed through
before the shutter was closed once
more. There is that, and the rose
in your hand. And history.

Gregory Warren Wilson

(1956–)

In a piquant twist, the poet and musician Gregory Warren Wilson holds Venice as a threat over the head of his lover in his poem 'Blindfold'.

Warren Wilson was born in London, and has pursued a threefold career in writing, dancing and music. Having trained at the Royal Ballet School, he then studied violin and composition at the Royal College of Music. He now performs internationally as a classical violinist.

If you ever take me for granted, I'll take you
by the hand, confound you this way and that
in a maze of Gothic passageways I memorised
year by year, nameplate by shutter by headstone,
to a place where the scent of crushed geranium
mingles with the sour lagoon — a blind alley
that comes to an end in three scooped steps
down to a green canal; there I'll unfasten
the muslin binding your eyes and say *Venice*
all Venice is lapping your feet
and darling you'd be lost without me.

City of Arts

ARTISTS AND WRITERS

By the light of a candle,
you do not judge women or paintings.

Deeds are men, words are women.

White walls, the paper of the mad.

VENETIAN PROVERBS

. . . for painting is the way Venetians write.

JOHN RUSKIN

Anyone who sets his little concoction in the triangle between the
Florian, San Giorgio and the Zattere is playing on velvet.

RÉGIS DEBRAY

All the principles of art are violated: and out of their violation
springs a new art, borrowed from the East but stamped with the
mark of Venice.

CHARLES YRIARTE

Pictures were there, replete with such enduring beauty and
expression: with such passion, truth, and power: that they
seemed so many young and fresh realities among a host of
spectres.

CHARLES DICKENS

Indeed, since the day when God created the heavens, never have
they been so fair . . . Nature, mistress of all masters! How
miraculous is her brush, how wonderful her pencil! I know that
your pencil, my Titian, is the rival of Nature and you her most
well beloved son: so I cried out three times, 'Titian, Titian,
Titian, where art thou?'

PIETRO ARETINO

Never before did any one surrender himself to such a debauch of the eye. We gazed fourteen hours each day without stopping.

THÉOPHILE GAUTIER

Their mastery over colour is the first thing that attracts most people to the painters of Venice. Their colouring not only gives direct pleasure to the eye but acts like music upon the moods . . .

BERNARD BERENSON

On one occasion a vain and foolish old nobleman wished to have his portrait painted, and would never have done urging the master to be careful to reproduce exactly the lace, gold, and rich stuffs with which he was adorned; at last Tintoretto, losing all patience, burst out, 'Go get yourself painted by Bassano,' who was universally known as an animal painter.

POMPEO MOLMENTI

Do you notice the variegated splendour of the walls and windows? It looks as if Genius had followed the caprices of a child, in the adornment of these singular temples.

HANS CHRISTIAN ANDERSEN

She entices each of us into the act that is the very genesis of our species: the effort to surpass ourselves unceasingly.

GABRIELE D'ANNUNZIO

But what a shame I didn't come here when I was a younger man, when I was full of daring!

CLAUDE MONET

At the San Luca, they gave us 'Elizabeth, the Exile of Siberia', tolerably acted: but there was one trait introduced very characteristic of the place and people: Elizabeth in a tremendous snow storm, is pursued by robbers; and finding a crucifix by the road side, embraces it for protection. The crucifix flies away with her in a clap of thunder, and sets her down safely at a distance from her persecutors . . . the men rose from their seats, clapped with enthusiasm, and shouted 'Bravo! Miracolo!'

ANNA JAMESON

Hearing even the worst performance at the Fenice is still a kind of luxury . . . flattering and coddling you simultaneously, but the Fenice *and* Verdi *and* Stiffelio – this is the very knickerbocker-glory of voluptuousness.

JONATHAN KEATES

Lorenzo Lotto

(c. 1480–1556)

'Lorenzo Lotto, when he is most himself . . . shows us people in want of the consolation of religion, of sober thought, of friendship and affection,' wrote the art historian Bernard Berenson.

It seems that this insecurity was something that the artist felt himself, for despite his success he described himself as 'of a most untranquil mind'.

He trained in the studio of Giovanni Bellini with Giorgione and Titian, with whom he had a cordial relationship, but his idiosyncratic style set him somewhat apart from central Venetian tradition. Lotto suffered great privations in order to pursue his art. He was reduced to painting comb-cases; was often paid in wine, cheese or ham. He took shelter with relatives or friends, and in hostelries. Then he suffered the worst affliction possible for an artist: he began to lose his sight. At this point he became a lay monk and ended his days in the monastery in Loreto.

While much of his life remains mysterious, there is much information to be gleaned from his account book of sundry expenses, which has survived and was published in 1894.

Lotto would have hired poor people to body-model for the figures of those noblemen and women whose portraits he painted: such important people could not be expected to pass long hours in his studio. Hence his paying a woman for 'undressing only to look' on 2 September 1541.

Note: There were 12 *bagattini* to the *soldo* and 20 *soldi* to the *lira*. A *ducat* was 6 *lire* and 4 *soldi*. A *lira* was worth around 10d in contemporary English currency.

1541		Lire	Soldi
15 February	For nails and purified linseed oil		4
	Mastic 2 ozs		10
	Kermes [red pigment] taken from Misser Sebastiano Serlio the Bolognese architect on account of certain credit that I have with him, 6 ozs at 6 ducats an oz	37	4
27 February	For transporting the pictures to decorate the house on Carnival Thursday . . . and for returning them to the workshop – boat and porters		2
8 March	Purified linseed oil		
12 March	For an undamaged vessel for purifying linseed oil		3½
	1½ lbs of lead white		6
	Vitriol		1
	½ lb of cinnibar in powdered form		
[. . .] April	For transporting the painting of the Graces and that of the Venus to the workshop and porters		9
	Linseed and walnut oil		5
2 September	For undressing a woman only to look		12
	On several occasions oil for working	1	4
	Oil for the lamp and for washing brushes and cleaning the stones used for grinding pigments		16
	Brushes		8
	3 lbs of lead white		12
October	Gums 2 ozs		10
	Tin foil and ink		2½

2 reams of thick blue paper for covering pictures

	Lire	Soldi
2 reams of thick blue paper for covering pictures		11
Contribution to the Guild		13
And on 13 August last Master Gasparo da Molin, the landlord of the studio was given 5½ ducats worth	34	2
Various pigments on several occasions		
Drawing-paper, oils and nails	3	0
To a woman for undressing	1	4

Albrecht Dürer

(1471–1528)

In late 1505, the great German artist Albrecht Dürer rode to Venice from his home town of Nuremberg, an arduous journey undertaken in ill-health. Various motives have been suggested: a pleasure trip, a search for patrons (Venetian artists were better paid than Germans), to combat Italian piracy of his own works, or even to escape the plague.

Dürer arrived just as Venice was rebuilding its Fondaco dei Tedeschi, the trading station for German merchants, which had been destroyed by fire. Titian and Giorgione were to decorate its façade by the Grand Canal near the Rialto. The Germans used the nearby Church of San Bartolomeo, and Dürer was commissioned to paint an altarpiece for their chapel.

Dürer felt deference and affection for Giovanni Bellini, then an old man. But he encountered hostility from the younger artists, and frequently complained that the cost of living in Venice was eating up his fees as fast as he could earn them.

These extracts are taken from two of many letters to his friend, Willibald Pirkheimer.

~~~

Venice, 7 Feb. 1506.

First my willing service to you, dear Master! . . .

How I wish you were here at Venice! There are so many nice men among the Italians who seek my company more and more every day — which is very pleasing to one — men of sense and knowledge, good lute-players and pipers, judges of painting, men of much noble sentiment and honest virtue, and they show me much honour and friendship. On the other hand there are also amongst them some of the most false, lying, thievish rascals; I should never have believed that such were living in the world. If one did not know them, one would think them the nicest men the earth could show. For my own part I cannot help laughing at them whenever they talk to me. They know that their knavery is no secret but they don't mind.

Amongst the Italians I have many good friends who warn me not to eat and drink with their painters. Many of them are my enemies and they copy my work in the churches and wherever they can find it; and then they revile it and say that the style is not *antique* and so not good. But Giovanni Bellini has highly praised me before many nobles. He wanted to have something of mine, and himself came to me and asked me to paint him something and he would pay well for it. And all men tell me what an upright man he is, so that I am really friendly with him. He is very old, but is still the best painter of them all.

Venice, 2 April, 1506.

First, my willing service to you, dear Herr Pirkheimer . . .

The painters here, let me tell you, are very unfriendly to me. They have summoned me three times before the magistrates and I have had to pay four florins to their school. You must also know that I might have gained a great deal of money if I had not undertaken to paint the German picture. There is much work in it and I cannot get it quite finished before Whitsuntide. Yet they only pay me 85 ducats for it. Now you know how much it costs to live, and then I have bought some things and sent some money away, so that I have not much before me now. But don't misunderstand me, I am firmly purposed not to go away hence till God enables me to repay you with thanks and to have a hundred florins over besides. I should easily earn this if I had not got the German picture to paint, for all men except the painters wish me well.

Palma il Giovane

(c. 1548–1628)

Jacopo Negreti was known as Palma il Giovane to distinguish him from his great-uncle Palma il Vecchio (another Jacopo Negreti). Il Giovane studied in Rome from 1567 until 1572, but returned to Venice for the rest of his career. His works are to be found throughout the city. The artist recorded his recollections of an eccentric Titian at work in old age. Here, in his recollections (recorded in Boschini, 1674), he describes how Titian, having sketched extraordinary figures, sometimes in just four strokes, would leave his work to mature like wine. Some of these sketches were so beautiful that customers wanted to carry them off as they were. Full of admiration for the master, Palma asserts: 'his brushstrokes always give birth to expressions of life'.

After he had laid these precious foundations, he turned the pictures round to face the wall, and there he left them, sometimes for months, without looking at them, and, when he then wanted to reapply the brushes, he examined them with a rigorous scrutiny as if they had been his mortal enemies, in order to see whether he could find fault with them. And, on discovering something that did not agree with his refined intention, he [treated] them like an effective surgeon who, in curing a patient, will – if it is necessary – cut out some swelling or superfluous flesh, straighten an arm if the bone structure is not quite correct, and set right the position of a foot which has become dislocated, without pitying his patient's pain, and so on. Thus Titian, working and revising those figures, brought them to the most perfect symmetry that the beauty of Nature and Art can represent, and after this was done he put his hand to other works until these were dry, and he did the same again and from time to time; he then covered these quintessential extracts with living flesh, creating them layer by layer, so that they only lacked breath.

Modesta Pozzo deí Zorzi,
known as Moderata Fonte

(1555–92)

Although Venice was the centre of European book production, and therefore many female-authored books were printed there, social strictures kept local women largely in seclusion and few were able to make their names as writers. The famed exception to the rule, Veronica Franco, was a courtesan, who lived a far freer life than the respectable Moderata Fonte.

Orphaned at an early age, Fonte was placed in a convent, where her intelligence soon became apparent. She was fortunate in a guardian, and later a husband, who encouraged her. Even before her marriage in 1582 she wrote several works of verse. Her only surviving prose work, *Il merito delle donne (The Worth of Women),* was published in 1592, the same year she died in childbirth, aged thirty-seven.

This engaging and witty work takes the form of a series of daily dialogues among seven Venetian noblewomen. In various ways they rebut the prevalent negative attitudes towards women, pointing out the vices and frailties of the men in their lives.

The scene that follows comes from the second day of discussions, when talk turns to the fashions of Venice.

Certainly, said Corinna, in Venice there are more beauties than in any other place; and speaking of dress, more grace and loveliness. Does it not seem that our fashion is truly feminine, because it shows a certain grace and delicacy that belongs exclusively to women and rightly so; whereas in contrast, the dress of women from outside Venice seems more mannish than feminine.

Above all, said Helena, this fashion of ours to wear our hair blonde not only looks sweetly feminine but also lends an air of nobility . . .

Oh, said Cornelia, if the men were to see us talking about such things, how they would laugh at us. For they already say in any case that we are good for nothing but to preen and polish ourselves.

Let them say what they like, replied Corinna, and they don't insult us with that anyway, for the sweetness and refinement of our looks comes from the nobility of our soul . . .

It's not unsuitable for women to show our natural refinement by feminine dress and ornamentation, said Corinna. Naturally men say that all this finery indicates a corrupt soul beneath, and can be a danger to our virtue. But they are completely in error, as I said before: the way women dress can scarcely endanger their virtue if men would only stop soliciting them and leave them in peace. And, as proof, just think how often one sees women of low estate importuned by men and coming to grief, even though they dress quietly and without any kind of adornment . . .

While we are on this course, added Leonora, many men also forbid their women to read and write, alleging that education is the downfall of many women. As if the pursuit of virtue (which is where learning leads) led straight to its opposite, vice! . . . we see from experience that far more illiterate women fall into vice than do educated women who use their minds. How many unlettered serving maids, how many country girls and working-class women submit to their lovers with a negligible struggle? And the reason is that they are more gullible than women like us, who have read their moral tales and learnt our lessons and so grown a love for virtue: we may still feel the temptations of our senses, but we know how to enforce discipline on our desires, and it's a rare thing for an educated woman to allow herself to be swept away by her desires . . .

It is really something, said Cornelia at this point, that men disapprove even our doing things that are obviously good. Would it not be possible for us simply to cast these men out of our lives, and escape their whining and mocking once and for all? Couldn't we live without them? Could we earn our own living and manage our lives without help from them?

Charles de Brosses

(1709–77)

The Venetian priest-composer Antonio Vivaldi became friendly with the eighteenth-century French traveller Charles de Brosses, who describes here some of the musical life in the city. The choirs of nuns and female orphans were among the major tourist attractions of the city. Both Vivaldi and Galuppi directed these choirs at the four *ospedali*, originally almshouses, which gradually came to house principally poor or illegitimate young girls. Music was such a major part of the education provided that, by the eighteenth century, the *ospedali* were virtually conservatories. Gabriel Bella has left a charming painting of an orphan-girl concert given to the Grand Duke Peter, heir to the Russian throne, who spent a week not-quite-incognito in Venice in January 1782.

Vivaldi, known as the *prete rosso* because of his red hair, was violin master and resident composer at the Church of the Pietà on the Riva degli Schiavoni. He also became a director of the Theatre of Sant'Angelo. But despite his success, Vivaldi, like Mozart, died a forgotten pauper.

Vivaldi has made himself one of my intimate friends, probably in order that he may sell me his concertos expensively.

Four of his compositions are good, and I have gained my wish, which was to hear him play and listen to good music; he is a *vecchio*, and is full of prodigious enthusiasm for his work. I have heard him compose a concerto with all its different parts more rapidly than a copyist could note it down. I am much surprised to discover that he is not much appreciated here, where everything depends upon the fashion of the day, and where his work has been so long known, and where last year's music is no longer the vogue. The famous Saxon composer is the man of the hour. I have heard him at his house, and also the famous Faustina Bordoni, his wife, who sings with much taste, and in a light and charming way, but her voice is no longer a young one. She is certainly a most delightful person, but that does not make her the greatest of songstresses.

The best music here is that of the charitable establishments. Of these there are four, all containing natural daughters, female orphans, or those girls whom their parents are unable to educate. They are maintained at the expense of the State, and their principal education is that of music. They can sing like angels, and play the violin, the flute, the organ, the hautboy, the violoncello, and the bassoon; the largest instrument of music has no terror for them. They are treated like nuns. They alone perform at these concerts; and at each of these, forty of the students play. I can assure you there can be nothing more charming than to see a young and pretty nun, dressed in white, with a bunch of pomegranate flowers in her hair, conducting the orchestra and beating time with the greatest skill and precision. Their voices are excellent, light, and well trained. The Zabetta, of the Hospital for Incurables, is remarkable for the extent of her voice and the high notes she commands. She has all the suffrages of the people here, and one would run the risk of being maltreated by the populace did one venture to compare her to any of the other musicians. But between ourselves, my dear friends, I think that Margarita of the Mendicanti is equal to the Zabetta, and she pleases me more.

Count Carlo Gozzi

(1720–1806)

'The epidemic of literature was always chronic in our household,' recalled Carlo Gozzi, one of eleven children, including two literary brothers.

In the family's country house was a little theatre, where the brothers and sisters would perform plays. But before long the aristocratic family fell into pecuniary difficulties, not helped by the arrival of Gozzi's sister-in-law, Luisa Pisana Bergalli.

Born in Venice in 1703, Bergalli had been educated by the painter Rosalba Carriera and the librettist and poet Apostolo Zeno. She had produced her first tragedy by the age of twenty-three and also an anthology of female poets. Her second tragedy was written by the age of twenty-five, and by thirty she had translated Terence and produced a comedy dedicated to her husband, Gozzi's brother, Gasparo, ten years her junior. In his memoirs Gozzi paints a highly unflattering portrait of Bergalli as an incompetent domestic tyrant.

Here Gozzi explains the genesis of his own literary career.

~~~

I learned to fence and dance; but books and composition were my chief pastime. Before a numerous audience in our literary assemblies, I felt no shyness. In private visits, among people new to me, the reserve of my demeanour often passed for savagery. My first sonnet of passable quality was written at the age of nine. Beside the applause it won me, I was rewarded with a box of comfits; and for this reason I have never forgotten it. The occasion of its composition was as follows. A certain Signora Angela Armano, midwife by trade, had a friend at Padua whose pet dog died and left her inconsolable. Signora Angela wished to comfort her friend; indulged in condolements for her loss; and sent a little spaniel of her own, called Delina, to replace the defunct pet. Delina was to be given as a present, and a sonnet was to accompany the gift, expressing all the sentiments which a lady of Signora Angela's profession might entertain in a circumstance of such importance. Though our family was a veritable lunatic asylum of poets, no one cared to translate the good creature's garrulity into verse. Moved by her entreaties, I undertook the task . . .

This trifling composition was read by the famous Apostolo Zeno . . . On my presenting myself, Signor Zeno politely expressed surprise at discovering a mere boy in the learned writer of the sonnet, treated me with kind attention, and placed his choice library at my disposal. The encouragement of this distinguished poet, true lover of pure style and foe to seventeenth-century conceits, added fuel to the fire of my literary passion. From that day forward not one of those collections of verses appeared in which marriages, the entrance of young ladies into convents, the election of noblemen to offices of state, the deaths of people, cats, dogs, parrots, and such events, are celebrated in Venice and other towns of Italy, but that it contained some specimen of my Muse in grave or playful verse.

Books, paper, pens and ink formed the staple of my existence. I was always pregnant, always in labour, giving birth to monsters in remote corners of our mansion. I scribbled furiously, God knows how, up to my seventeenth year . . .

My brother Gasparo had taken a wife in a fit of genial poetical abstraction. Even poetry has its dangers. This man, who was really singular in his absolute self-dedication to books, in his inde-fatigable labours as an author, and in certain philosophical temper or indolence, which made him indifferent to everything which was not literary, learned to fall in love from Petrarch . . . This woman, of fervent and soaring imagination, which fitted her for high poetic flights, undertook to regulate the disorder in our affairs . . .

Joshua Reynolds

(1723–92)

The English portrait painter Joshua Reynolds arrived in Venice on 23 July 1752, and embarked upon an exhaustive tour of her pictures, making copious notes in black-lead pencil, accompanied by sketches. He departed on 16 August, forever influenced by the techniques and colour of Titian, Veronese and Tintoretto. Extracts from his notebooks show that he was engaged in minute analysis of their methods of composition and use of light.

San Giovanni e Paolo
Observations on the 'Pietro Martire' di Titiano

The trees harmonize with the sky, *i.e.*, are lost in it in some places, and at others relieved smartly by means of white clouds. The angels' hair, wings, and the dark parts of their shadows, being the same colour as the trees – the trees of a brown tint. The shadows of the white drapery, the colour of the light ground. The light, the colour of the face of the saint. The landscape dark. Trees opposed to . . . of light; behind that, dark trees; behind that again, blue scumbled (ultramarine) mountains.

The drawing, in general, noble, particularly of the right leg of him who turns his head. The shadows of his eyes and nostrils determined and of a beautiful shape.

St. Maria della Salute

. . . In the sacristy, 'The Marriage of Cana, in Galilee,' by Tintoretto.

One sees by this picture the great use Tintoretto made of his pasteboard houses and wax figures for the distribution of his masses; it has the most natural light and shadow that can be imagined. All the light comes from several windows over the table.

The woman, who stands and leans forward to have a glass of liquor, is of great service: she covers part of the table-cloth, so that there is not too much white in the picture, and by means of her strong shadows, she throws back the table, and makes the perspective more agreeable. But, that her figure might not appear to be a dark inlaid figure on a light ground, her face is light, her hair masses with the ground, and the light of her handkerchief is whiter than the table-cloth. The shadows, blue, ultram –; strong shadows of the table-cloth, blueish; all the other colours of the draperies are like those of a washed drawing. One sees indeed a little lake of drapery here and there, and one strong yellow that receives the light. This picture has nothing of mistiness . . .

A. J. Finberg

(1866–?)

The art critic Alexander Finberg was commissioned by the National Gallery to catalogue its works by Turner. He brought to light many previously unknown works by the artist.

In his book, *In Venice with Turner* (1930), Finberg painstakingly follows the artist's steps, tracing the itineraries of his sketchbooks. In this extract, he fondly imagines that Turner and Byron could have been in Venice at the same moment in 1819.

Later in the book he attributes Turner's attraction to Venice to the cravings conjured by the poet's first famous work: 'I think Byron's 4th canto of "Childe Harold" must have had a good deal to do with it.'

When did Turner arrive in Venice, and on what date did he leave it? If he had not left before the 7th October he might have seen, or heard, two of his fellow-countrymen who made a rather noisy entrance into Venice during the evening of that day. These two men were Lord Byron and Mr Thomas Moore . . .

Moore tells us, 'the sun was just setting, and it was an evening such as Romance would have chosen for a first sight of Venice . . .'

As they 'turned into the dismal canal' and stopped before Byron's 'damp-looking mansion' Moore thought regretfully of a comfortable room in 'the Gran Bretagna', but Byron insisted that he should sleep in the palace. A dinner was ordered from a Trattoria, and while waiting for its arrival 'we stood', Moore says, 'out on the balcony, in order that, before the daylight was quite gone, I might have some glimpses of the scene which the Canal presented. Happening to remark, in looking up at the clouds, which were still bright in the west, that what had struck me in Italian sunsets was that peculiar rosy hue – I had hardly pronounced the word "rosy" when Lord Byron, clapping his hand on my mouth said, with a laugh, "Come, damn it, Tom, don't be poetical." Among the few gondolas passing at the time, there was one at some distance, in which sat two gentleman who had the appearance of being English; and observing them to look our way, Lord Byron putting his arms akimbo, said, with a sort of comic swagger, "Ah! If you John Bulls knew who the two fellows are, now standing up here, I think you *would* stare!"'

Now if Turner had not left Venice before the evening of the 7th of October he might possibly have heard the loud guffaws of Lord Byron and Mr Moore as their gondola passed through the canals;

or have seen them standing on the balcony of the Mocenigo palace; or even have been one of the two John Bulls to whom Lord Byron's playful remark was addressed. This seems almost too good to be true, but stranger things have happened in life, if not in fiction . . . I doubt if anyone could prove that Turner was not in Venice on the 7th of October.

Margaret Oliphant

(1828–97)

For centuries the key sources of information on the great Venetian artists were two colourful but deeply flawed works: *Lives of the Most Excellent Italian Architects, Painters and Sculptors* (1550), by the jealous gossip Giorgio Vasari, and Carlo Ridolfi's *Lives of the Venetian Painters* (1648).

In *The Makers of Venice* (1887), the Scottish writer and novelist Margaret Oliphant compares their accounts of how the technique of oil painting came to Venice.

It was not till a much later period, however, that an event occurred of the greatest importance in the history of art – the arrival in Venice of Antonello of Messina, a painter chiefly, it would seem, of portraits, who brought with him the great discovery of the use of oil in painting which had been made by Jan von Eyck in Bruges some time before. Antonello had got it, Vasari says, from the inventor himself; but a difficulty of dates makes it more probable that Hans Memling was the Giovanni di Bruggia whose confidence the gay young Sicilian gained, perhaps by his lute and his music and all his pleasant ways. Antonello came to Venice in 1473, and was received as a stranger, especially a stranger with some new thing to show, seems to have always been in the sensation-loving city. But when they first saw his work, the painter brotherhoods, the busy and rising *scuole*, received a sensation of another kind. Up to this time the only known medium of painting had been distemper, and in this they were all at work, getting what softness and richness they could, and that *morbidezza*, the melting roundness which the Italians loved, as much as they could, by every possible contrivance and exertion out of their difficult material. But the first canvas which the Sicilian set up to show his new patrons and professional emulators, was at once a revolution and a wonder . . .

This novelty created such a flutter in the workshops as no wars or commotions could call forth. How could that warmth and glow of life be got upon a piece of canvas? One can imagine the painters gathering, discussing in storms of soft Venetian talk and boundless argument, the Vivarini hurrying over in their boats from Murano and every lively *cena* and moonlight promenade upon the lagoon apt in a moment to burst into tempests of debate as to what was this new thing. And on their scaffoldings in the great hall of the palazzo, where they were dashing in their great frescoes, what a hum of commotion would run round. How did he get it, that light and lustre, and how could they discover what it was, and share the benefit?

The story which is told by Ridolfi, but which the historians of a more critical school reject as fabulous, is at all events in no way unlikely or untrue to nature, or the eager curiosity of the artists, or Venetian ways. These were the days, it must be recollected, when craftsmen kept the secret of their inventions and discoveries jealously to themselves, and it was a legitimate as well as a natural effort, if one could, to find them out. The story goes that Giovanni Bellini, by this time at the head of the painters in Venice, the natural and proper person to take action in any such matter, being unable to discover Antonello's secret by fair means, got it by what we can scarcely call foul, though it was a trick. But the trick was not a very bad one, and doubtless among men of their condition might be laughed over as a good joke when it was over. What Bellini did, 'feigning to be a gentleman,' was to commission Antonello to paint his portrait – an expedient which gave him the best opportunity possible for studying the stranger's method. If it were necessary here to examine this tale rigorously, we should say that it was highly unlikely so distinguished a painter as Bellini could be unknown to the new comer, who must, one would think, have been eager to make acquaintance on his first arrival with the greatest of Venetian artists. But at all events it is a picturesque incident . . .

There is another version of the manner in which Antonello's secret was discovered in Venice. Of this later story it is Vasari who is the author. He, on his side, develops out of the dim crowd of lesser artists a certain Domenico Veniziano who was the first to make friends with the Sicilian. Antonello, for the love he bore him, communicated his secret, Vasari says, to this young man, who for a time triumphed over all competitors; but afterwards coming to Florence was in turn cajoled out of the much-prized information by a Florentine painter, Andrea del Castegna, who, envious of Domenico's success, afterwards waylaid him, and killed him as he was returning from their usual evening diversions. This anecdote has been taken to pieces as usual by later historians jealous for exactness who have discovered that Domenico of Venice outlived his supposed murderer by several years.

James Abbott McNeill Whistler

(1834–1903)

The controversial American artist was born in Lowell, Massachusetts, but spent most of his adult life in Europe, particularly Paris and London.

Whistler was known for his eccentric and offensively domineering ways: he sometimes orchestrated conversations with a Japanese cane wand, and often referred to himself pompously in the third person.

When he arrived in Venice in the winter of 1879, aged forty-five, he was bankrupt and homeless. He was also freshly notorious from his libel action against the art critic John Ruskin, who had damned his work. (The court found in Whistler's favour but the damages were set at a derisory farthing, which Whistler thereafter wore on his watch-chain.)

Whistler had come to Venice to produce copperplate etchings commissioned by the Fine Arts Society. He also worked in pastels on brown paper, sketching real-life subjects showing ordinary Venetians in their day-to-day activities, rather than the traditional romantic views.

Otto H. Bacher, an etcher who befriended the artist during his times in the city, recalls him fondly in his book, *With Whistler in Venice*, published in 1908.

Initially staying near the Frari, in 1880 Whistler moved into a house full of art students, including Bacher, and lived with them on uncharacteristically friendly, if patronising, terms in their lodgings at the Casa Jankowitz on the Riva degli Schiavoni, with a view towards the Doge's Palace, San Giorgio and the Salute. While borrowing heavily from everyone, Whistler complained about the intense cold, having to eat chicken too often and that he missed the fogs and the gossip of London 'in this Opera Comique country'.

Dressed eccentrically ('Only Whistler could do this and pull it off,' he observed of himself), he was a popular guest in the houses of the rich American community, though forced to share the stage with Richard Wagner, George Eliot and her husband, Ouida, Robert Browning, Liszt and many other expatriate celebrities.

As Otto Bacher recalls in this extract, Whistler had strong opinions on everything Venetian, notably the artists.

～

His favourite themes were the old Venetian painters. 'Canaletto,' he said, 'could paint a white building against a white cloud. That was enough to make any man great.' He thought a great deal of Tintoretto. One day we were visiting the Scuola di San Rocco, where numerous Tintorettos are incased high up in the walls. He climbed up with great difficulty, in order to get a close look at the technique of that master, and was in great glee over it, perhaps because it coincided well with his own. Paul Veronese and Titian were, in his own words, 'great swells' . . . In speaking of certain things of Corot's, he remarked, 'They've been done before.'

I objected to that, saying, 'Who did them?'

'Whistler,' he observed.

. . . Once when I was at work at the Ponte del Pistor, Whistler joined me in my gondola, saying, 'This is a good subject. When you find one like this you should not do it, but come and tell Whistler.'

Mark Twain (Samuel Langhorne Clemens)

(1835–1910)

Mark Twain was not one to take his art too seriously. In this second extract from *The Innocents Abroad* he does not flinch at expressing the secret views of many an art-sodden traveller in Venice.

We have striven hard to learn. We have had some success. We have mastered some things, possibly of trifling import in the eyes of the learned, but to us they give pleasure, and we take as much pride in our little acquirements as do others who have learned far more, and we love to display them full as well. When we see a monk going about with a lion and looking tranquilly up to heaven, we know that that is St. Mark. When we see a monk with a book and pen, looking tranquilly up to heaven, trying to think of a word, we know that that is St. Matthew. When we see a monk sitting on a rock, looking tranquilly up to heaven, with a human skull beside him, and without other baggage, we know that that is St. Jerome. Because we know that he always went flying light in the matter of baggage. When we see a party looking tranquilly up to heaven, unconscious that his body is shot through and through with arrows, we know that that is St. Sebastian. When we see other monks looking tranquilly up to heaven, but having no trademark, we always ask who those parties are. We do this because we humbly wish to learn. We have seen thirteen thousand St. Jeromes, and twenty-two thousand St. Marks, and sixteen thousand St. Matthews, and sixty thousand St. Sebastians, and four millions of assorted monks, undesignated . . .

If I did not so delight in the grand pictures that are spread before me every day of my life by that monarch of all the old masters, Nature, I should come to believe, sometimes, that I had in me no appreciation of the beautiful, whatsoever.

It seems to me that whenever I glory to think that for once I have discovered an ancient painting that is beautiful and worthy of all praise, the pleasure it gives me is an infallible proof that it is *not* a beautiful picture and not in any wise worthy of commendation. This very thing has occurred more times than I can mention, in Venice. In every single instance the guide has crushed out my swelling enthusiasm with the remark:

'It is nothing – it is of the *Renaissance*.'

I did not know what in the mischief the Renaissance was, and so always I had to simply say:

'Ah! so it is – I had not observed it before.'

. . . But it occurred to me too often for even my self-complacency, did that exasperating 'It is nothing – it is of the *Renaissance*'. I said at last:

'*Who* is this Renaissance? Where did he come from? Who gave him permission to cram the Republic with his execrable daubs?'

City of Flavours

DINING IN VENICE

If your mouth is full you can't say no.

Rice is born in water and should die in wine.

Wine is the milk of the old.

There are more days than there are sausages.

At the table, and in bed, you don't need good manners.

VENETIAN PROVERBS

The cardinal sin of Venetian people is their gluttony; but it is a chatty and lively gluttony, and very different from the heavy and laborious digestion of many foreigners. Two glasses of wine, some bread and something on the side are able to generate an exuberant and playful inebriation.

PIETRO GASPARE MOROLIN

After having our hands washed . . . the servants and the carver came and the meal started: little doves and livers in their juices served in cups; stewed chicken in bowls; roasted chicken, kids and lambs in dishes and water with lemon in little cups; roasted pheasant with broad beans and peas; two courses of cakes, one black and one white cut into pieces and served on silver trays; boiled capon with salted tongues; boiled veal and kid with sausages and oiled herbs; another course of roasted veal and capon; scrambled eggs with milk and marzipan; cheese, parmesan, oranges, cherries, almonds, pine kernel cakes . . .

MARINO SANUDO, on the banquet of Doge Andrea Gritti

I recall also certain fishmongers' stalls covered with little fishes so white, so pearly, that I felt like swallowing them raw . . .

THÉOPHILE GAUTIER

. . . most of the Nobility content themselves with *Pilchards* and *Musles*, and such cheap stuff.

AMELOT DE LA HOUSSAIE

Better a dry biscuit every hour than a *frittole* once a week.

ANDREA CALMO

After making punch we amused ourselves eating oysters, exchanging them when we already had them in our mouths. She offered me hers on her tongue at the same time that I put mine between her lips; there is no more lascivious and voluptuous game between two lovers, it is even comic, but comedy does no harm, for laughter is only for the happy. What a sauce that is which dresses an oyster I suck in from the mouth of the woman I love! It is her saliva. The power of love cannot but increase when I crush it, when I swallow it.

GIACOMO GIROLAMO CASANOVA

We stopped at Florian's for a cooling drink, and thoughtlessly asked the waiter at what hour the café closed. 'Closed, sirs?' he said with astonishment. 'The doors of Florian's have not been shut for three hundred years.'

EUGENE SCHUYLER

Elio Zorzi

(1892–1955)

Elio Zorzi's *Osterie Veneziane* was published in 1928. Not just a guide to eating places, it also explains the historical origins of typical foods and dining habits of the Venetians.

To prevent the reckless dissipation of the city's wealth, Zorzi explains, the Venetian state was forced to act repeatedly to curb the luxurious tastes of her citizens. A special magistracy of *Provveditori alle Pompe*, or Luxury Commissioners, was established in 1514 to monitor conspicuous consumption.

A decree in 1562, for example, forbade the serving of oysters at private suppers for more than twenty people, and specified only 'modest confections' for dessert. (One wonders what the Renaissance lawmakers would have made of the Pasticceria Gobbetti by the Ponte dei Pugni. This glorious institution is famed for its glistening domes of chocolate mousse, without which it seems impossible to give a civilised dinner party in Venice.)

As well as food, the state tried to regulate excessive dowries and the adornment of women. The wearing of pearls, for example, was strictly controlled.

The state also attempted to control the ostentatious decoration of houses – with little success if one is to look at the Ca' d'Oro, Marino Contarini's fairy-tale extravaganza on the Grand Canal. Its roundels, shields, lions, arches, the foliation of its capitals, were literally gilded. The beams were painted in two coats of the costliest ultramarine, ground from lapis lazuli.

During the eleventh century, Princess Teodora, daughter of Alessio, married to Doge Domenico Selvo, was the first to introduce the use of the fork in Venice. She would never touch food with her fingers, but would have it cut by eunuchs first, and then she would lift it to her mouth using golden forks . . . This fact gained the poor *Dogaressa* Teodora the malediction of Saint Pier Damiano, and the scandalised reprobation of the Venetian people, who saw in the atrocious death of the *Dogaressa*, who perished in the spasms of gangrene, the just punishment from heaven for the laxity of her lifestyle. But the habit remained and the fork has kept its name of *piron*, given to it by the Venetians, as a sign of its Byzantine origin from the verb *peirein* (to stick) and from the neo-Greek *peironnion* (fork). A few hundred years later, in the sixteenth century, in Venice forks were used as cutlery by the person sitting at the table, unlike in all other countries where they were only used by the person doing the meat carving.

In the thirteenth century, laws to restrain food excesses started to be written. 'It is forbidden to have' – Molteni writes – 'from September all through Carnival, dinners and banquets with women who are not relatives of the host, and in order to avoid pointless penalties, it is ordered that nobody, from St. Michael's day to the first day of Lent, after the third sound of the bells, should entertain for dinner either men or women.

'In 1460,' he continues, 'luncheons where more than half a *ducato* per guest was spent were forbidden. This was decided in order to fight against the very expensive society banquets regarded as a shame towards God and the world.'

In 1473, according to Cecchetti in *The food of Venetians in the*

XIV Century, the Senate forbade the use of pheasants, peacocks, Indian roosters, mountain roosters, trout and other freshwater fish; it was forbidden to give sweets as presents, with the exception of *gelatine* and *frittole*.

Since it often happened that 'at parties and public lunches given by Companies, on top of *soleri* there were *spongade* and many other desserts served, all with great expense', those public luncheons were forbidden, and only private indoor feasts 'as it used to be done in the old times, and offering small almond sweets only [were permitted]. It was also proscribed to gild or cover with gold any kind of food, as was often done, because it was believed that gold would strengthen the heart . . .'

Obviously, restrictive laws are usually completely pointless, and Venetian cuisine became more and more opulent and succulent.

Thomas Coryate (or Coryatt)

(1577–1617)

Food is always of interest for the author of *Coryat's Crudities: Hastily Gobbled up in Five Moneth's Travels*. Coryate is most impressed with 'the marveilous affluence and exuberancy of all things tending to the sustentation of mans life' in Venice, particularly amazing in a city lacking arable land. Here he describes the fruit he most enjoyed during his stay. He also notes disapprovingly that, though even the noblest of Venetian men does not scorn to buy his own victuals from the bursting stalls at the Rialto, such 'inferior and sordid affaires' are, in his opinion, better left to the servants.

Likewise they had another special commodity when I was there, which is one of the most delectable dishes for a Sommer fruite of all Christendome, namely muske Melons. I wondered at the plenty of them; for there was such store brought into the citie every morning and evening for the space of a moneth together, that not onely St. Markes place, but also all the market places of the citie were super-abundantly furnished with them: insomuch that I thinke there were sold so many of them every day for that space, as yeelded five hundred pound sterling. They are of three sorts, yellow, greene, and redde, but the red is most toothsome of all. The great long banke whereof I have before spoken, which is interjected as a strong Rampier betwixt the Adriatique sea and the citie, even the Litto maggior, doth yeeld the greatest store of these Melons that are brought to Venice. But I advise thee (gentle Reader) if thou meanest to see Venice, and shall happen to be there in the sommer time when they are ripe, to abstaine from the immoderate eating of them. For the sweetnesse of them is such as hath allured many men to eate so immoderately of them, that they have therewith hastened their untimely death . . .

Also they have another excellent fruite called Anguria, the coldest fruit in taste that ever I did eate: the pith of it, which is in the middle, is as redde as blood, and full of blacke kernels. They finde a notable commodity of it in sommer, for the cooling of themselves in time of heate. For it hath the most refrigerating vertue of all the fruites of Italy.

Ludovico Pastò

(18th century)

This Italian poet prefaced his collection of poetry with the following self-portrait:

> Short and skinny
> With hair that used to be black
> Eyes like a cat, and a nose for tobacco
> Pale and yellow complexion.
>
> Great friend to wine
> Extremely unlucky in love,
> But still not disillusioned
> And full of zest all the time,
>
> Polite and discreet as a monk
> Sober when they give me nothing for dinner
> Stuffed full of ideas, but all crazy ones.

In his *Elogio sul vin, ditirambo burlesco, scritto in dialetto veneziano* (*In Praise of Wine, a Burlesque Dithyramb Written in the Venetian Dialect*, 1839), Pastò includes poems about wine, sketches of people, celebrations, marriages, and verses on bread and zabaglione, among other foodstuffs. The following is his dithyramb dedicated to polenta.

When I walk around Venice
And I find in the street
The chaps who sell polenta
One coin per slice . . .
All happy-happy and
All lovely-lovely
Under the wings of my cloak
I go around singing,
With my mouth full
So-so hot, and so-so greasy.

Carlo Goldoni

(1707–93)

Even the great Goldoni enjoyed singing the praises of polenta. In a Tom Jonesian moment of his play *The Charming Woman,* Goldoni has them linger on Rosaura's coral lips as she extends this mouth-watering invitation to the avid Bergamese servant, Arlecchino.

'. . . We will fill a beautiful pot of water and will put it on the fire. When the water starts to murmur I will take some of that ingredient in a powder that looks like gold called yellow flour and little by little I will pour it into the pot where, using a perfect stick, you will draw circles and lines. When the substance is thickened we will remove it from the fire and both of us together, each armed with a spoon, we will pour it from the pot into a dish. Then we will add slowly a generous portion of fresh, yellow, delicate butter and well-grated cheese, and then? And then *Arlecchino* and *Rosaura*, one on each side, with a fork in our hands, we will take two or three mouthfuls at once of that well-prepared *polenta* and we will eat it like an emperor.'

Antonio Sforza

(18th century)

For centuries, hot chocolate has been one of the supreme Venetian indulgences. Not the insipid milky froth now sold in fashionable chains of coffee-shops: *Venetian* hot chocolate is another experience entirely. With the consistency and colour of dark mud, this beverage is more food than drink, richer than the swarthiest mousse, recalling a time when chocolate was so highly valued that ten cocoa beans were worth one rabbit, one hundred a slave, and twelve a night with a courtesan.

Naturally, chocolate's charms have been serenaded by the city's creative talent: Longhi painted a society lady drinking her morning chocolate in bed; Casanova described travelling with sticks of chocolate in his strong box (he enjoyed supervising the maids who melted it down to make the drink) and the poet Antonio Sforza wrote his 'Sonnet in Praise of Hot Chocolate'.

Sforza also dedicated a poem to another well-known chocolate-lover of the eighteenth century, Rosalba Carriera, whose house, near the Guggenheim, is marked with a plaque on its Grand Canal wall. Carriera was famed for her delicate pastel portraits.

The modern *Carnevale* in Venice still celebrates hot chocolate with dedicated parties at the ancient Caffè Quadri in St Mark's Square. The Tiffany lamps, tall speckled mirrors, red damask walls, gilded Venetian chandeliers and refined atmosphere contrast with the antics of the throng below its windows. Participants, who are expected to arrive in full costume, are served traditional *Carnevale* pastries: *galani*, long sugared biscuits like crunchy doughnuts, and *fritelle* (the modern name for *frittole*). Tuxedoed waiters bearing white-crested jugs pour the thick chocolate into which they swirl a short stream of milk.

Hot chocolate also plays a part in one of the most endearing Venetian festivals, that of the *Epifania*, on 6 January. Through the morning mists that day improbable silhouettes appear, poling boats down the Grand Canal. Closer inspection reveals men dressed as old women, with carrots strapped to their noses. They are racing to the Rialto, some towing a stocking the size of a small whale. On the Riva di Carbon restaurants serve free cups of hot chocolate to the waiting crowds. An effigy of the old witch, the *Befana*, made entirely from cloves of garlic, also appears on the Rialto, as do large lumps of black sugar in the *pasticcerie*. The legend is that children who have not been good receive lumps of coal instead of sweets at this time of year.

The Venetian passion for chocolate is well captured in Sforza's effervescing poem to his favourite beverage.

Let it never be said that,
before going to bed,
I don't put my right
and my left hand together
without saying a requiem
for that good Christian
whose family gave him
the name Columbus.
Not just because he found
pure silver and gold,
because for me he did
that in vain;
Not because he conquered lands
for the Spanish king –
since I'm not so fond
of the Spanish myself;
But simply because he brought
from the new world
the sweet blessed potion
that we call Chocolate.
And for that I feel a
greater devotion than
have the Certosine Friars
for their wine-drenched fry-ups.
It has no beginning or end,
this love that I have for the
daughter of cocoa,
cinnamon, sugar and vanilla;
I would go three hundred miles
barefoot just to drink a

little cup of it,
I would pawn my Breviary
and my robe.
Truly my guts
are (And I wouldn't like to tell you
any wickedness) for chocolate
like a pig's lusting after acorns.
I would give up all beverages –
I would give up *tocai*, and *malvasia* –
and the whole genealogy of wines
if I could only be given
that holy liquor which
touches my heart,
which only to name it
makes my mouth water.
But there are lots of idiots
who believe that the Gods' ambrosia
would be a better drink than Chocolate . . .
He who never tries it could not believe
how many blessings it has for us,
delivering us first of all from all evils,
apart from death . . .
My soul, dead and buried,
will go begging that my flesh,
turning under the earth
till it becomes *earthenware*,
shall not be made into plates or urinals
but instead into little royal cups
for holding Chocolate
So that after death
I shall be still in my beatitude.

Antonio Lamberti

(1757–1832)

A popular song prescribes the perfect *frittole*, the classic Venetian bun:

> It has to be very tasty,
> Well cooked and well raised,
> Well sprinkled with sugar,
> Hot . . . or cold, as you like it.

At the time of the Republic, the corporation of *frittole* sellers counted seventy members and each of them was allocated a district. Sons followed fathers into the profession, which only a native Venetian might pursue.

An eighteenth-century account of a *frittole* emporium compares it to a military barracks. On one side the men kneaded the dough and on the other they fried it in a pan mounted on a tripod. Another man stood by armed with a sugar sprinkler. At the front of the shop was a table on which were laid big pewter or tin dishes, all polished to a shine and very tastefully decorated, some filled with pine kernels and grapes, and others with *frittole* and other sugar breads.

Lamberti, of 'La Biondina in Gondoleta' fame, was another poet who was as much at home dedicating a love song to a gustatory delicacy as to a delicate lady. The following extract is part of his piece on *frittoler*, the fryer of *frittole*.

During Lent,
And other solemn days,
There's an old custom
In our city,
Of a special fry-up
An abundant one,
Which in itself or because of the fashion
Is regarded as very tasty,
This we call the *frittole*,
And there is not even one little square,
(Which are called *campi*)
Where one does not find set up
A certain stall,
Where they are making
Those venerated *frittole*
Just one look at which would make you
breathless with delight . . .

Pietro Gaspare Morolin

(19th century)

The extract below comes from Morolin's beautiful illustrated book, formidably entitled *Venezia, ovvero quadro storico della sua origine, dei suoi progressi e di tutte le sue costumanze, scritta da un Viniziano adorna di incisioni topografiche e di litografie offerenti prospettive ritratti costumi antichi e moderni* (*Venice, a True Historical Picture from the Beginning of Her Story, and of All Her Customs, Written by a Venetian and Adorned with Topographical Engravings and Lithographs Offering Perspectives, Portraits and Costumes, both Antique and Modern*). Two volumes appeared in Venice between 1841 and 1843. It includes maps, views, battle scenes and even scores of gondolier songs – and this description of a kind of hostelry particular to the city.

~~~

In the old times there was in Venice a kind of shop called *malvasie*, because, among the liquors available, they mostly sold one called *malvasia*, a very delicate wine made from a small Greek grape known as *malvasia*. There were two types: the simple *malvasia* and the one called *garba*, which had a taste of *amaretto*.

In the *malvasie* one could also find *cipro*, *malaga*, *eleatico*, *scopulo*, *samos*, and all those wines that gave a sweet flavour back to the palate and which were all, almost without exception, imported from Greek islands.

Patrons of *malvasie* were people from all classes and all ranks. It was indeed beautiful to see such a picture of variety displayed in front of you and the constant coming and going taking place there. The nobleman would not mind, especially in the winter season, running into a *malvasia* to order his small glass of *garba*, gulp it down, and then leave to go back to his affairs; while there it was not uncommon for the nobleman to meet the *gondoliere* who, lifting his hat with respect towards him, would come in and before going to work would offer a small glass of liquor to the altar of Bacchus. According to the old *gondolieri*, it sometimes happened that when they met a nobleman in a *malvasia*, the grandee . . . would throw a coin to the shop owner and without saying a word he would give a nod meaning that he was paying for all the people around. The pantomime was brief and immediately understood, and all hats were lifted as a way of thanking the noble benefactor who, while still cleaning his lips from the libation, would leave the *malvasia* . . .

Luigi Plet

(19th century)

Luigi Plet, singing master at the Basilica's Musical Chapel, wrote a poem dedicated to *baccalà*, or dried salted cod. Bars in the town still serve rounds of bread heaped up with *baccalà mantecato*, the traditional Venetian delicacy of dried salted cod whipped up to a delicate mousse.

This poem, which appeared in April 1850, contains a complete list of recipes for cooking *baccalà*, including some quite unusual ways of preparing the fish.

It is likely that the poet's memory was still fresh from the 1849 siege of Venice – 146 days of Austrian bombardment and isolation – when *baccalà* proved to be the most delicious food Venetians could enjoy in those hungry times, and which has probably forever endeared it to them.

Boiled, stewed, roasted, and, if one wants
In four ways with a sauce; and then
Fried in another three ways; in pieces or in strips
With a turban, dressed or with ink,
Wrapped in paper, with tripe, turned over . . . one could
Make a list, and I do not know
Whether there is one who could claim to have eaten
Baccalà in all possible fashions.

William S. Rose

(1775–1843)

In this second extract from his *Letters from the North of Italy* William Rose, after spending Christmas in Venice, reflects on Venetian eating habits. In the extract here he describes, as a novelty to his nineteenth-century readers, the complicated confection known as *lasagna*, as well as a dish which is now familiar to us as *risotto*, and which was far more usual on humble tables in those days than pasta. *Lasagna*, as we know it today, usually omits the sweet ingredients listed here.

The fare of Christmas eve, though meagre, is, as I have said, magnificent, always bating a sort of pye-pottage, called 'torta de lasagne', which might, I suppose, pair off with plum-porridge itself . . .

It is composed of oil, onions, paste, parsley, pine-nuts, raisins, currants, and candied orange peel, a dish which, you will recollect, is to serve as a prologue to fish or flesh!

It ought, however, to be stated that the ordinary pottage of this country, and which is, generally speaking, that of all ranks in Venice, requires no prejudices of education or habit to make it go down, but may be considered as a dish to be eat at sight. It consists in rice boiled in beef broth, not sodden, and 'rari nantes', as in England and France, but firm, and in such quantity as to nearly, or quite, absorb the 'bouillon' in which they are cooked: To this is added grated Parmesan cheese. And the mess admits other additions, as tomatoes, onions, celery, parsley, etc. Rice thus dressed, which have drunk up the broth, are termed 'risi destirai', as capable of being spread, right or left, with the spoon. There is also a vulgar variety of the dish, termed 'risi a la bechera', or rice dressed butcher fashion. In this the principal auxiliary is marrow, which, if it is entirely incorporated in the grain, makes a pottage that (speaking after a friend) would almost justify the sacrifice of an Esau.

The mode of cooking the rice to a just degree of consistency, seems taken from the Turks, who have a saying that rice, as a proof of being well drest, should be capable of being counted. You will recollect the importance attached to this grain by the Janissaries, whose rice-kettles serve as standards . . . An almost equal degree of respect is attached to this food by the Venetians, and it is a common thing, on hiring a Venetian maid-servant, for her to stipulate for a certain monthly salary, and her rice.

T. Adolphus Trollope

(1810–92)

Sometimes it seems that almost every traveller to Venice has felt obliged to describe his own experience of her most famous café, Florian's, which spills out of the arches of the Procuratie Nuove into the heart of San Marco. It would be easier to enumerate the famous people who have *not* drunk a cup of expensive coffee in this faceted jewel-box of a café. This account of the Venetian institution comes from *A Family Party*, by T. Adolphus Trollope.

The son of a barrister, he had travelled to Italy in 1835 and remained there until 1890. He befriended many Italian revolutionaries, sympathising with their cause. In 1866 he settled in Rome as the Italian correspondent to the *Daily News*.

Floriano Francesconi opened his café, originally named Venice Triumphant, in 1720. Coffee had come to Venice in the previous century, but for many years it was used only as a medicine. The first establishment devoted to its recreational consumption opened in 1683, not far from Florian's.

One of many legends of Florian's concerns the great sculptor Canova, a regular customer. The patron suffered dreadfully from gout and Canova, no doubt settling his account in the process, modelled the man's leg in plaster so that he might have a shoe made to ease the pain.

What is Florian's? It is the principal, largest, and most fashionable caffè on the Piazza di San Marco. The caffè in itself is in many respects a speciality of Venetian life, and has been so since the days of Goldoni. The readers of his comedies, so abundantly rich in local colouring, will not have failed to observe that the caffè plays a larger part in the life of Venice than is the case in any other city. Probably no Venetian passes a single day without visiting once at least, if not oftener, his accustomed caffè. Men of business write their letters and arrange their meetings there. Men of pleasure know that they shall find their peers there. Mere loafers take their seats there, and gaze at the stream of life, as it flows past them, for hours together. And, most marked speciality of all, Venice is the only city in Italy where the native female aristocracy frequents the caffè. Indeed, I know no place in all the Peninsula where so large an amount of Italian beauty may be seen as among the fashionable crowd at Florian's on a brilliant mid-summer moonlight night.

Dorothy Menpes

(1883–1973)

Dorothy Menpes, accompanying her artist father on his travels, kept both an eye and an ear open in Venice when compiling her beautiful 1904 book about the city. Although a foreigner, Menpes was clearly in sympathy with the spirit of the town and could read the street cries as clearly as a written page.

~~~

If the streets of Venice are bewitching by night, they are certainly delightful in the early morning. It is then that one receives the most vivid impressions. There is a certain freshness in one's perceptions at the dawn . . . The great cisterns in the market-place are open, and the water is brought round to your house by dealers, stout young girls with broad backs and rosy cheeks; they carry it in two brass buckets attached to a pole, and empty it into large earthenware pots placed ready for its reception in the kitchen. These girls, called 'bigolanti,' supply the place of water-works. At this hour you see the shops opening like so many flowers before the sun. Butchers set forth their meat; fruit shops, crockery shops, bakers', cheap-clothing, and felt-hat shops, show their various wares. You see peasants at work among vegetables, building cabbages and carrots into picturesque piles, and decorating them with garlic and onions, while their masters are still sleeping on sacks of potatoes. Great barges arrive from Mestre, Chioggia, and Torcello, laden with vegetables and fruit. Eating-houses begin their trade. You see men and women taking their breakfast, and a savoury smell of spagettis and eels on gridirons fills the air . . . Picturesque old women, carrying milk in fat squat bottles, make the round of the hotels and restaurants at this early hour. They are good to look at, with their dark nut-brown faces and dangling gold earrings under their large straw hats. Their figures are much the shape of their bottles; and they bring a pleasant atmosphere into Venice, an atmosphere of fields and clover-scented earth. Fishermen, a handsome class, with weather-beaten faces, in blue clothing, come striding down the calle, shallow baskets of fish on their heads. They set up their stalls and display their soles and mackerel, chopping up their eels into sections and crying, 'Beautiful, and all alive!' . . .

The street cries are full of individuality, and the tradesman brings a little art to bear on the description of his wares. The song of the sweep, exquisitely sad, quite befits the warning, 'Beware of your chimney!' There is nothing gay about the sweep: he is a very melancholy person, and his expression is in sympathy with his music. The pumpkin-vendor is coy, and his cry has a winning pathos; his is not an easy vegetable to launch on the market, and he has developed into a very bashful person. His cry is cooing and subtle: he almost caresses you into buying, which is necessary, as no one in his right senses really desires a pumpkin. The fruiterer is different. He is handsome, fat-cheeked, and has scarlet lips, strong black hair curling in ringlets, and gold rings in his ears. His adjuration is a round, full, resonant roar, like a triumphant hymn; and there is altogether a certain Oriental splendour about his demeanour. It is not necessary for him to be subtle: there is always a sale for melons and pears, chestnuts and pomegranates. He uses colour as a stimulant to his customers, and dwells upon the hue of his fruit. 'Melons with hearts of fire!' he cries. Also he flatters. To a dear old gentleman passing by he will hold up a clump of melons, some of them sliced, or a group of richly coloured pomegranates, and say, 'Now, you as a man of taste will appreciate this marvellous colour; you are young enough to understand the fire and beauty of these melons'; and the old gentleman will go on his way feeling quite pleased and youthful. Some of the cries are quaint. I once heard a man say, 'Juicy pears that bathe your beard!'

Horatio F. Brown

(1854–1926)

The indefatigable chronicler of Venetian trivia explains the origin of another culinary speciality.

Beans have always formed an important ingredient, not just in the Venetian diet but also in the local superstitions. 'Casting the beans' (throwing them across the floor) enabled 'wise women' to predict the future of a romance, rather in the same way that other cultures read tea leaves. Here Horatio F. Brown describes how beans became one of the iconic foods of Venice.

Other Venetian pastries are still available, some prettily packaged for the tourists. One of the most picturesque kinds are the pairs of tiny meringues cemented with dark chocolate: these are known as 'Kisses in a Gondola'. Rumpled brown meringues are called 'Bones' and flat oval biscuits are sold variously as the tongues of cats or mothers-in-law. A *pasticceria* near San Tomà sells '*pallone di Casanova*', little balls of soft chocolate pastry rolled in brilliantly coloured candy sprinkles.

In Venice this custom of eating beans through the octave of All Souls' is extremely ancient. The monks of every cloister in the city used to make a gratuitous distribution of beans on All Souls' Day to any of the poor who chose to come for them. A huge caldron was placed in the middle of the courtyard and the food ladled out to the crowd. The gondoliers did not come with the rest, but had their portion sent down to them at their ferries. This grace was granted to them in consideration of the fact that all the year round they rowed the brothers across the canals for nothing. Indeed, though the customer is almost extinct, they still do so; and you may sometimes see a brown-cowled friar crossing a ferry with no other payment than a pinch of snuff or a benediction. As the Venetians grew more wealthy, true beans became distasteful to the palates of the luxurious, who were yet unwilling to break through the custom of eating them on All Souls' Day. The pastrycooks saw their opportunity, and invented a small round puff, coloured blue or red or yellow, and hollow inside; these they called *fave*, or beans; and these are to be seen at this time of the year in all the bakers' windows.

Francis Hopkinson Smith

(1838–1915)

The American writer, in his *Gondola Days* (1897), recalls a delightful breakfast shared with his gondolier Giorgio, all the more pleasurable for its leisurely nature. Hopkinson Smith had retired from a strenuous career in engineering, which saw him working on the foundations of both the Statue of Liberty and the Staten Island sea wall.

I say you have had all sorts of breakfasts out of doors in your time, but never yet in a gondola . . .

Giorgio draws all the curtains except the side next the oleanders, steps aft and fetches a board, which he rests on the little side seats in front of your lounging-cushions. On this board he spreads the cloth, and then the seltzer and Chianti, the big glass of powdered ice and the little hard Venetian rolls. (By the bye, do you know that there is only one form of primitive roll, the world over?) Then come the cheese, the Gorgonzola — active, alert Gorgonzola, all green spots — wrapped in a leaf; a rough-jacketed melon, with some figs and peaches. Last of all, away down in the bottom of the basket, there is a dish of macaroni garnished with peppers. You do not want any meat. If you did you would not get it. Some time when you are out on the canal, or up the Giudecca, you might get a fish freshly broiled from a passing cook-boat serving the watermen — a sort of floating kitchen for those who are too poor for a fire of their own — but never meat.

Giorgio serves you as daintily as would a woman; unfolding the cheese, splitting the rolls, parting the melon into crescents, flecking off each seed with his knife: and last, the coffee from the little copper coffee-pot, and the thin cakes of sugar, in the thick, unbreakable dumpy little cups.

There are no courses in this repast. You light a cigarette with your first mouthful and smoke straight through: it is that kind of a breakfast.

Carole Satyamurti

(1939–)

A completely different kind of repast is here described by the English poet and sociologist, Carole Satyamurti: a knowing, adult kind of nourishment, where food is not exactly the point. Any tourist who has dined expensively in Venice will find resonance in this subtle poem, called 'Il Contro'.

Satyamurti teaches at the University of East London and at the Tavistock Clinic, where her main academic interest is in the application of psychoanalytic ideas to a variety of social situations. She published three volumes of poetry and a *Selected Poems* with Oxford University Press, and her most recent collection is *Love and Variations* (Bloodaxe, 2000). She won the National Poetry Competition in 1986, and received a Cholmondeley Award for poetry in 2000. Her work has been widely anthologised and broadcast. She lives in London and Paris.

You pay for the fifteenth-century palazzo.
You pay for three smiles in evening dress,
for just the right degree of deference.

You pay for the dexterity of wrists,
the flattering chorale of glass and silver;
for the proffered chair, flourished napery,

the snowy acres of the sommelier's waistcoat.
You pay for the plush hush of the ladies' room,
tiny tablets of geranium soap.

Pasta that leaves a coating on your teeth
is not, you tell yourself, the point. You pay
for the precision sprinkling of *parmigiano*,

for the slick ripple of Gershwin; the magnetism
of Fame and Money at the other tables;
for candle-flame that gilds you, draws you in.

You pay for your reflection in the window
where Dukes' mistresses once leaned. You pay
for a starring role in your own Sweet Life.

And you pay for the centuries-old tact
with which you're not pressed to a second course,
with which the *portiere* averts his eyes.

The Haunting City

SADNESS AND MADNESS

Every evil comes from the intellect.

He who has a head of wax shouldn't go out in the sun.

*Everyone enjoys seeing a lunatic in the piazza
because he's not of the same breed.*

The first sign of madness is to remember proverbs.

VENETIAN PROVERBS

Venice is herself the ghost, her goblet brimming with a liquor that seems the drink of death, a perilous, grey, steely vapour.

BERYL DE SÉLINCOURT AND MAY STURGE HENDERSON

Don't take Venice, a drug that is only pleasurable on the first 'trip'.

RÉGIS DEBRAY

The poetry, the romance of the scene stole upon me unawares. I fell into a reverie, in which visionary forms and recollections gave way to dearer and sadder realities, and my mind seemed no longer in my own power. I called upon the lost, the absent, to share the present with me – I called upon past feelings to enhance that moment's delight. I did wrong – and memory avenged herself as usual. I quitted my seat on the balcony, with despair at my heart . . .

ANNA JAMESON

No rude sound disturbs your reveries; Fancy, therefore, is not put to flight. No rude sound distracts your self-consciousness. This renders existence intense.

BENJAMIN DISRAELI

The evening came; and when the moonbeams cast their uncertain light, and diffused broader shadows, I felt myself more at home; in the hour of the spirit-world, I could first become familiar with the dead bride.

HANS CHRISTIAN ANDERSEN

. . . the moonlight from behind, on the Salute, intense; but in my present tone of mind, ghastly like corpse light.

JOHN RUSKIN

A doctor friend . . . once told me that most deaths from violence in Rome are from passion, in Venice from suicide.

SEAN O'FAOLAIN

. . . the canals sickened him with their evil exhalations.

THOMAS MANN

Nevertheless, do not all fragile souls come here as to a place of refuge? Those who hide some secret wound, those who have accomplished some final renunciation, those whom a morbid love has emasculated, and those who only seek silence the better to hear themselves perish?

GABRIELE D'ANNUNZIO

Théophile Gautier

(1811–72)

Venice was a place of dark romance for Théophile Gautier, always alert for any sign of Gothic horror. Reading his travel sketches, it's easy to see that his first interest was in painting.

This French novelist, biographer, accomplished short-story writer and theatre critic arrived in Venice on a rainwashed summer night in 1850. He stayed at the Hotel Europa and later moved to rented lodgings. His first impressions of Venice were recorded in his *Voyage en Italie* (1852).

———

At every turn a night-lamp flickered before a Madonna. Strange
and guttural cries sounded around the canals; doors, whose
threshold the waves licked, opened to emblematic figures which
disappeared behind them; the parti-coloured posts to which the
gondolas are attached assumed, in the face of the sombre façades,
the attitude of spectres.

At the top of the arches human forms vaguely watched us pass
by, like the gloomy figures of a dream. Sometimes all the lights
were extinguished and we advanced in sinister fashion. All objects
in this obscurity touched by any wandering ray assumed appearances which were mysterious, fantastic, weird, and out of
proportion.

The water, always so formidable at night, added to the effect
by its dull lapping and its unresting life. The dark waves seemed
to spread their complaisant mantle over many a crime. We were
surprised not to hear some body fall down from a balcony or
from a half-opened door.

A cold horror, damp and dark as all that surrounded us, took
possession of us . . .

Each door which half opens has the air of permitting a lover or
a bravo to pass. Each gondola which glides silently by seems to
carry a pair of lovers or a corpse, with a stiletto in his heart . . .

Unknown

(early 16th century)

In Venice, as in all Italy, many bodily and emotional ills were traditionally blamed on the devil. A little manual on the subject was published in Venice in 1520, by Niccolò di Aristotile, otherwise known as Zoppino. Its title: *Incredible Exorcism to break every kind of curse and to cast out Demons, proved by a devout Divine.* Characteristically of many books of the period, the author is not attributed.

The signs to look for in someone possessed by the devil.
It is written that if someone cannot eat the flesh of a goat for thirty days then he is possessed by the devil. Some of those possessed by the devil have terrifying eyes: the demons agitate their limbs and wretched bodies; they soon perish if they are not given aid. Some pretend to be mad and change their comportment, but they can be discovered when they refuse to say the psalms . . . Another clear sign is when they speak in foreign tongues when they have never been out of their country, and when they are foul of tongue, and when they speak Latin and sing very musically or when they say something that they could never have known. Some of those possessed by the devil are dumb. Among other signs are also fears of being poisoned . . .

Ways to recognise that someone has been cursed.
Some people who have been cursed have faces the colour of green fruit. Their eyes are narrowed and all their flesh is tight. Their humours are dried up. These are two clear signs of constriction of the heart and the mouth of the stomach . . . Some feel as if they are being stabbed in the heart, as if by needles, and others feel their heart actually rotting. Some feel a great pain in the neck or in the kidneys. They feel as if dogs are devouring their flesh. Some feel as if they have a mouthful of food stuck in their throat, or a lump that rises and falls there . . . Others feel a cold wind blowing through their entire body; others still, a flame of fire.

Arthur Symons

(1865–1945)

The poet and critic Arthur Symons spent a great deal of time in Venice. In this extract from his *Cities of Italy* he explains the particular attractiveness of misery in Venice.

Symons was born of Cornish parents in Wales. He started writing at an early age and travelled around France and Italy. He was influenced by the French Symbolist movement and wrote a study of it in 1899, as well as translations of the poems of D'Annunzio and Baudelaire.

Melancholy . . . is an element in the charm of Venice; but a certain sadness is inherent in the very sound and colour of still water, and a little of the melancholy which we now feel must always have been a background of shadow . . . Why is it, then, that the melancholy of Venice is the most exquisite melancholy in the world? It is because that melancholy is no nearer to one's heart than the melancholy in the face of a portrait. It is the tender and gracious sadness of that beautiful woman who leans her face upon her hands in a famous picture in the Accademia. The feast is over, the wine still flushes the glass on the table, the little negro strikes his lute, she listens to the song, her husband sits beside her, proudly: something not in the world, a vague thought, a memory, a forgetfulness, has possessed her for the moment, setting those pensive lines about her lips, which have just smiled, and which will smile again when she has lifted her eyelids.

Sean O'Faolain
(1900–91)

Some travellers march through Venice like military invaders, ruthlessly efficient. Not so Sean O'Faolain, who owns up to idling there for weeks on end . . . Another extract from O'Faolain's 1950 book, *A Summer in Italy*, describes the addictive lassitude of the city and its deranging effect on a first-time visitor.

For the beginning and the end of Venice is that immediately you step into your first gondola the amiable pirate in browning straw hat with red ribbons, rowing behind your back, who lives in three rooms of Number 1576, Torreselle, two twists off the Grand Canal, with his wife, mother-in-law, sister and six water-rats, is not a gondolier, but the child of Circe and Silence; that he will hush you in his arms away from this mortal world as softly as the boat glides from the pier; that it will be well with you if you can ever return to it; or if you do, ever bear to live in it again. People say that anybody who travels in Japan is never the same person after. I once knew of a man who had made love to an Indian priestess and after that Western women meant nothing to him. Browning's fish went from cool to warm water and was never after happy in either. One's first visit to Venice is a climb to a Mount of Revelation. It unseats the reason.

My reason told me that men and women in Venice have to pay the grocer's bills, go to the movies, suffer toothaches, have trouble with the kid's school reports, the maid, the stove and the choked drains, but though my reason told me all this, it did so over a flying shoulder. When next I met the poor thing it had a shivering hand and bloodshot eye. It never quite recovered from the hunted life it had been leading in the meantime.

Octavio Paz

(1914–98)

Born in Mexico City, Paz devoted his life to both politics and poetry, once describing the latter as 'the secret religion of the modern age'. He wrote extensively on literary, aesthetic and political issues, but also took an active role in the causes he so fervently supported in his writings. He fought on the Republican side in the Spanish Civil War and served as Mexico's ambassador to India in the 1960s.

The wild and delusional qualities of Venice are perfectly evoked in his poem 'Masks of Dawn'. In common with many other writers, Paz chooses to interpret the city as a waking nightmare.

Over the chessboard of the piazza
the last stars linger on their way.
Castles of light and shimmering thin bishops
surround these spectral monarchies.
The empty game, yesterday's war of angels!

Brilliance of stagnant water whereon float
a few small joys, already green,
the rotten apple of desire,
a face nibbled in places by the moon,
the wrinkled minute of an eagerness,
everything life itself has not consumed,
leavings of the orgy of impatience [. . .]

A young girl, tamer of the lightning-bolt,
and the woman slipping away along under
the glittering fine edge of the guillotine;
the gentleman who from the moon descends
with a sweet-smelling branch of epitaphs;
the frigid sleepless woman sharpening
the wornout flint-stone of her sex;
the man of purity, within whose forehead
the golden eagle makes his nest,
the monomaniac hunger of obsession;
the tree that has eight interlocked branches
struck by the bolt of love, set on fire
and burned to ash in transitory beds;
the man buried in life among his grief;
the young dead woman who prostitutes herself

and goes back to her grave at the first cock;
the victim searching out his murderer;

he who has lost his body, and he his shadow,
he who escapes himself and he who hunts himself,
who pursues himself and never finds himself, all those,
the living corpses on the edge of the moment,
wait suspended. Time itself in doubt,
day hesitates.
                    Moving in dream,
upon her bed of mire and water, Venice
opens her eyes and remembers: canopies,
and a high soaring that has turned to stone!
Splendor flooded over . . .
The bronze horses of San Marco
pass wavering architecture,
go down in their green darkness to the water
and throw themselves in the sea, toward Byzantium.

Volumes of stupor and stone, back and forth
in this hour among the few alive . . .
But the light advances in great strides,
shattering yawns and agonies.
Exultance, radiances that tear apart!
Dawn throws its first knife.

Anthony Hecht

(1923–2004)

The Venetian Vespers, a novella in verse by the American writer
Anthony Hecht, tells the story of a man spellbound by the city. As
does all Hecht's poetry, it weaves together history and myth while
exploring the endless confrontations between good and evil.

Like Octavio Paz, Hecht saw active service in World War II,
and his experiences are perhaps reflected in a grim fascination
with death. Here he identifies with another writer deranged by
the city, the Anglo-Swiss painter and writer Henri Fuseli
(1741–1825).

Hecht's second collection, *The Hard Hours*, about the
Holocaust, won the Pulitzer Prize for poetry. He has received
many other awards.

Probably I shall die here unremarked
Amid the albergo's seedy furniture,
Aware to the last of the faintly rotten scent
Of swamp and sea, a brief embarrassment
And nuisance to the management and the maid.
That would be bad enough without the fear
Byron confessed to: 'If I should reach old age
I'll die "at the top first," like Swift.' Or Swift's
Lightning-struck tree. There was a visitor,
The little Swiss authority on nightmares,
Young Henry Fuseli, who at thirty-one
Suffered a fever here for several days
From which he recovered with his hair turned white
As a judicial wig, and rendered permanently
Left-handed. And His Majesty, George III,
Desired the better acquaintance of a tree
At Windsor, and heartily shook one of its branches
Taking it for the King of Prussia. Laugh
Whoso will that has no knowledge of
The violent ward. They subdued that one
With a hypodermic, quickly tranquilized
And trussed him like a fowl. These days I find
A small aperitif at Florian's
Is helpful, although I do not forget.
My views are much like Fuseli's who described
His method thus: 'I first sits myself down.
I then works myself up. Then I throws in
My darks. And then I takes away my lights.'
His nightmare was a great success, while mine
Plays on the ceiling of my rented room
Or on the bone concavity of my skull
In the dark hours when I take away my lights.

City of Birds and Beasts

CATS, RATS AND MYTHICAL CREATURES

With bread, you can make dogs dance.

Lice come from Christians and fleas from dogs.

The cat used to have a field, but he sold it for a fish.

He who runs with the pigs learns to grunt.

VENETIAN PROVERBS

The dragon . . . a creature formidable rather by its gluttony than its malice, and degraded beneath the level of all other spirits of prey; its wings having wasted away into mere paddles or flappers, having in them no faculty or memory of flight; its throat stretched into the flaccidity of a sack, its tail swollen into a molluscous encumbrance, like an enormous worm . . .

> JOHN RUSKIN, on the bas-relief over the door of
> the Scuola Dalmata dei Santi Giorgio e Trifone

One has heard of a horse being exhibited there, and yesterday I watched the poor people paying a penny a-piece for the sight of a stuffed one.

> HESTER PIOZZI

The mosquitoes are perfectly infernal – and you can't say more for Venice than that you are willing, at this moment, for the sake of the days she bestows, to endure the nights she inflicts.

> HENRY JAMES

When I was young and seeing Venice through the eyes of its bards, one of its terrible mosquitoes bit me around six o'clock in the evening in the Eden garden where I suppose I was seeking at the 'Giudecca' the ghosts of Gabriele D'Annunzio and Madame Eleanora Duse. For several years a malignant fever came each evening to carry through my veins a disagreeable memory of my romantic pilgrimage. It is thus possible that mosquitoes had a part in the reputation attributed to Venice of a sick and fever-ridden city, in the fable of an aged Ophelia floating on stagnant water and spreading mournful miasmas around her.

JEAN COCTEAU

In Venice, it is the ambition of every dog to look as much like the Lion of St. Mark as the nature of the case will permit.

WILLIAM DEAN HOWELLS

Countess Giustina Renier Michiel

(1755–1832)

The presence of pigeons in San Marco, according to the Italian
blue-stocking *Dosetta* (consort to the Doge) Giustina Renier
Michiel, can be explained by a certain innovation which was insti-
tuted one Palm Sunday during a time when the people of the city
were poor and lacked meat in their diet.

While they were singing *Gloria, Laus et honor*, some sacristans would ascend to the external *loggia* and set free some birds of various species, but in particular many pairs of pigeons, with cardboard tied to their claws so that they could not fly very high and would soon be forced to land, so it was easy for the people gathered in the square to catch them and take them away as a delicious meal for Easter Day.

This ceremony would be repeated three times during the procession, after which the Doge and his entourage retired. Many, no doubt, would go to the Piazza to enjoy this happy hunt with the populace, which ended swiftly because of the efforts made by the birds trying to escape from the hands of their persecutors and from yells of the crowds who were drunk with joy, and who, in the act of grabbing them, would also stop to clap their hands for those birds that managed to evade the hunt. The applause, alternately bestowed on those birds who achieved permanent freedom and those who fell to the ground to become victims of Evil Fates, gave an idea of the flexible spirit of humanity, agitated first one way and then the other by successive passions . . .

But Nature provided the birds with a very effective means of defence against which man is impotent unless he borrows from technology and chemistry some kind of superior strength. Without this help the pride of dominant Man would be humiliated in front of these harmless beasts, which, flying as fast as a glance, can conquer unknowable distances, leaving the king of the world ashamed of his heaviness, and of his weak vision that loses sight of them when they go near the sun, where he cannot fix his eye. It happened that every year a few pairs of these timid pigeons, terrified of the tumult and the yells, but careful enough not to waste their energy, would fly up looking for a refuge.

And where could they find one more safe, appropriate or happy than in the place of peace sacred to Him, who had been so pleased to create them? In the roof of the famous Church of San Marco the pigeons would find sanctuary, some of them even under the lead-roofed prisons of the Doge's Palace, as if they wished, with their soft cries, to give the relief of some sweet entertainment to the unhappy inhabitants of those jails.

These feathered colonists formed a Republic, the keystone of which was freedom without controversies, a community without invasions, and spiced with all the delights of Love. From that moment onwards they regarded themselves as free from any persecutions and almost forgetful of the troubles they had suffered, and were to be seen flaunting themselves among the populace that only a little while before had been their enemy.

Enjoying this amiable intimacy, the Venetians decided to make it a holy duty for themselves never to disturb again the tranquillity of those Republicans, and naturally they pushed this affectionate feeling to a point that they wanted to respect the whole species and on the day of Palm Sunday they contented themselves with the other birds that were presented to them, and excepted the pigeons. You see in this the general character of the people, a feeling of sweetness and goodness that attracts them spontaneously to favour and support those who are weak; if they are sometimes cruel then it is a foreign impulse that pushes them to it.

Théophile Gautier
(1811–72)

Less charitable to certain creatures of Venice were the feelings of Théophile Gautier, tormented by mosquitoes on his trip in 1850. These days the *Gazzettino* often reports invasions of the dreaded tiger mosquitoes, particularly at Mestre, but Gautier seemed to be dealing with something altogether more ferocious . . .

As well as pigeons, Venice hosts a plentiful and daring population of mice and water rats, known as *pantegane*, the biggest of which are the size of a small cat.

The *pantegane* are celebrated in Venice's maddest shop window: that of Fiorella in Campo San Stefano. The eponymous designer paints luminous green rats on her trademark velvet clothes that are draped over androgynous high-heeled wooden mannequins wearing the Doge's *corno*.

The *Gazzettino* has also reported in recent years new infestations in the *acque dolce* of the Lagoon, which now dramatically change colour for days on end with the arrival of millions of lurid algae.

The great business before going to bed is to hunt for the *zinzares*, the atrocious mosquitoes which especially torment foreigners, upon whom they throw themselves with the pleasure that a gourmet takes in relishing exotic and rare viands.

The grocers and pharmacists sell a fumigating powder that, burned on a chafing dish, all windows being closed, drives away or suffocates the terrible insects. We believe this powder to be more disagreeable to human beings than to mosquitoes . . .

The wisest plan is not to place a light near one's bed and to wrap oneself hermetically in the gauze of the mosquito net. Fortunately we have a southern skin, tanned by the air, burned by travel, which repulses the proboscis and the borings of these nocturnal drinkers of blood; the skin is inflamed and covered with pustules; the face swells under these venomous pustules which cause an insufferable itching.

George Augustus Sala

(1828–95)

The lapdog or *cagnetta / cagnolino* was an essential accessory for the Venetian lady of fashion in the eighteenth century. Languorous ladies enduring the attentions of their hairdresser were invariably accompanied by a pampered and bejewelled little dog. Goldoni wrote a poem about Babiole, the estimable dog of the French ambassador's wife.

Less fortunate were the dogs that took part in the bear-baitings that entertained the populace on high days and holidays. Or those delicate hounds squeezed into elaborate costumes to dance on their back legs at the side-shows on the Riva degli Schiavoni, not to mention the unfortunate creatures in the menagerie Lord Byron kept in the dank, dark *androne* of the Palazzo Mocenigo. It was said to include three dogs, a wolf, a fox, several cats and a monkey.

Byron was fascinated by an elephant that went on the rampage in Venice. Escaping from a circus, the desperate animal took refuge in the Church of San Antonin. The Austrian soldiers dragged a cannon to the door and shot it. Byron recorded how it 'broke loose, ate up a fruit shop, killed his keeper . . . I saw him dead the next day, a stupendous fellow. He went mad for want of a She, it being his rutting month.'

Casanova described a rhinoceros – 'an appalling animal' – which came to Venice in 1751 and was immortalised by Pietro Longhi, who painted it enfolded in plates of dark armoured flesh, no sign of a horn, and surrounded by piles of its own dung. The beast, tame as a cow, munches meekly on straw with a shame-faced expression, as if, like Casanova, it knows that more was expected of it. The entrepreneur who had brought it to Venice tethered it at the Ponte della Paglia and charged ten *soldi* a look.

It's impossible not to feel a pang for the pig who still plays an honorary role in the *Regatta Storica*. Several times during the day a coloured gondola passes up and down the Grand Canal. On a platform inside the boat is a little cage. Inside is a live piglet whose fate is to nourish the winning gondolier team in the races. This sacrifice, of course, recalls the old ceremony of firing twelve live pigs from a cannon in San Marco during *Carnevale* . . .

Nowadays there's an annual summer parade for *amici a quattro zampfe* (friends with four paws) and competitions for the prize for the oldest, the fattest and the best-behaved dogs and cats.

A lone poodle in San Marco attracted the attention of the English journalist George Augustus Sala, in the depressed and silent days of the Austrian occupation.

~~~

Once I remember seeing a solitary poodle with the whole of the
Piazza San Marco to himself. I saw a kindred bow-wow once in
the middle of the Admiralty-square, at St. Petersburg, by moonlight. The Russian dog squatted down on his haunches, and,
lifting his head towards the moon, howled at it dismally. The
Venetian poodle trotted about the deserted stones of St. Mark's,
worn to glassy smoothness by so many millions of human footsteps. He trotted to the three tall masts which stood all of a row
in front of St. Mark's, bannerless. He sniffed at Alessandro
Leopardi's bronze bases, as though to inquire what had become of
the three gonfalons of the Republic – of Venice, Cyprus, and the
Morea. He did not howl, or seem to lament that, like Ichabod, his
glory had departed. He fell, instead, into a merry mood, and happening to remember that he had a tail, began an exciting chase
after that caudal appendage, gambolling in unseemly and unpa-
triotic gyrations, as though all were going as merrily as a
marriage-bell – as though Marino Faliero's head had never rolled
upon the scaffold, and the Two Foscari had never lived – as
though the Most Serene Republic had never come to grief and
shame, and the Austrian eagle, cruellest of birds, had not clawed
out the eyes of the Lion of St. Mark. An inconsequent poodle; but
he had the whole of the Piazza to himself.

William Dean Howells

(1837–1920)

Sadly, the cats of Venice are less evident than they used to be. Many street-cats have been rescued by DINGO, the local animal charity, which used to house them in excellent facilities on the island of San Clemente, once the lunatic asylum for women. Evicted from those premises some years ago, DINGO now operates from a sanctuary on the Lido, through which it is possible to adopt a Venetian cat long-distance for a small annual outlay.

In certain quiet corners of the city, DINGO has placed honeycomb complexes of shelters for the remaining wild felines, and there never seems to be a shortage of old ladies bringing daily offerings of meat to such cat-haunted squares as San Lorenzo, where the pigeons and seagulls compete with the scrawny *gatti* for the juiciest portions.

Other well-known cats hold individual court in different parts of the city. There's the handsome white cat at the bar near San Polo, and the enormous tabby that sleeps in a cardboard box on the counter of the haberdashery near San Silvestro. 'Private' cats are to be seen gazing down impassively from first-floor balconies.

Much has been made of the correspondence between San Marco's lion and the cats of Venice, but the latter have not always occupied such a privileged position. In the February festivities at Santa Maria Formosa, at least until the late eighteenth century, it was traditional to tie a cat to a board. Men would line up to beat it to death with their bare heads. In the last few years isolated outbreaks of cat-poisonings have shocked the city, always provoking editorials about these little Venetian lions and their important part in city life.

William Dean Howells observed more fortunate felines in his *Venetian Life* . . .

I have repeatedly found sleek and portly cats in the churches, where they seem to be on terms of perfect understanding with the priests, and to have no quarrel even with the little boys who assist at mass. There is, for instance, a cat in the sacristy of the Frari, which I have often seen in friendly association with the ecclesiastics there, when they came into his room to robe or disrobe, or warm their hands, numb with supplication, at the great brazier in the middle of the floor. I do not think this cat has the slightest interest in the lovely Madonna of Bellini which hangs in the sacristy; but I suspect him of dreadful knowledge concerning the tombs in the church. I have no doubt he has passed through the open door of Canova's monument, and that he sees some coherence and meaning in Titian's; he has been all over the great mausoleum of the Doge Pesaro, and he knows whether the griffins descend from their perches at the midnight hour to bite the naked knees of the ragged black caryatides. This profound and awful animal I take to be a blood relative of the cat in the church of San Giovanni e Paolo, who sleeps like a Christian during service, and loves a certain glorious bed on the top of a bench, where the sun strikes upon him through the great painted window, and dapples his tawny coat with lovely purples and crimsons.

Sir Max Beerbohm
(1872–1956)

Known as 'the incomparable Max', Beerbohm was born in London, the son of a Lithuanian corn merchant. Educated at Charterhouse and Merton College, Oxford, he was a writer and a caricaturist, broadcaster and drama critic for the *Saturday Review* until 1910, when he married the American actress Florence Kahn and went to live with her in Rapallo, Italy.

Beerbohm had first visited Italy in 1906, recording his impressions in a series of articles for the *Daily Mail*. Six of these were about Venice and became the basis of 'A Stranger in Venice', which was published in his 1928 volume *A Variety of Things*.

In this extract from 'A Stranger in Venice', Beerbohm writes of lions past and present in Venice, recalling Pietro Longhi's painting of the *casotto del leone*, which depicts the king of the jungle sadly run-down and tethered to a sideshow stage during the *Carnevale* of 1762.

They had a live lion in Venice, once. That was in the great days of conquest. They dedicated him to S. Mark, and gave him a gilded cage in the Piazza. He licked off the gilding, and died. It was thought that S. Mark, had he been pleased by the lion, would not have let him be killed even by kindness. The Senate passed a decree that in future no live lion should be brought into the city . . .

But on a certain Michaelmas morning in the fifteenth century, and in the Campo San Zaccaria, was seen a live imitation lion; and thenceforth, and always on that day and in that place, such lions abounded; and one of them, at least, was there on that day in the year of grace 1906.

Nowhere in Venice is a more Venetian thing than this little, melancholy shabby Campo . . . And the brightlier shines the sun the sadder seems the Campo San Zaccaria, seeming, indeed, to shrink away from the sun's rays, like a woman who has been beautiful, or like a woman who is ill.

Yet I think the place would not have thrown such a spell on me in its time of grandeur. Time was when always the greatest servants of the Venetian Republic were laid to rest here. Always on Easter Day the Doge came, in remembrance of a favour done to Venice by the nuns of San Zaccaria . . . It was here, too, that most of the great marriages were solemnised. And it was here, on the aforesaid Michaelmas morning, that a devil, in the guise of a very beautiful youth, came and, smiling, plucked by the sleeve the bride of Sebastiano Morosini, and whispered in such sweet wise that she let go the arm of her bridegroom and gave her hand to the stranger. Sebastiano would have drawn his sword, but, under a spell that the devil had cast, it stayed in its scabbard. By a frantic inspiration of the moment, he went down on his hands and knees, and, crawling, roared, insomuch that the devil (having, like all the devils of that day, a share of simplicity) mistook him for the lion of St. Mark, and instantly vanished. Nor, so far as we know, did he ever reappear. But Sebastiano's stratagem, S. Mark's miracle, had laid such hold on the hearts of the Venetians that every man who was soon to be married would come on Michaelmas morning to the Campo San Zaccaria, and crawl once around the well-head, roaring. Thereby, it was thought, he assured for himself happiness of wedlock: his wife would never be inconstant to him, even in thought . . .

It is a far cry from this century to the fifteenth. But Venice, in the long interval, has stood still . . . It seemed to me not so very strange, on Michaelmas morning, to see mimicked in all simple earnestness the action of Sebastiano Morosini.

My Venetian friends had laughed, told me there was no chance of seeing any such thing. But I, with an obstinacy foreign to my nature, rose very early on Michaelmas morning, and went to my beloved Campo. If any bridegroom came, he would not care to have a tourist's eye on him. So I posted myself well within the shadow of the arch where the Doge was murdered . . . A fool's errand it seemed to be, after I had waited half an hour or so; and I (determined to say nothing of the matter to my Venetian friends) was on the point of going away, when through the other gateway, came a small party of peasants, all in their Sunday best. There were six of them – two middle-aged men, two middle-aged women, and a young man, and a girl. For a minute or so they stood talking. Then the young man detached himself from the group, tossing his sombrero to an elder, and came across to the well-head. There, having crossed himself, he went down on his hands and knees, and did as Sebastiano had done before him; and, little though the roaring may have been like a lion's, I did not once smile on my way home along the Riva Schiavoni.

Hans Habe (János Békessy)
(1911–77)

A final word on the omnipresent pigeons of Venice, this time from the extraordinary novel *Palazzo* by the German writer, Hans Habe, also author of the famous memoir *A Thousand Shall Fall*. *Palazzo* is the story of the ageing Signora Anna-Maria Santarato, defending her way of life and her decaying home on the Grand Canal against the insolence and ignorance of her family, the Italian bureaucracy, the onslaught of the industrialists in the Lagoon and the encroaching tide.

Her struggle is paralleled in essays and anecdotes about the city, a kaleidoscope of finely observed impressions, bittersweet revelations and ironic asides.

Here Habe inhabits the soul of a gentle Venetian entrusted with exterminating the 'winged rats' of Venice. These days, a month rarely passes without a new idea for liberating the city from this plague: peregrine falcons have been suggested, as well as sonic scarers, contraception and poisoning. In December 2000, an ill-wisher made a massacre of pigeons in San Marco. Hundreds of poisoned birds were found limp and dying, with *schiuma dal becco* (foaming from the beak). Other casualties occur each *Redentore*, when dozens of pigeons die of heart failure during the fireworks.

Professor Achille Santi, forty six, head of the Venice Health Department, is sitting on the roof of the Procuratie Vecchie. A small wooden shed has been built for him there, and boards have been laid on the roofs. What acrobats and building workers can do isn't going to scare Professor Santi.

He eats a sandwich, the last of his provisions. He has spent seventy-two hours on the roofs of St Mark's Square. He looks down on the piazza and contemplates the end of a daring enterprise. It was called: *Operation Pigeon*.

Below, thousands of travellers, many in typical knee-bending positions, are photographing women and children as they feed the pigeons. Little stalls, folding chairs alongside, where corn is sold in bags, for the pigeons. There are a hundred and eighty thousand pigeons in Venice, about twice as many as there are people. It seems to Professor Santi as if they were all assembled in St Mark's Square today, a gigantic demonstration, against him, Professor Santi. He, their enemy? Achille Santi, a Venetian, grew up among pigeons. He fed them from the balcony, he gave them names, he felt he knew each and every one of them. Now he is called the Genghis Khan of the Pigeons. His three children look askance at him. His wife reproaches him sadly.

At least sixty thousand pigeons are ill. They die during the night, in the morning they are cleared away. Many of them are unaware that it is night; they are blind. Overfed. Disease carriers, a danger for the people. And for the works of art. Their excrement bites into the statues, particularly those on the roofs which are spared by the flood. The ground can be cleaned, but not the angels.

On the roofs of St Mark's Square, Professor Santi has been looking for pigeon's eggs. In seventy-two hours he has only found one.
That was the last resort.

He has proceeded very humanely. He thinks the contraceptive
pill, now modestly called the pill, is a humane thing. It cannot be
mixed into the food for the Indians, because the Indians have
nothing to eat. The pigeons have too much to eat. They got the
pill. It was a fruitless effort, the pigeons remained fertile. The
anti-pigeon preparation from France! It causes aversion to
pigeon-feed. Similar preparations have been tried on men to
stop them smoking. Because the man who smokes less dies later.
The pigeons would have died earlier, without pain. But they had
no appetite for the appetite-spoiler. Then there was the Society
for the Prevention of Cruelty to Animals, and deportation. The
deportation of pigeons cannot be compared to the deportation of
people. Nobody wants to take the deported people. New York
City and Tokyo and Berlin applied to take the pigeons. Genuine
Venetian pigeons for Times Square, the Ginza, the
Kurfürstendamm. But the stupid pedestrians couldn't distinguish
the Venetian pigeons from the others. Now nobody wants to
have the exiled pigeons any more, like the exiled people. Besides,
pigeons do not thrive any better in foreign squares than people on
foreign soil. Japan Air Lines don't fly them any more.

The city council had traps set up; five thousand pigeons were
trapped and poisoned. Against the Professor's will, although his
wife doesn't believe him. And although nobody knows what the
pigeons would do to sick people if they had the power.

Professor Santi wanted to spare the lives of fifty thousand
pigeons. Fifty thousand were to stay in Venice, in the ghetto. Just
like the Jews in former times. Professor Santi had special bins
made. Far away from the works of art and the tourist racket, the

pigeons were to be given their feed and water. But pigeons, unlike Jews, can fly. Next day they were sitting on the roofs of the Ducal Palace.

The professor on the roof smiles bitterly, like a defeated commander at his command post. He has not found a single egg today . . .

Who in hell appointed him the Genghis Khan of the pigeons? The city council has led him on to slippery ground. Venice employs enough statisticians. No one, so far, has worked out how much damage the pigeons actually cause. Probably less than a single chimney in Marghera. Does the petty dirt get cleared away all over the world, so that nobody need mention the big mess? Few benefit from the oil storage tanks in Marghera. Millions enjoy seeing the pigeons. Perhaps his wife is right.

He should have thought about this earlier. And perhaps he would never have thought about it if he had found more than one pigeon's egg. Failure makes one wiser. Sometimes even more humane.

Two workers climb up the ladder to fetch the Professor.

Pigeons have settled at Achille Santi's feet. They have discovered the crumbs — from his last sandwich. The victors always feed on the vanquished. The Professor hopes they'll enjoy their meal.

Anthony Hecht

(1923–2004)

Here, in another extract from *The Venetian Vespers*, Hecht tumbles
us through the literal dog-ends of the city.

～～～

　　　　　　　　But here in Venice,
The world's most louche and artificial city,
(In which my tale some time will peter out)
The summons comes from the harsh smashing of glass.
A not unsuitable local industry,
Being the frugal and space-saving work
Of the young men who run the garbage scows.
Wine bottles of a clear sea-water green,
Pale, smoky quarts of *acqua minerale*,
Iodine-tinted liters, the true-blue
Waterman's midnight ink of Bromo Seltzer,
Light-bulbs of packaged fog, fluorescent tubes
Of well-sealed, antiseptic samples of cloud,
Await what is at once their liquidation
And resurrection in the glory holes
Of the Murano furnaces. Meanwhile
Space must be made for all ephemera,
Our cast-offs, foulings, whatever has gone soft
With age, or age has hardened to a stone,
Our city sweepings. Venice has no curbs
At which to curb a dog, so underfoot
The ochre pastes and puddings of dogshit
Keep us earthbound in half a dozen ways,
Curbing the spirit's tendency to pride.
The palaces decay. Venice is rich
Chiefly in the deposits of her dogs.
A wealth swept up and gathered with its makers.
Canaries, mutts, love-birds and alley cats
Are sacked away like so many Monte Cristos,

There being neither lawns, meadows nor hillsides
To fertilize or to be buried in.
For them the glass is broken in the dark
As a remembrance by the garbage men.
I am their mourner at collection time
With an invented litany of my own.
Wagner died here, Stravinsky's buried here,
They say that Cimarosa's enemies
Poisoned him here. The mind at four AM
Is a poor, blotched, vermiculated thing.
I've seen it spilled like sweetbreads, and I've dreamed
Of Byron writing, 'Many a fine day
I should have blown my brains out but for the thought
Of the pleasure it would give my mother-in-law.'
Thus virtues, it is said, are forced upon us
By our own impudent crimes. I think of him
With his consorts of whores and countesses
Smelling of animal musk, lilac and garlic,
A *ménage* that was in fact a menagerie,
A fox, a wolf, a mastiff, birds and monkeys,
Corbaccios and corvinos, *spintriae*,
The lees of the Venetian underworld,
A plague of iridescent flies. Spilled out.
O lights and livers. Deader than dead weight.
In a casket lined with tufted tea-rose silk.

The Past and Future City

SOME CONCLUSIONS

Tell me who I am, but not who I was.

Distancing is the child of forgetting.

VENETIAN PROVERBS

I conclude, these are bad times: we see our ruin ahead, and nobody does anything . . .

MARINO SANUDO

Venice . . . is still left for our beholding in the final period of her decline: a ghost upon the sands of the sea, so weak – so quiet – so bereft of all but her loveliness, that we might well doubt, as we watched her faint reflection in the mirage of the lagoon, which was the City, and which the Shadow.

JOHN RUSKIN

> Venice shall die: and all the seas that filled
> Her streets and at the touch of love-oars thrilled
> Shall wash around the dead.

GEORGE BARLOW

Indeed, it seemed a very wreck found drifting on the sea; a strange flag hoisted in its honourable stations, and strangers standing at its helm.

CHARLES DICKENS

Over balustrades of marble, where once beauty loved to lean, float the unseemly nether garments suspended to be dried.

MARGUERITE, COUNTESS OF BLESSINGTON

Meanwhile the 'restorations' went on in Venice '*more solito*,' and the ignorant proprietors of most beautiful ancient houses allowed them to be demolished and replaced by ugly modern buildings. Window frames, doors, balconies, staircases, well-heads, etc, found their way to the antiquaries' shops and then emigrated.

ALVISE PIETRO ZORZI who battled with John Ruskin to save the stones of Venice, and particularly those of San Marco, from the depredations of uninformed restorers

. . . a parasite bureaucracy that has an effect like gangrene . . .

PIERO PAZZI

. . . she deserves something better than to be kept as an antiquated toy, for the amusement of travelling ladies and gentlemen, in the rococo line of research.

FRANCES TROLLOPE

In a museum there is ample room for beauty, but only rats can live in a museum.

HANS HABE

Venetian life, in the large old sense, has long since come to an end, and the essential present character of the most melancholy of cities resides simply in its being the most beautiful of tombs. Nowhere else has the past been laid to rest with such tenderness . . .

HENRY JAMES

She has paid for her mistakes with all save her inextinguishable life; she has expiated her sins of ill-faith, of injustice and ingratitude, by the loss of everything but her imperishable charm.

FRANCIS MARION CRAWFORD

But then, just when you begin to experience a sense of horror at being alone in this dead city, you are treated to a series of glimpses – through windows that are invariably barred – of a family sitting around a table to eat *risotto alle vongole*, risotto with clams, which is being brought to it in a cloud of steam, of children doing their homework, of someone working later in an archive . . . like a series of realistic pictures hung in the open air on walls of crumbling brick and flaking stone.

ERIC NEWBY

Under the wave, or lava, of millions of tourists we'll have to go searching for *something* among the crowded *calli*, the secret chasms, the rims, the canals and ravines. We'll have to go look for the city, present in its stones and its waters, yet vanished, invisible.

PAOLO BARBARO

Acknowledgements

Virago gratefully acknowledges the following for permission to reprint copyright material.

Venice Revealed: An Intimate Portrait by Paolo Barbaro, translated by Tami Calliope, published by Souvenir Press. Copyright © 1998 Marsilio Editore. English translation copyright © 2001 Steerforth Press.

A Stranger in Venice by Max Beerbohm, published by Robert Booth at the Winged Lion. Copyright © 1993 the Estate of Max Beerbohm. Reprinted courtesy of London Management.

The Ghetto of Venice by Riccardo Calimani, translated by Katherine Silberblatt Wolfthal, published by M. Evans and Company, Inc. Copyright © 1985 Rusconi Libri S. P. A. Translation copyright © 1987 M. Evans and Company.

'Venice' from *All of Us, The Collected Poems of Raymond Carver*, published by the Harvill Press. Copyright © 1996, Tess Gallagher. Reprinted courtesy of the Random House Group Ltd. and International Creative Management.

History of My Life, volumes 1 and 2, by Giacomo Casanova. English translation by Willard R. Trask. Copyright © 1966, 1994 Harcourt, Inc. Reprinted courtesy of the publishers.

History of My Life, volume 3, by Giacomo Casanova. English translation by Willard R. Trask. Copyright © 1967 Harcourt, Inc. Reprinted courtesy of the publishers.

History of My Life, volume 7, by Giacomo Casanova. English translation by Willard R. Trask. Copyright © 1969, 1997 Harcourt, Inc. Reprinted courtesy of the publishers.

History of My Life, volume 11, by Giacomo Casanova. English translation by Willard R. Trask. Copyright © 1971 Harcourt, Inc. Reprinted courtesy of the publishers.

'King and Pen' from *Approach to Murano* by Jack Clemo, published by Bloodaxe Books. Copyright © 1993 Jack Clemo.

Il Fuoco by Gabriele D'Annunzio, translated by Kassandra Vivaria, published by William Heinemann in 1900.

The Venice I Love by André Fraigneau, with an introduction by Jean Cocteau, published by Tudor Publishing Company. Copyright © 1957 Editions Sun Paris (France).

Italy: The Unfinished Revolution by Matt Frei, published by Sinclair-Stevenson. Copyright © 1996 Matt Frei. Reprinted courtesy of A. M. Heath & Co. Ltd. and the Random House Group Ltd.

Dream Cities by Douglas Goldring, published by T. Fisher Unwin in 1913. Copyright © Patrick Goldring. Reproduced courtesy of Polly Bird, literary executor.

Palazzo by Hans Habe, translated by Salomé Hangartner, published by W. H. Allen. Copyright © 1975 Hans Habe. English translation copyright © 1977 W. H. Allen & Co. Ltd. Reprinted courtesy of Virgin Books Ltd.

Eustace and Hilda by L. P. Hartley, published by Putnam & Co. Ltd in 1947. Reprinted courtesy of the Society of Authors as the Literary Representative of the Estate of L. P. Hartley.

The Venetian Vespers by by Anthony E. Hecht, published in the UK by Oxford University Press and reprinted by permission of Carcanet Press Limited. Copyright © 1979 Anthony E. Hecht. Published in North America in *Collected Earlier Poems* by Anthony Hecht, copyright © 1990 Anthony E. Hecht. Used by permission of Alfred A. Knopf, a division of Random House, Inc.

Carnevale by M. R. Lovric, published by Virago Press. Copyright © 2001 M. R. Lovric.

Surfaces and Masks. A Poem by Clarence Major, published by Coffee House Press. Copyright © 1988 Clarence Major. Reprinted courtesy of Coffee House Press, Minneapolis.

Venice Observed by Mary McCarthy, published by William Heinemann. Copyright © 1956 Mary McCarthy. Reprinted courtesy of A. M. Heath & Co. Ltd.

Journal of a Visit to Europe and the Levanti, October 11, 1856–May 6, 1857 by Herman Melville, published by Princeton University Press. Copyright © 1955 Princeton University Press.

Venice by Mortimer Menpes with text by Dorothy Menpes, published by Adam & Charles Black in 1900. Reprinted by permission of the publishers.

'Two Venetian Pieces' from *New Poems, A Selection from Satura and Diario del '71 e del '72* by Eugenio Montale, translated by G. Singh, published by Chatto & Windus. Copyright © 1971, 1972 Eugenio Montale. English translation copyright © 1976 Chatto & Windus. Reprinted courtesy of Professor G. Singh.

On the Shores of the Mediterranean by Eric Newby, published by Harvill Press. Copyright © 1984 Eric Newby.

A Summer in Italy by Sean O'Faolain, published by Eyre & Spottiswoode. Copyright © 1949 the Estate of Sean O'Faolain. Reprinted courtesy of Rogers, Coleridge & White Ltd.

'Masks of Dawn' from *Selected Poems* by Octavio Paz, translated by Muriel Rukeyser, published by Indiana University Press in 1963. Copyright © 1963, 1973 Octavio Paz and Muriel Rukeyser.

'Night Litany' from *Collected Early Poems* by Ezra Pound, copyright © 1926, 1935, 1954, 1965, 1967, 1976 the Ezra Pound Literary Property Trust. Reprinted by permission of New Directions Publishing Corporation and Faber & Faber Ltd.

'Il Conto' from *Striking Distance* by Carole Satyamurti, published by Oxford University Press. Copyright © 1994 Carole Satyamurti. Reprinted courtesy of the author.

Winters of Content and Other Discursions on Mediterranean Art and Travel by Osbert Sitwell, published by Gerald Duckworth & Co. Ltd in 1932. Reprinted courtesy of David Higham Associates Ltd.

'Venetian Night' from *Poems*, volume 2, by Arthur Symons, published by William Heinemann in 1924.

The History of Italy by William Thomas, edited by George B. Parks, published by Cornell University Press. Copyright © 1963 the Folger Shakespeare Library.

Extracts from *Venice: A Documentary History, 1450–1630*, edited by David Chambers and Brian Pullan, with Jennifer Fletcher, published by Blackwell Publishers. Copyright © David Chambers and Brian Pullan, 1992.

'Blindfold' by Gregory Warren Wilson. Copyright © 2003 Gregory Warren Wilson. Reprinted courtesy of the author.

Osterie Veneziane by Elio Zorzi, published by Zanichelli Editore S. P. A. in 1928.

Select Bibliography

ANDERSEN, Hans Christian, *The Improvisatore, or, Life in Italy*, translated by M. Howitt, London, 1845.

ANDERSEN, Hans Christian, *Pictures of Travel*, New York, 1871.

ANON., *Venetian Tales, Or, A Curious Collection of Entertaining Novels and Diverting Tales, Designed for the Amusement of the Fair Sex, Faithfully Translated from the Italian*, London, 1737.

ARSLAN, Antonia, CHEMELLO, Adriana, and PIZZAMIGLIO, Gilberto, *Le Stanze Ritrovate: Antologia di Scrittici Venete dal Quattrocento al Novecento*, Eidos, Venice, 1991.

BACHER, Otto H., *With Whistler in Venice*, New York, 1908.

BAFFO, Giorgio, *Le Poesie di Giorgio Baffo*, Catania, 1926.

BANDELLO, Matteo, *The Novels of Matteo Bandello*, translated by John Payne, London, 1890.

BARBARO, Paolo, *Venice Revealed: An Intimate Portrait*, translated by Tami Calliope, Steerforth Press, South Royathon, Vermont, 2001.

BARBIERA, Raffaello, *Poesie Veneziane*, Florence, 1886.

BARLOW, George, *The Poetical Works of George Barlow*, London, 1902–1914.

BATILLANA, Marilla, *English Writers and Venice 1350–1950*, Stamperia di Venezia, Venice, 1981.

BECKFORD, William, *Dreams, Waking Thoughts and Incidents*, London, 1783.

BEERBOHM, Max, *A Stranger in Venice*, The Winged Lion, London, 1993.

BERENSON, Bernard, *The Venetian Painters of the Renaissance*, 4 volumes, Oxford, 1894–1907.

BIDERA, Giovanni Emmanuele, *Marino Faliero (tragedia lirica in tre atti)*, Milan, 1837.

BLACKIE, John Stuart, *Messis Vitae: Gleanings of Song from a Happy Life*, London, 1886.

BLESSINGTON, Lady Marguerite, *The Idler in Italy*, London, 1839–40.

BOSCHINI, M., *Le Breve Istruzione Premesse a le Ricche Minere della Pittura Veneziana*, Venice, 1674.

BOTERO, Giovanni, *Della relatione della Repubblica Venetiana*, Venice, 1605, translated by R. Peterson: *The Greatness of Cities* (translation first published 1606), with *The Reason of State*, translated by P. J. and D. P. Waley, Routledge & Kegan Paul, London, 1956.

BRADDON, Mary, *The Venetians*, London, 1892.

BROWN, Horatio F., *Life on the Lagoons*, London, 1894.

BROWN, Horatio F., *In and Around Venice*, London, 1905.

BULL, George, *Venice, the Most Triumphant City*, Folio Society, London, 1981.

BURTON, Lady Isabel, *The Romance of Isabel Lady Burton: The Story of Her Life*, told in part by herself and in part by W. H. Wilkins, London, 1897.

BYRON, George Gordon, Lord, *The Selected Letters of Lord Byron*, edited by Jacques Barzun, Farrar, Straus & Giroux, New York, 1953.

BYRON, George Gordon, Lord, *The Works of Lord Byron*, The Wordsworth Poetry Library, London, 1994.

CALIMANI, Riccardo, *The Ghetto of Venice*, translated by Katherine Silberblatt Wolfthal, M. Evans & Company, Inc., New York, 1987.

CALMO, Andrea, *Le Lettere, riprodotte sui testi migliori* (A cura di Vittorio Rossi), Turin, 1888.

CALÒ, Giuseppe, *Ciò, Zibaldone Veneziano*, Corbo e Fiore Editori, Venice, 1992.

CALVINO, Italo, *Invisible Cities*, translated by W. Weaver, Secker & Warburg, London, 1974.

CARVER, Raymond, *All of Us: The Collected Poems*, The Harvill Press, London, 1996.

CASANOVA, Giacomo Girolamo, *History of My Life*, translated by Willard R. Trask, The Johns Hopkins University Press, Baltimore, 1966–71.

CASOLA, Pietro, *Canon Pietro Casola's Pilgrimage to Jerusalem in the year 1494*, translated by M. Margaret Newett, Manchester, 1907.

CECCHETTI, Bartolomeo, *La Vita dei Veneziani fino al 1200*, Venice, 1870.

CHEKHOV, Anton, *Letters of Anton Chekhov*, selected and edited by Avrahm Yarmolinksy, Jonathan Cape, London, 1974.

CIBOTTO, Giovanni Antonio, *Proverbi del Veneto*, Giunti Editore, Florence, 1995.

CINTHIO, Gian Battista Giraldi, *The Story of the Moor of Venice*, translated from the Italian by Wolstenholme Parr, with 'Two Essays on Shakespeare', and 'Preliminary Observations', London, 1795.

CLAMPITT, Amy, *The Collected Poems of Amy Clampitt*, Alfred A. Knopf, New York, 1997.

CLEMO, Jack, *Approach to Murano*, Bloodaxe Books, Newcastle, 1993.

CLOUGH, Arthur Hugh, *Poems*, London, 1862.

CONWAY, William Martin, *Literary Remains of Albrecht Dürer*, Cambridge, 1889.

COOK, Thomas, *Cook's Tourist Handbook for Northern Italy*, London, 1875.

COOPER, James Fenimore, *The Bravo*, New York, 1859.

CORNARO, Luigi, *The Art of Living Long*, Milwaukee, 1903.

CORONELLI, Vincenzo, *Guida dei Forestieri*, Venice, 1700.

CORYATE, Thomas, *Coryate's Crudities*, London, 1611.

COTTON, William, *Sir Joshua Reynolds' Notes and Observations on Pictures*, London, 1859.

CRAWFORD, Francis Marion, *Marietta, A Maid of Venice*, London, 1901.

CRAWFORD, Francis Marion, *Gleanings from Venetian History*, London, 1905.

CROSS, J. W., *George Eliot's Life*, London, 1885.

DAMERINI, Gino, *La Gondola*, Nuova Editoriale, Venice, 1956.

D'ANNUNZIO, Gabriele, *Il Fuoco*, translated by Kassandra Vivaria, London, 1900.

DA PONTE, Lorenzo, *Memoirs of Lorenzo da Ponte*, translated by Elizabeth Abbott, J. B. Lippincott, New York, 1929.

DAY, John, *Humour Out of Breath*, London, 1608.

DE BLASI, Marlena, *A Thousand Days in Venice*, Virago Press, London, 2003.

DEBRAY, Régis, *Contre Venise*, Gallimard, Paris, 1995.

DE BROSSES, Charles, *Letters from Italy*, translated by Lord Ronald Sutherland Gower, London, 1839.

DESSAIX, Robert, *Night Letters*, Pan Macmillan Australia Pty Ltd, Sydney, 1996.

DI ARISTOTILE, Niccolò, *Exorcismo Mirabile*, Venice, 1520.

DICKENS, Charles, *Pictures from Italy*, London, 1846.

DI POGGIBONSI, Niccolò, *Libro di Oltramare, A Voyage Beyond the Seas*, translated by Fr. T. Bellorini OFM and Fr. E. Hoade OFM, Franciscan Press, Jerusalem, 1945.

DISRAELI, Benjamin, *Contarini Fleming: A Psychological Romance*, London, 1832.

EMERSON, Ralph Waldo, *The Journals and Miscellaneous Notebooks*, Cambridge (Mass.), 1960.

EQUIVOCA, Mario (attrib.), *Il Novo Cortigiano de Vita Cauta e Morale*, Venice, 1530.

EVELYN, John, *The Diary*, edited by E. S. de Beer, London, 1905.

FINBERG, A. J., *In Venice with Turner*, The Cotswold Gallery, London, 1930.

FONTE, Moderata, *Il Merito delle Donne*, Venice, 1600.

FRAIGNEAU, André, *The Venice I Love*, Tudor Publishing Company, New York, 1957.

FREI, Matt, *Italy: The Unfinished Revolution*, Sinclair-Stevenson, London, 1996.

FUSINATO, Arnaldo, *Poesie Complete,* Milan, 1909.

GAUTIER, Théophile, *Journeys in Italy*, translated by Daniel B. Vermilye, London, 1903.

GOETHE, Johann Wolfgang von, *Italian Journey 1761–88*, translated by W. H. Auden and Elizabeth Mayer, Pantheon Books, New York, 1962.

GOLDONI, Carlo, *The Liar, a Comedy in Three Acts*, translated from the Italian by Grace Lovat Fraser, London, 1922.

GOLDRING, Douglas, *Dream Cities: Notes of an Autumn Tour in Italy and Dalmatia*, T. Fisher Unwin, London, 1913.

GOZZI, Count Carlo, *The Memoirs of Count Carlo Gozzi*, translated from the Italian by John Addington Symonds, London, 1889.

GRAY, David, *The Poetical Works of David Gray*, edited by H. G. Bell, Glasgow, 1874.

HABE, Hans, *Palazzo*, translated by Salomé Hangartner, W. H. Allen, London, 1977.

HARTLEY, L. P., *Eustace and Hilda*, Putnam & Co., London, 1947.

HECHT, Anthony, *The Venetian Vespers*, Alfred A. Knopf, New York, 1980.

HOUSSAIE, Amelot de la, *The History of the Government of Venice*, London, 1677.

HOWELL, James, *The Familiar Letters of James Howell*, volume 1, Houghton Mifflin & Co., Boston and New York, 1907.

HOWELLS, William Dean, *Venetian Life*, New York, 1866.

HULL, Thomas, *Select Letters between The Late Duchess of Somerset, Lady Luxborough, Miss Dolman, Mr Whistler, Mr R. Dodsley, William Shenstone, Esq. and Others*, London, 1778.

HUTTON, Edward, *Pietro Aretino, the Scourge of Princes*, London, 1922.

HYATT, Alfred A., *The Charm of Venice: An Anthology*, London, 1924.

JAMES, Henry, *Letters from Palazzo Barbaro*, edited by Rosella Mamoli Zorzi, Pushkin Press, London, 1998.

JAMES, Henry, et al., *The Great Streets of the World*, London, 1892.

JAMESON, Anna, *Visits and Sketches at Home and Abroad*, London, 1834.

JONSON, Ben, *Volpone*, London, 1605.

KEATES, Jonathan, *Italian Journeys*, William Heinemann, London, 1991.

LITHGOW, William, *The Totall Discourse of the Rare Adventures and Painful Peregrinations of Long Nineteene Yeares Travayles, etc*, Glasgow, 1906.

LITTLEWOOD, Ian, *A Literary Companion to Venice*, Penguin Books, London, 2001.

LOVRIC, M. R., *Carnevale*, Virago Press, London, 2001.

LUBBOCK, Percy, *Elizabeth Barrett Browning in her Letters*, London, 1906.

LUMBROSO, Alberto, *Pagine Veneziane*, Rome, 1905.

MAJOR, Clarence, *Surfaces and Masks*, Coffee House Press, Minneapolis, 1988.

MANN, Thomas, *Death in Venice*, translated by H. T. Lowe-Porter, Penguin Books, London, 1971.

MARANGONI, Giovanni, *La Bibbia dei Poveri Diavoli*, Filippi Editore, Venice, 1975.

MARINETTI, Tommaso Filippo, *Contro Venezia Passatista*, Venice, 1910, printed in English in *Marinetti*, Selected Writings, translated by R. W. Flint and Arthur A. Coppotelli, Martin Secker & Warburg, London, 1972.

MARQUSEE, Michael, *Venice: An Illustrated Anthology*, Conran Octopus, London, 1988.

MARTINELLI, Domenico, *Il Ritratto di Venezia*, Venice, 1684.

McCARTHY, Mary, *Venice Observed*, William Heinemann, London, 1961.

MELVILLE, Herman, *Journal of a Visit to Europe and the Levant, October 11, 1856–May 6, 1857*, Princeton University Press, Princeton, 1955.

MENPES, Dorothy, and MENPES, Mortimer, *Venice*, Adam & Charles Black, London, 1904.

MICHIEL, Countess Giustina Renier, *Origine delle Feste Veneziane*, Milan, 1829.

MICHIELE, Pietro, *Novelle Amorose, dei Signori Academici Incogniti*, Venice, 1641.

MOLMENTI, Pompeo, *Venice: An Individual Growth from the Earliest Beginnings to the Fall of the Republic*, translated by Horatio F. Brown, London, 1906.

MOLMENTI, Pompeo, *Venice*, London, 1926.

MONET, Claude, *Monet by Himself*, translated by Richard Kendell, Macdonald & Co., London, 1989.

MONTAGU, Mary Wortley, *The Selected Letters of Lady Mary Wortley Montagu*, edited by Robert Halsbrand, St Martins Press, New York, 1970.

MONTALE, Eugenio, *New Poems*, translated and introduced by G. Singh, Chatto & Windus, London, 1976.

MORAND, Paul, *Venises*, Gallimard, Paris, 1971.

MORGAN, Lady Sydney, *Italy*, London, 1821.

MOROLIN, Pietro Gasparo, *Venezia ovvero quadro storico della sua origine, dei suoi progressi e di tutti le sue costumanze*, Venice, 1841.

MOROSINI, Francesco, *A Journal of the Venetian Campaign*, Venice, 1687.

MORRIS, Jan, *Venice*, Faber & Faber, London, 1960.

MOZART, Wolfgang Amadeus, *The Letters of Wolfgang Amadeus Mozart 1769–91*, translated, from the collection of Ludwig Nohl, by Lady Wallace, New York, 1867.

MUTINELLI, Fabio, *Del Costume Veneziano*, Venice, 1831.

NASHE, Thomas, *The Unfortunate Traveller*, London, 1594.

NEVILL, Lady Dorothy, *The Reminiscences of Lady Dorothy Nevill*, edited by her son Ralph Nevill, London, 1906.

NEWBY, Eric, *On the Shores of the Mediterranean*, The Harvill Press, London, 1984.

NEWETT, M. N., *Canon Pietro Casola's Pilgrimage to Jerusalem in the Year 1494*, Manchester, 1907.

O'FAOLAIN, Sean, *A Summer in Italy*, Eyre & Spottiswoode, London, 1949.

OLIPHANT, Margaret, *The Makers of Venice: Doges, Conquerors, Painters and Men of Letters*, London, 1887.

ONGANIA, Ferdinand, *Calli, Canali a Venezia e Isole della Laguna*, Venice, 1898.

PAZ, Octavio, *Selected Poems*, translated by Muriel Rukeyser, Indiana University Press, Bloomington, 1963.

PAZZI, Piero, *Calendario dei Gondolieri*, Venice, 2003.

POUND, Ezra, *A Lume Spento and Other Early Poems*, Faber & Faber, London, 1965.

READE, Charles, *The Cloister and the Hearth*, London, 1861.

ROLFE, Frederick, *The Desire and Pursuit of the Whole: A Romance of Modern Venice*, Cassell & Co., London, 1934.

ROSE, William, *Letters from the North of Italy addressed to Henry Hallam, esq.*, London, 1819.

RUSKIN, John, *The Stones of Venice*, London, 1851–3.

RUSKIN, John, *Fors Clavigera*, London, 1871–84.

RUSKIN, John, *Praeterita*, London, 1889.

RUSKIN, John, *The Diaries of John Ruskin*, selected and edited by Joan Evans and John Howard Whitehouse, Clarendon Press, Oxford, 1956.

SALA, George Augustus, *Wanderings in Italy 1866–7*, London, 1869.

SAND, George, *The Uscoque*, translated by Juliette Bauer, London, 1850.

SAND, George, *Lettres d'un Voyageur*, Paris, 1857.

SANSOVINO, Francesco, *Delle Cose Notabili che Sono in Venetia*, Venice, 1592, translated by Lewes Lewkenor and published in English in 1599.

SANUDO, Marino, *I Diarii di Marino Sanuto*, edited by R. Fulin et al., Venice, 1879–1903.

SARPI, Fra Paolo, *The Maxims of the Government of Venice in an Advice to the Republick*, translated from the Italian, London, 1707.

SATYAMURTI, Carole, *Striking Distance*, Oxford University Press, Oxford, 1994.

SCHUYLER, Eugene, *Italian Influences*, New York, 1901.

SÉLINCOURT, Beryl de, and HENDERSON, May Sturge, *Venice*, London, 1907.

SFORZA, Antonio, *Rime di Antonio Sforza*, Venice, 1736.

SHARP, Samuel, *Letters from Italy*, London, 1766.

SHELLEY, Mary, *The Letters of Mary Wollstonecraft Shelley*, edited by Betty T. Bennett, The Johns Hopkins University Press, Baltimore, 1980.

SHELLEY, Percy Bysshe, *The Complete Poetical Works of Percy Bysshe Shelley*, London, 1878.

SITWELL, Osbert, *Winters of Discontent*, Gerald Duckworth & Co. Ltd., London, 1932.

SMITH, Francis Hopkinson, *Gondola Days*, London, 1897.

SPENCE, Joseph, *Letters from the Grand Tour*, edited by Slava Klima, McGill-Queen University Press, Montreal, 1975.

STARKE, Mariana, *Information and Directions for Travellers on the Continent*, London, 1824.

SULLIVAN, Alan, *Venice and Other Verse*, 1893.

SYMONS, Arthur, *Cities of Italy*, J. M. Dent & Co., London, 1907.

SYMONS, Arthur, *Poems*, volume 2, William Heinemann, London, 1924.

TASSINI, Giuseppe, *Curiosità Veneziane*, Venice, 1897.

THOMAS, William, *The History of Italy*, Cornell University Press, New York, 1963.

THRALE-PIOZZI, Hester, *A Journey Through Italy*, London, 1785.

TROLLOPE, Frances, *A Visit to Italy*, London, 1842.

TROLLOPE, Thomas Adolphus, *A Family Party in the Piazza of St. Peter, and Other Stories*, London, 1877.

TWAIN, Mark, *The Innocents Abroad*, New York, 1869.

VILLARI, Linda, *On Tuscan Hills and Venetian Waters*, London, 1885.

WERNER, A., *The Humour of Italy*, London, 1892.

WOOLSON, Constance Fenimore, *The Front Yard and Other Italian Stories*, New York, 1895.

YRIARTE, Charles, *Venise*, Paris, 1878.

ZANE, Zuane di Andrea, petition dated 31 July 1550, Archivio di Stato, Venice, Terra, filza 11.

ZAMPETTI, Pietro, *Lorenzo Lotto: Il 'Libro di Spese Diverse'*, Venice and Rome, 1969.

ZORZI, Elio, *Osterie Veneziane*, Bologna, 1928.

Of related interest from Virago

A THOUSAND DAYS IN VENICE

by Marlena de Blasi

When Fernando spots her in a Venice café and knows immediately that she is The One, Marlena de Blasi is caught off guard. A divorced American woman travelling through Italy, she thought she was satisfied with her life. Yet within a few months, she quits her job as a chef, sells her house, kisses her two grown-up children goodbye, and moves to Venice. Once there, she finds herself sitting in sugar-scented pasticcerie, strolling through sixteenth-century palazzi, renovating an apartment overlooking the seductive Adriatic Sea, and preparing to wed a virtual stranger in an ancient stone church.

As she learns the hard way about the peculiarities of Venetian culture, De Blasi treats us to an honest, often comic view of how two middle-aged people, both set in their ways but also set on being together, build a life.

Recipes included.

'You will be swept away' Adriana Trigiani,
author of *Big Stone Gap*

'A luxurious story of sudden love' *Kirkus Reviews*

'Enchanting' *Publishers Weekly*

Travel
1 84408 020 X
£7.99

CARNEVALE

by M.R. Lovric

When I think of Venice as she was in 1782, *I think of a hundred thousand souls all devoted to pleasure. Souls like that become insubstantial and faintly luminous. You see, we were in the* phosphorescent *stage of decay* . . .

Richly imagined and as irresistible as its magical setting, *Carnevale* evokes the three great loves of the celebrated painter Cecilia Cornaro: Casanova, Byron, and La Serenissima herself.

'Lovric immerses us in the life and loves of beautiful Cecilia, the artistic daughter of an 18th-century Venetian merchant. The setting is faded yet decadent – think gondolas, palazzi, delicate food and amorous trysts. It's a lavish description of a sensual education that drips detail and drama' *Elle*

'A dazzling baroque tale' *Sunday Tribune*

'This novel mixes fiction with reality as surely as water mixes with the air and stone in that strange, floating city. Part love story, part lesson in aesthetics, part history lesson, this is a fascinating book' *Tatler*

'A lush book, dripping with opulent descriptions and elegant imagery . . . Ambitiously imagined'
Australian Book Review

'Think gondolas and pigeons and
A Room with a View . . . a dreamy, fantastical novel'
Sunday Business Post

Fiction
1 86049 866 3
£7.99

THE FLOATING BOOK

by Michelle Lovric

Venice, 1468. Sosia Simeon, a free spirit with a strange predilection for books and Venetians is making her mark on the fabled city. On the other side of the Grand Canal, Wendelin von Speyer is setting up the first printing press in Venice, and looking for the book that will make his fortune.

A love triangle develops between Sosia, Wendelin's young editor, and the seductive scribe Felice Feliciano, a man who loves the crevices of the alphabet the way other men love the crevices of women. Before long, a dark magic begins to haunt Sosia and the printers: an obsessive nun and a book-hating priest conspire against them, and soon their fate hangs in the balance. For binding them all together is the poet Catullus — whose desperate and unrequited love inspired the most tender erotic poems of antiquity.

Brilliantly imagined and richly poetic, *The Floating Book* is an extraordinary recreation of the human drama behind one of the defining moments of western culture.

Praise for *Carnevale*:

'Mixes fiction with reality as surely as water mixes with the air in that strange, floating city . . . a fascinating book' *Tatler*

'Of all the fictional lives of 2002, none is so covetable as that of Cecilia Cornaro' *The Times*

Fiction
1 84408 002 1
£7.99

THE REMEDY

by Michelle Lovric

So at fifteen, spread belly-down upon the floor, a black sheet hunched over me and a candle at my foot and head, my lips pressed on stone, litanies in my ears, as the priest broke and entered my shocked fist to slide the ring on my finger, I promised to take no other husband than Christ. I almost meant it. In that heady moment the vow itself seemed no great sacrifice: I'd never known a man, but I had tasted chocolate.

One unforgettable night in 1785, in a theatre in Drury Lane, the heady alchemy of love and murder suddenly fuses the lives of a Venetian actress and the prince of London's medical underworld. Dangerous secrets and elaborate lies soon send the lovers spinning in different directions, desperate for the truth not just about one another but also their own pasts. Their quest takes them from the dank environs of London's Bankside to the enigmatic city of Venice: her playhouses and brothels, her apothecaries and quack doctors, her spies and noblemen, her convents and her crypts.

'A pacy, atmospheric narrative that exposes the dark
secrets of Enlightenment Venice and London'
Mary Laven, author of *Virgins of Venice*

'Prose as luminous as a Venetian dawn'
Philadelphia Inquirer of
The Floating Book

Fiction
1 84408 135 4
£10.99